Mometrix
TEST PREPARATION

STAAR

Test Prep Guide
Grade 8
Science

DEAR FUTURE EXAM SUCCESS STORY

First of all, **THANK YOU** for purchasing Mometrix study materials!

Second, congratulations! You are one of the few determined test-takers who are committed to doing whatever it takes to excel on your exam. **You have come to the right place.** We developed these study materials with one goal in mind: to deliver you the information you need in a format that's concise and easy to use.

In addition to optimizing your guide for the content of the test, we've outlined our recommended steps for breaking down the preparation process into small, attainable goals so you can make sure you stay on track.

We've also analyzed the entire test-taking process, identifying the most common pitfalls and showing how you can overcome them and be ready for any curveball the test throws you.

Standardized testing is one of the biggest obstacles on your road to success, which only increases the importance of doing well in the high-pressure, high-stakes environment of test day. Your results on this test could have a significant impact on your future, and this guide provides the information and practical advice to help you achieve your full potential on test day.

Your success is our success

We would love to hear from you! If you would like to share the story of your exam success or if you have any questions or comments in regard to our products, please contact us at **800-673-8175** or **support@mometrix.com**.

Thanks again for your business and we wish you continued success!

Sincerely,
The Mometrix Test Preparation Team

Written and edited by the Mometrix Exam Secrets Test Prep Team
Printed in the United States of America

Table of Contents

Introduction

Thank you for purchasing this resource! You have made the choice to prepare yourself for a test that could have a huge impact on your future, and this guide is designed to help you be fully ready for test day. Obviously, it's important to have a solid understanding of the test material, but you also need to be prepared for the unique environment and stressors of the test, so that you can perform to the best of your abilities.

For this purpose, the first section that appears in this guide is the **Success Strategies**. We've devoted countless hours to meticulously researching what works and what doesn't, and we've boiled down our findings to the four most impactful steps you can take to improve your performance on the test. We start at the beginning with study planning and move through the preparation process, all the way to the testing strategies that will help you get the most out of what you know when you're finally sitting in front of the test.

We recommend that you start preparing for your test as far in advance as possible. However, if you've bought this guide as a last-minute study resource and only have a few days before your test, we recommend that you skip over the first two Success Strategies since they address a long-term study plan.

If you struggle with **test anxiety**, we strongly encourage you to check out our recommendations for how you can overcome it. Test anxiety is a formidable foe, but it can be beaten, and we want to make sure you have the tools you need to defeat it.

Strategy #1 – Plan Big, Study Small

There's a lot riding on your performance. If you want to ace this test, you're going to need to keep your skills sharp and the material fresh in your mind. You need a plan that lets you review everything you need to know while still fitting in your schedule. We'll break this strategy down into three categories.

Information Organization

Start with the information you already have: the official test outline. From this, you can make a complete list of all the concepts you need to cover before the test. Organize these concepts into groups that can be studied together, and create a list of any related vocabulary you need to learn so you can brush up on any difficult terms. You'll want to keep this vocabulary list handy once you actually start studying since you may need to add to it along the way.

Time Management

Once you have your set of study concepts, decide how to spread them out over the time you have left before the test. Break your study plan into small, clear goals so you have a manageable task for each day and know exactly what you're doing. Then just focus on one small step at a time. When you manage your time this way, you don't need to spend hours at a time studying. Studying a small block of content for a short period each day helps you retain information better and avoid stressing over how much you have left to do. You can relax knowing that you have a plan to cover everything in time. In order for this strategy to be effective though, you have to start studying early and stick to your schedule. Avoid the exhaustion and futility that comes from last-minute cramming!

Study Environment

The environment you study in has a big impact on your learning. Studying in a coffee shop, while probably more enjoyable, is not likely to be as fruitful as studying in a quiet room. It's important to keep distractions to a minimum. You're only planning to study for a short block of time, so make the most of it. Don't pause to check your phone or get up to find a snack. It's also important to **avoid multitasking**. Research has consistently shown that multitasking will make your studying dramatically less effective. Your study area should also be comfortable and well-lit so you don't have the distraction of straining your eyes or sitting on an uncomfortable chair.

The time of day you study is also important. You want to be rested and alert. Don't wait until just before bedtime. Study when you'll be most likely to comprehend and remember. Even better, if you know what time of day your test will be, set that time aside for study. That way your brain will be used to working on that subject at that specific time and you'll have a better chance of recalling information.

Finally, it can be helpful to team up with others who are studying for the same test. Your actual studying should be done in as isolated an environment as possible, but the work of organizing the information and setting up the study plan can be divided up. In between study sessions, you can discuss with your teammates the concepts that you're all studying and quiz each other on the details. Just be sure that your teammates are as serious about the test as you are. If you find that your study time is being replaced with social time, you might need to find a new team.

Strategy #2 – Make Your Studying Count

You're devoting a lot of time and effort to preparing for this test, so you want to be absolutely certain it will pay off. This means doing more than just reading the content and hoping you can remember it on test day. It's important to make every minute of study count. There are two main areas you can focus on to make your studying count.

Retention

It doesn't matter how much time you study if you can't remember the material. You need to make sure you are retaining the concepts. To check your retention of the information you're learning, try recalling it at later times with minimal prompting. Try carrying around flashcards and glance at one or two from time to time or ask a friend who's also studying for the test to quiz you.

To enhance your retention, look for ways to put the information into practice so that you can apply it rather than simply recalling it. If you're using the information in practical ways, it will be much easier to remember. Similarly, it helps to solidify a concept in your mind if you're not only reading it to yourself but also explaining it to someone else. Ask a friend to let you teach them about a concept you're a little shaky on (or speak aloud to an imaginary audience if necessary). As you try to summarize, define, give examples, and answer your friend's questions, you'll understand the concepts better and they will stay with you longer. Finally, step back for a big picture view and ask yourself how each piece of information fits with the whole subject. When you link the different concepts together and see them working together as a whole, it's easier to remember the individual components.

Finally, practice showing your work on any multi-step problems, even if you're just studying. Writing out each step you take to solve a problem will help solidify the process in your mind, and you'll be more likely to remember it during the test.

Modality

Modality simply refers to the means or method by which you study. Choosing a study modality that fits your own individual learning style is crucial. No two people learn best in exactly the same way, so it's important to know your strengths and use them to your advantage.

For example, if you learn best by visualization, focus on visualizing a concept in your mind and draw an image or a diagram. Try color-coding your notes, illustrating them, or creating symbols that will trigger your mind to recall a learned concept. If you learn best by hearing or discussing information, find a study partner who learns the same way or read aloud to yourself. Think about how to put the information in your own words. Imagine that you are giving a lecture on the topic and record yourself so you can listen to it later.

For any learning style, flashcards can be helpful. Organize the information so you can take advantage of spare moments to review. Underline key words or phrases. Use different colors for different categories. Mnemonic devices (such as creating a short list in which every item starts with the same letter) can also help with retention. Find what works best for you and use it to store the information in your mind most effectively and easily.

Strategy #3 – Practice the Right Way

Your success on test day depends not only on how many hours you put into preparing, but also on whether you prepared the right way. It's good to check along the way to see if your studying is paying off. One of the most effective ways to do this is by taking practice tests to evaluate your progress. Practice tests are useful because they show exactly where you need to improve. Every time you take a practice test, pay special attention to these three groups of questions:

- The questions you got wrong
- The questions you had to guess on, even if you guessed right
- The questions you found difficult or slow to work through

This will show you exactly what your weak areas are, and where you need to devote more study time. Ask yourself why each of these questions gave you trouble. Was it because you didn't understand the material? Was it because you didn't remember the vocabulary? Do you need more repetitions on this type of question to build speed and confidence? Dig into those questions and figure out how you can strengthen your weak areas as you go back to review the material.

Additionally, many practice tests have a section explaining the answer choices. It can be tempting to read the explanation and think that you now have a good understanding of the concept. However, an explanation likely only covers part of the question's broader context. Even if the explanation makes perfect sense, **go back and investigate** every concept related to the question until you're positive you have a thorough understanding.

As you go along, keep in mind that the practice test is just that: practice. Memorizing these questions and answers will not be very helpful on the actual test because it is unlikely to have any of the same exact questions. If you only know the right answers to the sample questions, you won't be prepared for the real thing. **Study the concepts** until you understand them fully, and then you'll be able to answer any question that shows up on the test.

It's important to wait on the practice tests until you're ready. If you take a test on your first day of study, you may be overwhelmed by the amount of material covered and how much you need to learn. Work up to it gradually.

On test day, you'll need to be prepared for answering questions, managing your time, and using the test-taking strategies you've learned. It's a lot to balance, like a mental marathon that will have a big impact on your future. Like training for a marathon, you'll need to start slowly and work your way up. When test day arrives, you'll be ready.

Start with the strategies you've read in the first two Success Strategies—plan your course and study in the way that works best for you. If you have time, consider using multiple study resources to get different approaches to the same concepts. It can be helpful to see difficult concepts from more than one angle. Then find a good source for practice tests. Many times, the test website will suggest potential study resources or provide sample tests.

Test-Taking Strategies

This section contains a list of test-taking strategies that you may find helpful as you work through the test. By taking what you know and applying logical thought, you can maximize your chances of answering any question correctly!

It is very important to realize that every question is different and every person is different: no single strategy will work on every question, and no single strategy will work for every person. That's why we've included all of them here, so you can try them out and determine which ones work best for different types of questions and which ones work best for you.

Question Strategies

✓ Read Carefully

Read the question and the answer choices carefully. Don't miss the question because you misread the terms. You have plenty of time to read each question thoroughly and make sure you understand what is being asked. Yet a happy medium must be attained, so don't waste too much time. You must read carefully and efficiently.

✓ Contextual Clues

Look for contextual clues. If the question includes a word you are not familiar with, look at the immediate context for some indication of what the word might mean. Contextual clues can often give you all the information you need to decipher the meaning of an unfamiliar word. Even if you can't determine the meaning, you may be able to narrow down the possibilities enough to make a solid guess at the answer to the question.

✓ Prefixes

If you're having trouble with a word in the question or answer choices, try dissecting it. Take advantage of every clue that the word might include. Prefixes can be a huge help. Usually, they allow you to determine a basic meaning. *Pre-* means before, *post-* means after, *pro-* is positive, *de-* is negative. From prefixes, you can get an idea of the general meaning of the word and try to put it into context.

✓ Hedge Words

Watch out for critical hedge words, such as *likely, may, can, often, almost, mostly, usually, generally, rarely*, and *sometimes*. Question writers insert these hedge phrases to cover every possibility. Often an answer choice will be wrong simply because it leaves no room for exception. Be on guard for answer choices that have definitive words such as *exactly* and *always*.

✓ Switchback Words

Stay alert for *switchbacks*. These are the words and phrases frequently used to alert you to shifts in thought. The most common switchback words are *but, although*, and *however*. Others include *nevertheless, on the other hand, even though, while, in spite of, despite*, and *regardless of*. Switchback words are important to catch because they can change the direction of the question or an answer choice.

⊘ Face Value

When in doubt, use common sense. Accept the situation in the problem at face value. Don't read too much into it. These problems will not require you to make wild assumptions. If you have to go beyond creativity and warp time or space in order to have an answer choice fit the question, then you should move on and consider the other answer choices. These are normal problems rooted in reality. The applicable relationship or explanation may not be readily apparent, but it is there for you to figure out. Use your common sense to interpret anything that isn't clear.

Answer Choice Strategies

⊘ Answer Selection

The most thorough way to pick an answer choice is to identify and eliminate wrong answers until only one is left, then confirm it is the correct answer. Sometimes an answer choice may immediately seem right, but be careful. The test writers will usually put more than one reasonable answer choice on each question, so take a second to read all of them and make sure that the other choices are not equally obvious. As long as you have time left, it is better to read every answer choice than to pick the first one that looks right without checking the others.

⊘ Answer Choice Families

An answer choice family consists of two (in rare cases, three) answer choices that are very similar in construction and cannot all be true at the same time. If you see two answer choices that are direct opposites or parallels, one of them is usually the correct answer. For instance, if one answer choice says that quantity *x* increases and another either says that quantity *x* decreases (opposite) or says that quantity *y* increases (parallel), then those answer choices would fall into the same family. An answer choice that doesn't match the construction of the answer choice family is more likely to be incorrect. Most questions will not have answer choice families, but when they do appear, you should be prepared to recognize them.

⊘ Eliminate Answers

Eliminate answer choices as soon as you realize they are wrong, but make sure you consider all possibilities. If you are eliminating answer choices and realize that the last one you are left with is also wrong, don't panic. Start over and consider each choice again. There may be something you missed the first time that you will realize on the second pass.

⊘ Avoid Fact Traps

Don't be distracted by an answer choice that is factually true but doesn't answer the question. You are looking for the choice that answers the question. Stay focused on what the question is asking for so you don't accidentally pick an answer that is true but incorrect. Always go back to the question and make sure the answer choice you've selected actually answers the question and is not merely a true statement.

⊘ Extreme Statements

In general, you should avoid answers that put forth extreme actions as standard practice or proclaim controversial ideas as established fact. An answer choice that states the "process should be used in certain situations, if..." is much more likely to be correct than one that states the "process should be discontinued completely." The first is a calm rational statement and doesn't even make a definitive, uncompromising stance, using a hedge word *if* to provide wiggle room, whereas the second choice is far more extreme.

☑ Benchmark

As you read through the answer choices and you come across one that seems to answer the question well, mentally select that answer choice. This is not your final answer, but it's the one that will help you evaluate the other answer choices. The one that you selected is your benchmark or standard for judging each of the other answer choices. Every other answer choice must be compared to your benchmark. That choice is correct until proven otherwise by another answer choice beating it. If you find a better answer, then that one becomes your new benchmark. Once you've decided that no other choice answers the question as well as your benchmark, you have your final answer.

☑ Predict the Answer

Before you even start looking at the answer choices, it is often best to try to predict the answer. When you come up with the answer on your own, it is easier to avoid distractions and traps because you will know exactly what to look for. The right answer choice is unlikely to be word-for-word what you came up with, but it should be a close match. Even if you are confident that you have the right answer, you should still take the time to read each option before moving on.

General Strategies

☑ Tough Questions

If you are stumped on a problem or it appears too hard or too difficult, don't waste time. Move on! Remember though, if you can quickly check for obviously incorrect answer choices, your chances of guessing correctly are greatly improved. Before you completely give up, at least try to knock out a couple of possible answers. Eliminate what you can and then guess at the remaining answer choices before moving on.

☑ Check Your Work

Since you will probably not know every term listed and the answer to every question, it is important that you get credit for the ones that you do know. Don't miss any questions through careless mistakes. If at all possible, try to take a second to look back over your answer selection and make sure you've selected the correct answer choice and haven't made a costly careless mistake (such as marking an answer choice that you didn't mean to mark). This quick double check should more than pay for itself in caught mistakes for the time it costs.

☑ Don't Rush

It is very easy to make errors when you are in a hurry. Maintaining a fast pace in answering questions is pointless if it makes you miss questions that you would have gotten right otherwise. Test writers like to include distracting information and wrong answers that seem right. Taking a little extra time to avoid careless mistakes can make all the difference in your test score. Find a pace that allows you to be confident in the answers that you select.

☑ Keep Moving

Panicking will not help you pass the test, so do your best to stay calm and keep moving. Taking deep breaths and going through the answer elimination steps you practiced can help to break through a stress barrier and keep your pace.

Final Notes

The combination of a solid foundation of content knowledge and the confidence that comes from practicing your plan for applying that knowledge is the key to maximizing your performance on test day. As your foundation of content knowledge is built up and strengthened, you'll find that the strategies included in this chapter become more and more effective in helping you quickly sift through the distractions and traps of the test to isolate the correct answer.

Now that you're preparing to move forward into the test content chapters of this book, be sure to keep your goal in mind. As you read, think about how you will be able to apply this information on the test. If you've already seen sample questions for the test and you have an idea of the question format and style, try to come up with questions of your own that you can answer based on what you're reading. This will give you valuable practice applying your knowledge in the same ways you can expect to on test day.

Good luck and good studying!

Matter and Energy

Properties of Matter

Matter is anything that takes up space and has weight. Even air has weight and takes up space. All types of matter have different properties that can be observed or measured. Properties of matter include temperature, mass, density, and magnetism.

Basic Organization of Matter

An **element** is the most basic type of matter. It has unique properties and cannot be broken down into other elements. The smallest unit of an element is the **atom**. A chemical combination of two or more types of elements is called a compound. **Compounds** often have properties that are very different from those of their constituent elements. The smallest independent unit of an element or compound is known as a **molecule**. Most elements are found somewhere in nature in single-atom form, but a few elements only exist naturally in pairs. These are called diatomic elements, of which some of the most common are hydrogen, nitrogen, and oxygen. Elements and compounds are represented by chemical symbols, one or two letters, most often the first in the element name. More than one atom of the same element in a compound is represented with a subscript number designating how many atoms of that element are present. Water, for instance, contains two hydrogens and one oxygen. Thus, the chemical formula is H_2O. Methane contains one carbon and four hydrogens, so its formula is CH_4.

Atom

A **neutral atom** consists of an extremely dense **nucleus** composed of one or more positively-charged **protons** and a varying number of uncharged **neutrons**, except for hydrogen-1 which contains no neutrons, surrounded by a cloud of one or more negatively-charged **electrons**. This cloud is also called the **electron cloud**. In a neutral atom, the number of electrons equals the number of protons in the nucleus. The protons and neutrons are bound together by the strong nuclear force, which overcomes the repulsive force the positive charges of the protons have for each other. The negatively-charged electrons are bound to the positively-charged protons by the attractive electromagnetic force. The number of protons, or the atomic number, determines the chemical element the atom represents. The number of electrons in the outermost shell determines how the atom interacts with other atoms or molecules.

Protons, Neutrons, and Electrons

The three major subatomic particles are the proton, neutron, and electron. The **proton**, which is located in the nucleus, has a relative charge of +1. The **neutron**, which is located in the nucleus, has a relative charge of 0. The **electron**, which is located outside the nucleus, has a relative charge of −1. The proton and neutron, which are essentially the same mass, are much more massive than the electron and make up the mass of the atom. The electron's mass is insignificant compared to the mass of the proton and neutron.

Review Video: Structure of Atoms
Visit mometrix.com/academy and enter code: 905932

EXAMPLE

Neon is a chemical element belonging to the Noble Gases, which have very low reactivity. A typical neon atom contains 10 protons, 10 neutrons, and 10 electrons. Which of the following best explains why neon has such low reactivity?

a. It has an equal number of protons, neutrons, and electrons.
b. It has a full outer electron shell.
c. It has an empty outer electron shell.
d. It has an overall charge of zero.

Choice A states that having an equal number of protons, neutrons, and electrons makes an atom more stable. However, most atoms have a balanced number of protons and electrons, and many have the same number of neutrons as well. This does not explain neon's low reactivity, making it incorrect.

Choice B states that neon has a full outer electron shell. When atoms react with one another, they do so to gain or lose electrons. Having a full outer shell makes an element less reactive because it does not need to bond with another atom in order to have a stable number of electrons. This could be the correct answer.

Choice C states that neon has an empty outer electron shell. Having a full outer shell makes an element less reactive, so this does not make sense. This answer is incorrect.

Choice D states that neon has an overall charge of zero. This is true because the charge of the protons and the charge of the electrons cancel one another out. However, reactivity is a result of how many electrons are in an element's outer shell and is unrelated to its overall charge.

Choice B is the correct answer because the number of electrons in an atom's outer shell is the most important factor in the element's reactivity. Because neon has a full outer electron shell, it is unlikely to react with other elements.

Atomic Number and Mass Number

The **atomic number** of an element is the number of protons in the nucleus of an atom of that element. This is the number that identifies the type of an atom. For example, all oxygen atoms have eight protons, and all carbon atoms have six protons. Each element is identified by its specific atomic number.

The **mass number** is the number of protons and neutrons in the nucleus of an atom. Although the atomic number is the same for all atoms of a specific element, the mass number can vary due to the varying numbers of neutrons in various isotopes of the atom.

EXAMPLE

An atom has an atomic mass of 81, 40 protons, and an overall neutral charge. Which of the following configurations is possible?

a. 40 protons, 40 neutrons, 40 electrons
b. 40 protons, 41 neutrons, 40 electrons
c. 40 protons, 41 neutrons, 41 electrons
d. 40 protons, 40 neutrons, 41 electrons

Choice A proposes that the atom would contain 40 neutrons and 40 electrons. The information given in the prompt explains that the atomic mass of the atom is 81 atomic mass units (AMU).

Because we know the number of protons is 40, we can find the number of neutrons by subtracting 40 from 81, resulting in 41. Choice A is incorrect because the atom would have 41 neutrons rather than 40.

Choice B proposes an atom with 41 neutrons and 40 electrons. The atomic mass of an atom with 40 protons and 41 neutrons is 81, matching the atomic mass in the description. The atom should also have an overall neutral charge. Since the positive and negative charges of protons and electrons cancel out, a neutral atom would have 40 electrons. Choice B has the correct number of neutrons and electrons.

Choice C proposes an atom with 41 neutrons and 41 electrons. As shown above, an atom with 41 neutrons would have the given atomic mass. However, an atom with 40 protons and 41 electrons would have an overall charge of negative 1. Choice C is incorrect.

Choice D proposes an atom with 40 neutrons and 41 electrons. This does not match the atomic mass or overall charge of the atom described in the question, so Choice D is incorrect.

Choice B is the correct answer because it is the only atomic configuration that results in an atomic mass of 81 and an overall neutral charge.

Periodic Table

The **periodic table** groups elements with similar chemical properties together. The grouping of elements is based on atomic structure. It shows periodic trends of physical and chemical properties and identifies families of elements with similar properties. It is a common model for organizing and understanding elements. In the periodic table, each element has its own cell that includes varying amounts of information presented in symbol form about the properties of the element. Cells in the table are arranged in rows (periods) and columns (groups or families). At minimum, a cell includes the symbol for the element and its atomic number. The cell for hydrogen, for example, which appears first in the upper left corner, includes an "H" and a "1" above the letter. Elements are ordered by atomic number, left to right, top to bottom.

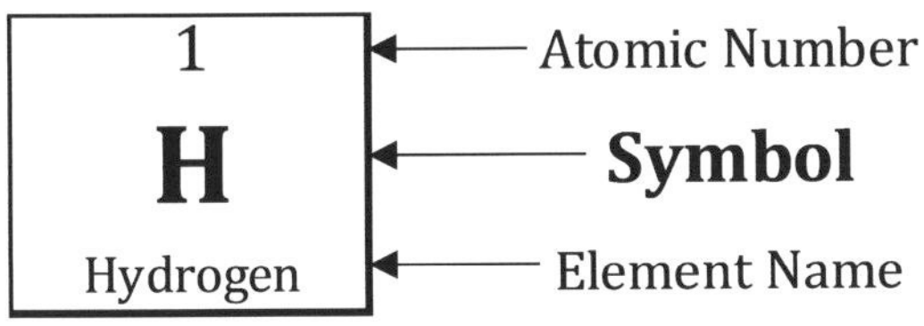

Review Video: Periodic Table
Visit mometrix.com/academy and enter code: 154828

In the periodic table, the groups are the columns numbered 1 through 18 that group elements with similar outer electron shell configurations. Since the configuration of the outer electron shell is one of the primary factors affecting an element's chemical properties, elements within the same group have similar chemical properties. Previous naming conventions for groups have included the use of Roman numerals and upper-case letters. Currently, the periodic table groups are: Group 1, alkali metals; Group 2, alkaline earth metals; Groups 3-12, transition metals; Group 13, boron family; Group 14; carbon family; Group 15, pnictogens; Group 16, chalcogens; Group 17, halogens; Group 18, noble gases.

In the periodic table, there are seven periods (rows), and within each period there are blocks that group elements with the same outer electron subshell (more on this in the next section). The number of electrons in that outer shell determines which group an element belongs to within a given block. Each row's number (1, 2, 3, etc.) corresponds to the highest number electron shell that is in use. For example, row 2 uses only electron shells 1 and 2, while row 7 uses all shells from 1-7.

Groups and Periods in the Periodic Table

A **group** is a vertical column of the periodic table. Elements in the same group have the same number of **valence electrons**. For the representative elements, the number of valence electrons is equal to the group number. Because of their equal valence electrons, elements in the same groups have similar physical and chemical properties. A period is a horizontal row of the periodic table. Atomic number increases from left to right across a row. The **period** of an element corresponds to the **highest energy level** of the electrons in the atoms of that element. The energy level increases from top to bottom down a group.

Period ↓ / Group →	1	2	3	4	5	6	7	8	9	10	11	12	13	14	15	16	17	18
1	1 H																	2 He
2	3 Li	4 Be											5 B	6 C	7 N	8 O	9 F	10 Ne
3	11 Na	12 Mg											13 Al	14 Si	15 P	16 S	17 Cl	18 Ar
4	19 K	20 Ca	21 Sc	22 Ti	23 V	24 Cr	25 Mn	26 Fe	27 Co	28 Ni	29 Cu	30 Zn	31 Ga	32 Ge	33 As	34 Se	35 Br	36 Kr
5	37 Rb	38 Sr	39 Y	40 Zr	41 Nb	42 Mo	43 Tc	44 Ru	45 Rh	46 Pd	47 Ag	48 Cd	49 In	50 Sn	51 Sb	52 Te	53 I	54 Xe
6	55 Cs	56 Ba	*	72 Hf	73 Ta	74 W	75 Re	76 Os	77 Ir	78 Pt	79 Au	80 Hg	81 Tl	82 Pb	83 Bi	84 Po	85 At	86 Rn
7	87 Fr	88 Ra	**	104 Rf	105 Db	106 Sg	107 Bh	108 Hs	109 Mt	110 Ds	111 Rg	112 Cn	113 Uut	114 Fl	115 Uup	116 Lv	117 Uus	118 Uuo

*	57 La	58 Ce	59 Pr	60 Nd	61 Pm	62 Sm	63 Eu	64 Gd	65 Tb	66 Dy	67 Ho	68 Er	69 Tm	70 Yb	71 Lu
**	89 Ac	90 Th	91 Pa	92 U	93 Np	94 Pu	95 Am	96 Cm	97 Bk	98 Cf	99 Es	100 Fm	101 Md	102 No	103 Lr

Atomic Number and Atomic Mass in the Periodic Table

The elements in the periodic table are arranged in order of **increasing atomic number** first left to right and then top to bottom across the periodic table. The **atomic number** represents the number of protons in the atoms of that element. Because of the increasing numbers of protons, the atomic mass typically also increases from left to right across a period and from top to bottom down a row. The **atomic mass** is a weighted average of all the naturally occurring isotopes of an element.

Using Mass and Density to Identify an Unknown Substance

Density is a **physical property** that measures how much matter is contained within a certain amount of space. Different substances have their own unique densities, which means scientists can determine the identity of an unknown substance by calculating its density. Density is calculated using the equation **density = mass / volume**. **Mass** can easily be measured using tools like a triple-beam balance. Finding the **volume** of a substance depends on its phase of matter. For example, to calculate the volume of a liquid, scientists use glassware such as a graduated cylinder. However, to calculate the volume of a solid, scientists use equations based on the shape of the sample. They can also submerge the sample in water and calculate how much the volume has changed, which is called the **water displacement method**. Using measurements for mass and volume along with the equation above, scientists can calculate an unknown substance's density and compare it to the average densities of known substances in order to identify it. For example, a substance with a density of 2.7 g/cm^3 is likely to be aluminum, while a value of 11.3 g/cm^3 is likely to be lead.

Atomic Symbols

The **atomic symbol** for many elements is simply the first letter of the element name. For example, the atomic symbol for hydrogen is H, and the atomic symbol for carbon is C. The atomic symbol of other elements is the first two letters of the element name. For example, the atomic symbol for helium is He, and the atomic symbol for cobalt is Co. The atomic symbols of several elements are derived from Latin. For example, the atomic symbol for copper (Cu) is derived from *cuprum,* and the atomic symbol for iron (Fe) is derived from *ferrum.* The atomic symbol for tungsten (W) is derived from the German word *wolfram.*

ARRANGEMENTS IN THE PERIODIC TABLE

The three main sections of the periodic table are metals, nonmetals, and metalloids. There are also further subcategories for each section such as alkaline earth metals, transition metals, noble gases, etc.. The **metals** are located on the left side and center of the periodic table, and the **nonmetals** are located on the right side of the periodic table. The **metalloids** or **semimetals** form a zigzag line between the metals and nonmetals as shown below. Metals include the alkali metals such as lithium, sodium, and potassium and the alkaline earth metals such as beryllium, magnesium, and calcium. Metals also include the transition metals such as iron, copper, and nickel and the inner transition metals such as thorium, uranium, and plutonium. Nonmetals include the chalcogens such as oxygen and sulfur, the halogens such as fluorine and chlorine, and the noble gases such as helium and argon. Carbon, nitrogen, and phosphorus are also nonmetals. Metalloids or semimetals include boron, silicon, germanium, antimony, and polonium.

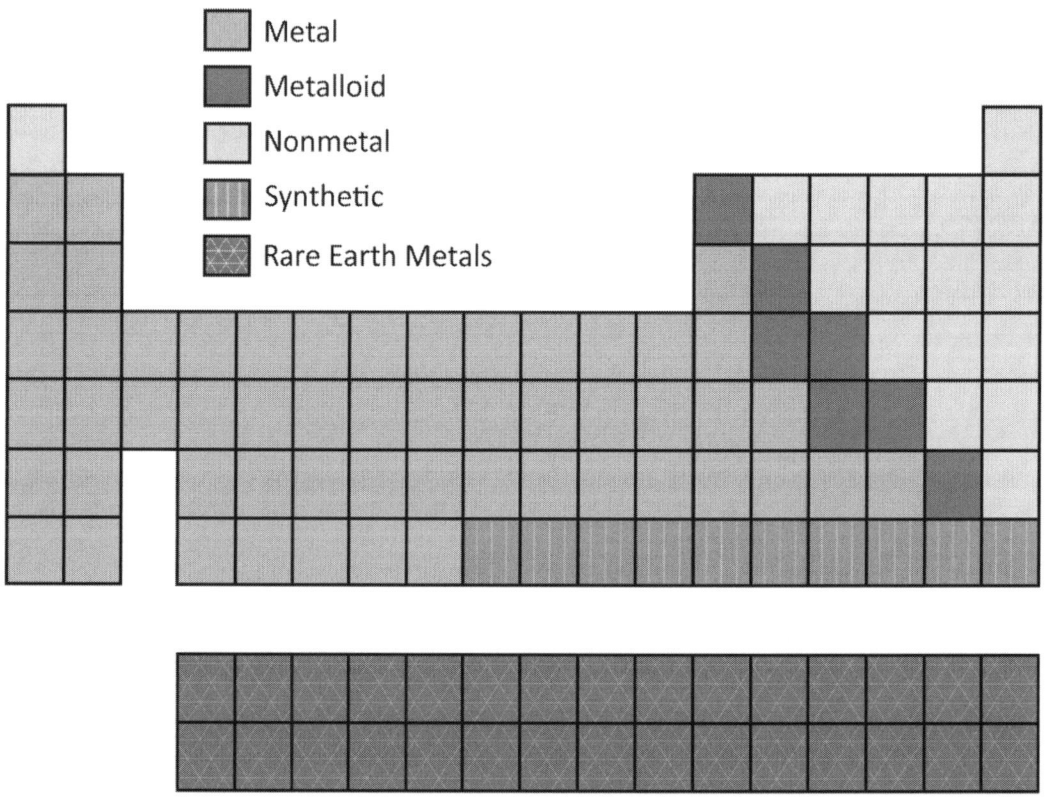

TRANSITION ELEMENTS

The **transition elements** belong to one of two categories—transition metals or inner transition metals. The **transition metals** are located in the middle of the periodic table, and the inner transition metals are typically set off as two rows by themselves at the bottom of the periodic table. The transition metals correspond to the "*d* block" for orbital filling, and the inner transition metals correspond to the "*f* block" for orbital filling. Examples of transition metals include iron, copper, nickel, and zinc. The inner transition metals consist of the *lanthanide* or *rare-earth series*, which corresponds to the first row, and the *actinide series*, which corresponds to the second row of the inner transition metals. The *lanthanide series* includes lanthanum, cerium, and praseodymium. The *actinide series* includes actinium, uranium, and plutonium.

Physical Properties of the Elements in Relation to the Periodic Table

The **boiling point**, **melting point**, and **conductivity** of the elements depend partially on the number of valence electrons of the atoms of those elements. For the representative elements in groups 1A–8A, the number of valence electrons matches the group number. Because all of the elements in each individual group contain the same number of valence electrons, elements in the same groups tend to have similar boiling points, melting points, and conductivity. Boiling points and melting points tend to decrease moving down the column of groups 1A–4A and 8A but increase slightly moving down the column of groups 5A–7A.

Physical Properties of Metals, Nonmetals, and Metalloids

The periodic table separates elements based on the physical and chemical properties of their pure forms. Elements fall into one of three categories based on their properties: **metals**, **nonmetals**, or **metalloids**. One of these key properties is **luster**, which describes how well a material reflects light. Other examples include **conductivity**, or how easily the material conducts heat or electricity, and **malleability**, meaning how easily the material can be molded and shaped. Metals, such as copper and gold, are easily identified as having high luster, high conductivity, and high malleability. Comparatively, solid nonmetals are dull or low luster, poor conductors, and easily break when bent. Lastly, metalloids are substances that possess a combination of the properties that are characteristic of metals and nonmetals. For example, silicon has high luster like a metal, is a moderate conductor of electricity, and has a brittle consistency like that of a nonmetal.

Chemical Reactivity in Relation to the Periodic Table

Atoms of elements in the same **group** or **family** of the periodic table tend to have **similar chemical properties** and **similar chemical reactions**. For example, the alkali metals, which form cations with a charge of +1, tend to react with water to form hydrogen gas and metal hydroxides. The alkaline earth metals, which form cations with a charge of +2, react with oxygen gas to form metal oxides. The halogens, which form anions with a charge of −1, are highly reactive and toxic. The noble gases are unreactive and never form compounds naturally.

Example

Copper (atomic number 29), silver (atomic number 47), and gold (atomic number 79) are soft and shiny metals that are useful for creating coins, jewelry, and electrical wiring. Which of the following explains these metals' shared properties?

a. They belong to the same period of the periodic table.
b. They belong to the same group of the periodic table.
c. They contain the same number of protons.
d. They contain the same number of total electrons.

Choice A states that these elements belong to the same period of the periodic table, resulting in their similar properties. A period, or row, on the periodic table is organized by atomic number. For example, copper is followed by zinc (30) and gallium (31). Elements in the same period do not share the same properties. Thus, choice A is incorrect.

Choice B states that these three elements belong to the same group. A group on the periodic table is a vertical column of elements that share similar properties. Elements are grouped based on how many electrons exist in their outer shell, which influences the properties of the element. If copper, silver, and gold were in the same group, then it would make sense that they share properties. Choice B could be the answer.

Choice C states that these elements have the same number of protons. An element's number of protons is equal to its atomic number, which is different for each element. For example, copper has 29 protons, making its atomic number 29. It is impossible for three different elements to have the same number of protons, so choice C is incorrect.

Choice D states that the elements contain the same number of total electrons. For a neutral atom, the number of electrons is equal to the number of protons. In this case, copper should have 29 electrons while silver should have 47. Copper, silver, and gold do have the same number of electrons in their outer shell. However, this answer specifies "total electrons," making it incorrect. Choice D is not the answer.

Choice B is the correct answer because elements in the same group of the periodic table share similar properties.

Chemical Formulas

A chemical formula is a set of letters, numbers, and symbols that describe the elemental composition of a particular substance. Elements are listed by their periodic table symbol. A subscript number after the element symbol indicates the number of that type of element's atoms in the formula. If there is no subscript, there is only one atom of that type of element. There are three common types of chemical formulas to be familiar with:

1. The *molecular formula* describes the elemental composition of a single molecule of a substance. For instance, the molecular formula for glucose is $C_6H_{12}O_6$, because each molecule of glucose contains six atoms of carbon and oxygen, and twelve atoms of hydrogen.
2. The *empirical formula* is a reduced form of the molecular formula that gives only the ratios of the elements in a substance. For instance, the empirical formula for glucose is CH_2O, because the ratio of carbon to hydrogen to oxygen in glucose is 1 to 2 to 1. The empirical formula will be the same as the molecular formula for many simple substances.
3. The *structural formula* is an expanded formula that gives information about the way that the atoms in a molecule are bonded. Below is an example of the structural formula for ethane:

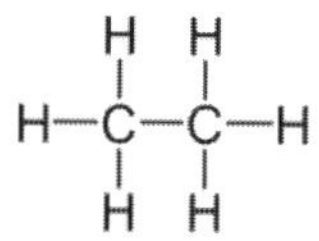

Example

Sulfuric acid is a strong acid composed of hydrogen, sulfur, and oxygen atoms. The chemical formula for sulfuric acid is H_2SO_4. Which of the following correctly describes the number of hydrogen, sulfur, and oxygen atoms in sulfuric acid?

a. 2 hydrogen; 4 sulfur; 4 oxygen
b. 2 hydrogen; 1 sulfur; 4 oxygen
c. 8 hydrogen; 1 sulfur; 4 oxygen
d. 8 hydrogen; 4 sulfur; 8 oxygen

Choice A: 2 hydrogen; 4 sulfur; 4 oxygen. When counting the number of atoms in a chemical formula, each element is represented by its atomic symbol. In this case, we have H, S, and O representing hydrogen, sulfur, and oxygen, respectively. The number next to the atomic symbol, called a subscript, denotes how many atoms of that element are in the molecule. In H_2SO_4, there is no subscript next to the S, which means there is only one sulfur atom. Choice A is incorrect because there is only one sulfur atom in sulfuric acid, not four.

Choice B: 2 hydrogen; 1 sulfur; 4 oxygen. This option has one sulfur atom, making it a possible correct answer. The number of hydrogen atoms is denoted next to the H in H_2SO_4. Therefore, there are 2 hydrogen atoms in H_2SO_4. Lastly, the four next to the O in H_2SO_4 means there are four oxygen atoms in H_2SO_4. In summary, H_2SO_4 consists of two hydrogen atoms, one sulfur atom, and four oxygen atoms. Choice B is correct.

Choice C: 8 hydrogen; 1 sulfur; 4 oxygen. This answer is incorrect because it does not have the correct number of hydrogen atoms. Choice C is not the answer.

Choice D: 8 hydrogen; 4 sulfur; 8 oxygen. This answer has the incorrect number of all three atoms. The subscript only affects the element directly before it. Choice D is not the answer.

Choice B is the answer because it has the correct number for all three elements. The subscript to the right of the element denotes how many atoms there are, and having no subscript means there is only one atom of that element.

Pure Substances and Mixtures

Pure Substances

Pure substances are substances that cannot be further broken down into simpler components or pieces and still retain their characteristics. Pure substances are categorized as either **elements** or **compounds**. Elements consist of only one type of atom may be monatomic, diatomic, or polyatomic. For example, helium (He) and copper (Cu) are monatomic elements, and hydrogen (H_2) and oxygen (O_2) are diatomic elements. Phosphorus (P_4) and sulfur (S_8) are polyatomic elements. Compounds consist of molecules of more than one type of atom. For example, pure water (H_2O) is made up of molecules consisting of two atoms of hydrogen bonded to one atom of oxygen, and glucose ($C_6H_{12}O_6$) is made up of molecules of six carbon atoms and twelve hydrogen atoms bonded together with six oxygen atoms.

Mixtures

Mixtures can be classified as either homogeneous or heterogeneous. The molecules of a **homogeneous mixture** are distributed uniformly throughout the mixture, whereas the molecules of a **heterogeneous mixture** are not. Air is an example of a homogeneous mixture, and a pile of sand and rock is an example of a heterogeneous mixture. Solutions are homogeneous mixtures consisting of a **solute** (the substance that is dissolved) and a **solvent** (the substance doing the dissolving).

Mixtures with Compounds

Mixtures are similar to compounds in that they are produced when two or more substances are combined. However, there are some key differences as well. Compounds require a chemical combination of the constituent particles, while mixtures are simply the interspersion of particles. Unlike compounds, mixtures may be **separated** without a chemical change. A mixture retains the chemical properties of its constitutent particles, while a compound acquires a new set of properties. Given compounds can exist only in specific ratios, while mixtures may be any ratio of the involved substances.

Acids and Bases and Water

One property of matter is its pH value. A **pH value** tells whether a chemical is an **acid** or a **base**. Acids, such as lemon juice, tend to taste sour. Bases, such as soap, tend to taste bitter. Some chemicals, such as water, are called **neutral** because they are neither an acid nor a base. An acid or a base can be mixed with water to change the pH. Lemon juice tastes very sour if it is not mixed with water. However, lemon juice can taste sweet instead of sour when mixed with sugar and water. Adding water to reduce the strength of a solution is called **dilution.** Dilution is another example of how the ingredients in a solution keep their physical properties. Lemon juice tastes less sour when mixed with water, but that is because the water is also being tasted. However, the flavor and color of the lemon juice can still be observed in the solution.

	Very Acidic			**Neutral**			**Very Basic**
pH value	0-2	2-4	5-7	7	7-9	10-12	12-14
	Hydrochloric acid and stomach Acid	Vinegar, fruit juice, and sodas	Tomatoes and bananas	water	Eggs and baking soda	Soap and ammonia	Bleach and drain cleaner

Physical Changes

Physical changes are those that do not affect the chemical properties of a substance. Changes in state are **physical changes**. For example, a liquid can freeze into a solid or boil into a gas without changing the chemical nature of the substance. It is all still the same substance. Ice, steam, and liquid water are all still water, H_2O. Physical properties include such features as shape, texture, size, volume, mass, and density. Cutting, melting, dissolving, mixing, breaking, and crushing are all types of physical changes.

Chemical Changes

Chemical changes occur when chemical bonds are broken and new ones are formed. The original substances are **transformed** into different substances. If vinegar and baking soda are mixed together, a lot of bubbles (carbon dioxide) and water will form. Burning wood in a fireplace is another type of chemical change. The carbon in the wood reacts with oxygen in the air to make ash, carbon dioxide, smoke and energy that we feel as heat and see as light.

Examples of chemical changes include the following:

- (a) The temperature of a system changes without any heating or cooling.
- (b) The formation of a gas (bubbles).
- (c) The formation of a precipitate (solid) when two liquids are mixed.
- (d) A liquid changes color.

A **chemical change** occurs when two or more substances come together and interact in such a way that they become completely new substances. For example, two hydrogen atoms and one oxygen atom combine to make a new compound—a water molecule, H_2O. Likewise, two oxygen atoms and one carbon atom combine to make one molecule of carbon dioxide—CO_2. The two substances that combine are called **reactants,** and the new compound that emerges is the **product**. Chemical reactions (changes) can be much more complicated than this.

Properties of Water

Cohesion-Tension Theory

The **cohesion-tension theory** was advanced to explain the method of transport of water from the roots of a plant, where it receives its water supply, to its uppermost leaves, even in the tallest trees. Hydrogen bonds in water molecules form strong bonds with the oxygen atoms in all nearby water molecules. Water moves from plant cells into leaf pores one molecule at a time. As one molecule exits a cell, another water molecule from lower in the plant enters the same cell. This movement, caused by the cohesive properties of the water molecule, creates a tension among all of the (connected) water molecules in the plant and even those in the soil about to enter the plant's roots. This tension provides the force needed to move water upward through a plant from its roots.

Surface Tension of Water

Cohesive forces are attractive forces that act between the molecules of a liquid. **Adhesive forces** are attractive forces that act between the molecules in a liquid and other substances' molecules. In most areas of a liquid, the molecules experience these forces equally from all directions. On the surface of a liquid, however, the molecules are drawn inward toward the center of the liquid's mass but experience no equal force from the outside. This causes the surface to contract and behave like a stretched elastic membrane. This property of a liquid is referred to as its surface tension. Water has a relatively high surface tension; this means that it forms stable, spherical droplets when placed on a nonporous surface. The high surface tension of water is what allows denser objects to float and insects (such as the water skater) to walk atop water bodies.

Law of Conservation of Mass

The **law of conservation of mass** is also known as the **law of conservation of matter**. This basically means that in a closed system, the total mass of the products must equal the total mass of the reactants. This could also be stated that in a closed system, mass never changes. A consequence of this law is that matter is never created or destroyed during a typical chemical reaction. The atoms of the reactants are simply rearranged to form the products. The number and type of each specific atom involved in the reactants is identical to the number and type of atoms in the products. This is the key principle used when balancing chemical equations. In a balanced chemical equation, the number of moles of each element on the reactant side equals the number of moles of each element on the product side.

Law of Conservation of Energy

The **law of conservation of energy** states that in a closed system, energy cannot be created or destroyed but only changed from one form to another. This is also known as the first law of thermodynamics. Another way to state this is that the **total energy in an isolated system is constant**. Energy comes in many forms that may be transformed from one kind to another, but in a closed system, the total amount of energy is conserved or remains constant. For example, potential energy can be converted to kinetic energy, thermal energy, radiant energy, or mechanical energy. In an isolated chemical reaction, there can be no energy created or destroyed. The energy simply changes forms.

Example

A group of 8th-grade science students mixed 100 grams of blue copper (II) chloride solution ($CuCl_2$) with 1 gram of aluminum foil. Which of the following observations could be used as evidence that a chemical reaction occurred?

a. The reaction took 20 minutes.
b. The mass after the reaction occurred was 97 grams.
c. The reaction produced a copper-red crumbly solid.
d. A phase change did not occur.

Choice A: This answer describes how long the reaction takes, which is an example of a scientific observation and could be useful information. However, this information alone does not tell us whether or not a chemical reaction occurred. Choice A can be eliminated.

Choice B: This answer describes the mass of the reaction's products, which does not tell us whether or not a chemical reaction occurred. In addition, this piece of data shows that the mass of the products (97 grams) was less than the mass of the reactants (100 grams). Because chemical reactions follow the Law of Conservation of Mass, the mass before and after a chemical reaction must be the same. This choice does not provide evidence that a chemical reaction occurred.

Choice C: This option describes the product of the reaction, a copper-red crumbly solid. This is different from the reactants the students mixed together: a blue solution and aluminum foil, which is a shiny silver metal. The substance produced had different properties than the original substances, such as a new copper color and a crumbly texture. Chemical reactions always produce a new substance with different properties than the reactants, so this could be evidence that a chemical reaction occurred. Choice C might be the answer.

Choice D: This option states that a phase change did not occur. A phase change is the transformation from one state of matter to another, such as ice melting into water. While a phase change is not a chemical reaction, simply stating that a phase change did not occur does not necessarily mean that a chemical reaction did occur. This choice can be eliminated because it is not evidence of a chemical reaction.

Choice C is the best answer because it describes a new substance with different properties that was produced, indicating that a chemical reaction has occurred.

Producers, Consumers, and Decomposers

Producers are organisms that can make their own food. Most producers are plants. Through photosynthesis plants make sugars that provide energy. Plants only need sunlight, water, and the proper minerals and other nutrients to live, grow, and reproduce themselves. **Consumers** are organisms that eat other organisms. Consumers are animals that eat plants or other animals that eat plants. Decomposers are organisms that feed on decaying plant and animal matter. Since decomposers cannot make their own food they are classified as consumers. Fungi such as mushrooms are **decomposers** that break down the tissues and wood of living or dead plants or the bodies of dead animals.

Energy Pyramid

Energy flow through an ecosystem can be tracked through an energy pyramid. An **energy pyramid** shows how energy is transferred from one trophic level to another. **Producers** always form the base of an energy pyramid, and the consumers form successive levels above the producers. Producers only store about 1% of the solar energy they receive. Then, each successive level only uses about 10% of the energy of the previous level. That means that **primary consumers** use about 10% of the energy used by primary producers, such as grasses and trees. Next, **secondary consumers** use 10% of primary consumers' 10%, or 1% overall. This continues up for as many trophic levels as exist in a particular ecosystem.

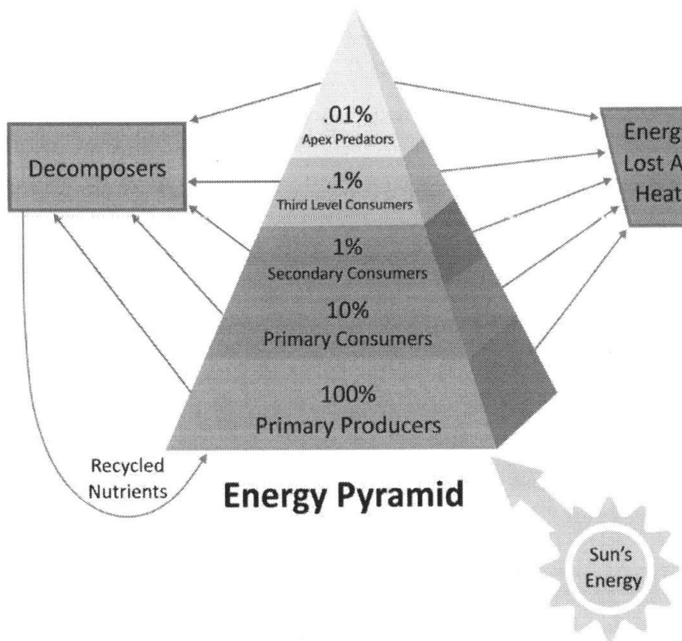

Food Web

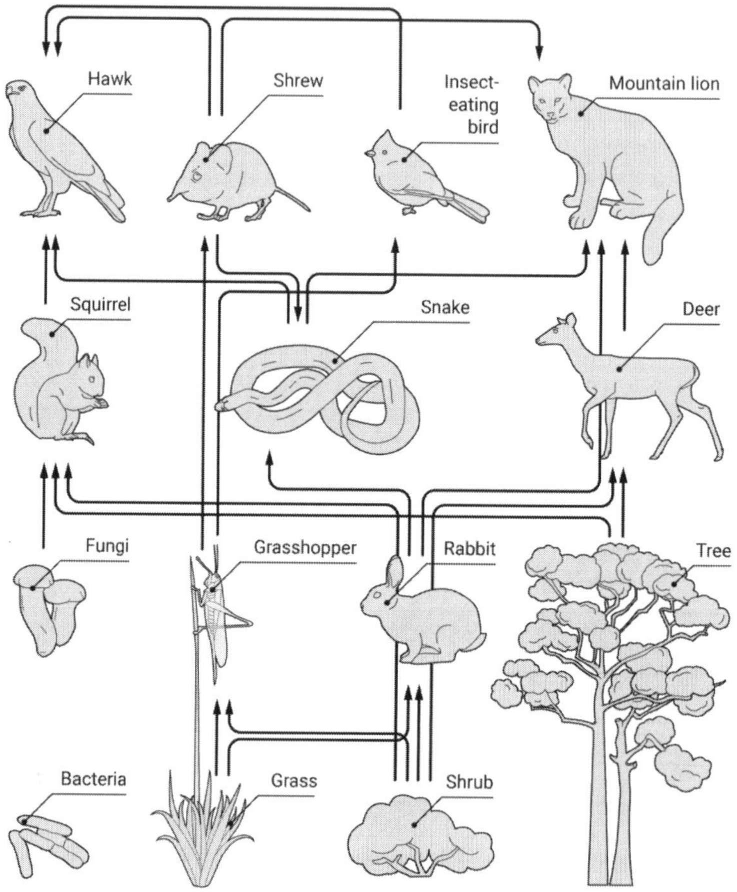

Energy flow through an ecosystem can be illustrated by a **food web**. Energy moves through the food web in the direction of the arrows. In the food web, **producers** such as grass, trees, and shrubs use energy from the Sun to produce food through photosynthesis. **Herbivores** or **primary consumers** such as squirrels, grasshoppers, and rabbits obtain energy by eating the producers. **Secondary consumers**, which are carnivores such as snakes and shrews, obtain energy by eating the primary consumers. **Tertiary consumers**, which are carnivores such as hawks and mountain lions, obtain energy by eating the secondary consumers.

Review Video: Food Webs
Visit mometrix.com/academy and enter code: 853254

Chapter Quiz

1. Which of the following is the most basic type of matter?

a. Proton
b. Element
c. Atom
d. Molecule

2. The atomic number of an element is the number of ____________ in the nucleus of an atom of that element.

a. protons
b. neutrons
c. electrons
d. protons and neutrons

3. Which of the following is typically set off as two separate rows at the bottom of the periodic table?

a. Metals
b. Transition metals
c. Inner transition metals
d. Nonmetals

4. Which of the following is considered a neutral because it is neither an acid nor a base?

a. Baking soda
b. Water
c. Bleach
d. Vinegar

5. What type of chemical formula gives information about the way that the atoms in a molecule are bonded?

a. The molecular formula
b. The empirical formula
c. The structural formula
d. All of the above

6. Producers (organisms that can make their own food) only store about _______ of the solar energy they receive.

a. 10%
b. 1%
c. .1%
d. .01%

Chapter Quiz Answer Key

1. D: See section **Basic Organization of Matter**

2. A: See section **Atomic Number and Mass Number**

3. C: See section **Arrangement of Transition Elements**

4. B: See section **Acids and Bases and Water**

5. C: See section **Chemical Formulas**

6. B: See section **Energy Pyramid**

Force, Motion, and Energy

Motion and Force

Sir Isaac Newton observed three major laws explaining how the motion of an object works. The term **motion** refers to the movement of an object and the term **force** refers to physical energy that is applied to an object. Newton also referred to objects that are not moving as being in a state of **rest**.

- **Newton's First Law of Motion** - a body will remain at **rest** or in **motion** until a **force** is applied to it.
  - A bowling ball continues to roll in the same direction it was thrown until friction eventually slows it down.
  - A ball sitting on the ground will not move unless a force is applied to it.
- **Newton's Second Law of Motion** -the amount of **acceleration** is determined by the amount of **force** and the **mass** of the object being moved.
  - A soccer ball will accelerate more if kicked harder.

  - A shopping cart is much easier to push than a car because it is much less massive.

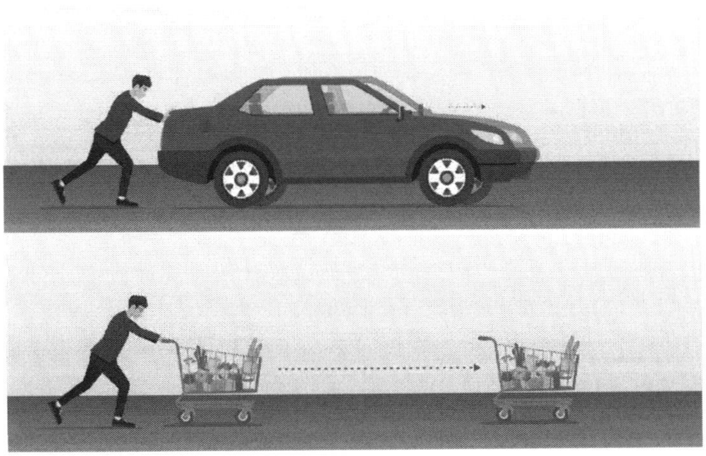

- **Newton's Third Law of Motion** – For every **action**, there is an equal and opposite **reaction**.
    - The floor applies force upward to hold up the weight of a person standing on it.
    - A dog pulls against a leash that his owner is holding.

Directions of Motion

Motion can be either linear, rotational, or oscillating.

- **Linear motion** - a single direction, like a bowling ball rolling down the lane or a train moving in one direction down its tracks.
- **Rotational motion** – rotating or spinning in a circular motion, such as a top spinning, a merry-go-round, or the Earth rotating around the Sun.
- **Oscillating motion** – bouncing up and down repeatedly, such as a yo-yo on a string or a spring. This also includes waves as they rise and fall.

Examples of Newton's Laws in the Real World

- **Vehicle restraints** – seat belts and air bags all work to slow down the acceleration applied to the body in a car wreck. When a car hits another car, it slows down almost immediately, but the body and objects inside have inertia of their own, so they want to continue moving forward. Acceleration is directly related to force, so stopping immediately with the car would be harmful. Instead, the safety features help slow down the acceleration to keep the people inside safe.
- **Amusement park rides** – Rollercoasters apply Newton's laws in many ways. Rollercoasters tend to go very fast, but before you see them do so, they often climb a tall hill before falling very fast. In this way, they use gravity to their advantage to gain as much speed as possible before performing stunts like loop-the-loops and twists. Rollercoasters and other rides seem to defy gravity sometimes, making people feel like they are floating when they are only falling slower than the rollercoaster itself. If a rollercoaster goes down quickly, the body tries to stay in the air, causing this type of effect.
- **Earth's tectonic activities** – The theory of plate tectonics says that there are moving layers of the Earth's crust called plates. These plates are very slow moving, but enormous. When these plates bump into each other or slide past each other, they cause massive amounts of force because of Newton's laws. Every action produces an equal and opposite reaction. This is the cause of earthquakes, mountain volcano formation, and some forms of tidal waves.
- **Rocket launches** – When rockets are launched, many forces are at play. The rockets are huge, and they require a great amount of force to lift them into the air and into space. To do so, the rockets ignite fuel underneath and push downwards to cause lift upwards. These forces must be carefully calculated, however, so that the rocket does not veer off in the wrong direction and so that the humans and cargo inside don't accelerate fast enough that they are harmed in the process.

Example

Newton's third law of motion states that forces come in pairs of equal size and opposite direction. In which of the following scenarios does an object move as a result of Newton's third law?

a. A soccer player kicks a ball with a force of 25 Newtons.
b. Someone pushes a car, but it does not move.
c. A rocket launches from Earth.
d. An astronaut can jump higher on the Moon.

Choice A describes a soccer player kicking a ball. The action force in this case is the player's foot kicking the ball. According to Newton's third law, the soccer ball exerts an equal and opposite force on the player's foot. This does not cause the player to move, so Choice A can be eliminated.

Choice B describes pushing a car that does not move. The action force in this scenario is the push applied to the car, while a reaction force is applied to the person. Neither the car nor the person moves, so Choice B can be eliminated.

Choice C describes a rocket being launched from Earth. When a rocket is launched, large amounts of hot gas are shot out from the bottom of the rocket. When the gases push the air molecules behind them, there is an equal and opposite reaction force that pushes back on the rocket and causes it to move. Choice C could be the answer.

Choice D has to do with an astronaut jumping higher on the Moon due to the Moon's lower gravity. In this case, the Moon exerts a gravitational force on the astronaut, which pulls the astronaut toward the Moon. The reaction force exerted by the astronaut does not cause the Moon to move, so Choice D can be eliminated.

Choice C is the best answer because it is the only situation in which a reaction force causes something to move.

UNBALANCED FORCES AND SPEED AND VELOCITY

A **force** can cause an object to move and accelerate. **Newton's first law** of motion states that an object will not change its motion unless acted on by an unbalanced force. When forces of the same strength or magnitude are applied to the same object in opposite directions, they cancel out, resulting in a **balanced force**. When two people of the same size and strength pull on either end of a tug-of-war rope with the same force, this results in a balanced force, and neither the rope nor the people will move. An **unbalanced force** is one that is not fully canceled out by an opposing force. For example, if there are two people pulling on one end of the rope and only one person pulling on the other, the two people would most likely exert a stronger pulling force than the person pulling alone. In this example, the rope would move in the direction of the stronger force because the direction of motion is always the same as the direction of the unbalanced force.

EXAMPLE

A group of students in P.E. play tug-o-war. The group of students on the left side pulls with a force of 250 Newtons (N), while the group on the right pulls with a force of 200 Newtons. Which of the following accurately describes the size and direction of the net force?

a. 50 Newtons to the left
b. 50 Newtons to the right
c. 450 Newtons to the left
d. 450 Newtons to the right

Choice A: 50 Newtons to the left. The net force is the force left over when multiple forces are acting on an object and one force is bigger than the other. In this case, the group on the left side pulls the rope with more force (250 N) than the group on the right (200 N). To calculate net force, you can subtract the smaller force from the bigger force, resulting in a net force of 50 Newtons. The direction of the net force is the same as the direction of the bigger force. In this case, the direction of the net force is to the left. Thus, the net force is 50 Newtons to the left, making this answer correct.

Choice B: 50 Newtons to the right. This answer has the correct net force, 50 N, because the 200 N to the right cancels out part of the 250 N force to the left. However, the direction of the net force should be in the same direction as the larger force, which is to the left in this case. This answer is incorrect.

Choice C: 450 Newtons to the left. To calculate net force, it is important to keep in mind the direction of the forces at play. In this case, because the forces are in opposite directions, they partially cancel out and we can subtract one from the other. Forces are only added together if they are applied in the same direction, such as two people pushing an object together. This answer is incorrect.

Choice D: 450 Newtons to the right. This answer is incorrect because the size of the force should be 50, not 450. The direction is also incorrect because it should be in the direction of the larger force.

Choice A is the correct answer.

Speed and Velocity

Speed is a scalar quantity. That is, it has a **magnitude** but the **direction** does not matter. The formula for speed is the distance traveled within a certain amount of time. Velocity is a **vector quantity,** which means it has both magnitude and **direction**. For example, if you drive your car at a constant 70 kilometers per hour in any direction, you will be traveling at the **same speed**. Even if you drive around a curve and change your direction of travel, you are still traveling at the same speed as long as the car remains at 70 km/h. However, if you change your direction of travel, you have changed your velocity. **Velocity** is a specified speed in a specified direction. When you go around a corner in your car, even though you maintain the same speed, you have changed velocity because the direction has changed. Any change in velocity, such as a change in speed, direction, or both, constitutes acceleration and requires that a net unbalanced force act upon the moving system.

Calculating Speed

Speed measures the distance an object moves in a certain amount of time. For instance, if a car is moving at a speed of 65 miles per hour, then that car will travel 65 miles in one hour. To calculate average speed, you can divide the total distance traveled over the time that has passed: **speed = distance / time**. For example, consider the speed of a runner who runs an 800-meter race in 2 minutes. To calculate the runner's average speed, use the following formula:

$$\text{speed} = \text{distance} / \text{time}$$

$$800 \text{ meters} / 2 \text{ minutes}$$

$$400 \text{ m/min}$$

When dividing two different units, such as meters and minutes, the units of the answer calculated will reflect the original units of the numerator and denominator. Example units for speed include miles per hour (mi/hr or mph), kilometers per hour (km/hr or km/h), or meters per second (m/s).

Acceleration

Acceleration is the **change in the velocity** of an object. Acceleration will be expressed in units of distance divided by time squared; for instance, meters per second squared. Like position and velocity, acceleration is a vector quantity and will therefore have both magnitude and direction.

Graphing Changes in Motion

A **velocity graph** shows how an object or being's **velocity** changes over the course of a certain time period. Scientists obtain this data by measuring velocity at specific intervals, such as once every minute. When an object is speeding up, or **accelerating**, its velocity is increasing. On a graph, an object that is speeding up is represented by a line with an upward or positive slope. In contrast, an object that is slowing down, or **decelerating,** is represented by a line with a downward or negative slope. When an object is moving at a constant speed, its velocity is not changing. This is represented by a flat or horizontal line on the graph. Lastly, an object that is not moving will have a velocity of zero, which is represented on the graph as a flat line at the horizontal axis, or zero.

Energy

Performing work or moving an object is a function of **energy**. The **law of conservation of energy** states that energy cannot be created or destroyed. Energy can only be changed to another form. Therefore, energy is always part of a pattern, cycle, or system. Two common forms of energy are potential energy and kinetic energy. **Potential energy** is energy that is **stored** in matter. If an object or organism moves or is moved, its potential energy will become kinetic energy. **Kinetic energy** is the energy of **motion**. Therefore, energy used during movement is always kinetic energy. A change from one type of energy to another is called a **conversion**.

Kinetic Energy

The **kinetic energy of an object** is that quality of its motion that can be related in a qualitative way to the amount of work performed on the object. Kinetic energy can be defined as $KE = mv^2/2$, in which m is the mass of an object and v is the magnitude of its velocity. Kinetic energy cannot be negative, since it depends on the square of velocity. Changes in kinetic energy occur when a force does work on an object, such that the speed of the object is altered.

Potential Energy

Potential energy is based on position. There are a couple of different kinds of potential energy. **Gravitational potential energy** is the energy associated with the separation of bodies that are attracted to one another by gravity. Any time you lift an object, you are increasing its gravitational potential energy. Another kind of potential energy is **elastic potential energy**; elastic potential energy is associated with the compression or expansion of an elastic, or spring-like, object. **Chemical potential energy** is associated with the chemical bonds and intermolecular forces of the matter contained in the system. Physicists will often refer to potential energy as being **stored** within a body, which implies that the energy may be used or converted later.

Review Video: Potential and Kinetic Energy
Visit mometrix.com/academy and enter code: 491502

Mechanical Energy

Mechanical energy is the term for the total potential and kinetic energy of an object. Another way to say that is with the equation:

$$mechanical\ energy = potential\ energy + kinetic\ energy$$

Mechanical energy can be increased by increasing either the potential energy, the kinetic energy, or both. For example, lifting a block or squishing a spring increases potential energy. In contrast, throwing a ball or swinging a hammer increases kinetic energy. In each of those examples, mechanical energy is increased.

Thermal Energy

Thermal energy is energy that is produced when particles move and give off **heat**. The Sun is the main source of the thermal energy on Earth. Fire is another natural source of thermal energy. Many devices, such as hair dryers, can also produce thermal energy using parts that are designed to heat up when they are powered using electrical energy.

Electrical Energy

Electrical energy is energy that is produced when **electrons** or **electric charges** move from one place to another. Items that need **electricity**, such as lights and household appliances, use electrical energy.

Light and Sound Energy

Light travels in waves, and the light visible to humans is an example of **light energy**. Most of the light energy on Earth comes from sunlight or bulbs powered by electricity.

Sound energy is caused by **vibrations**. When something moves or has an electrical current moving through it, it will vibrate. This creates waves that move through the space around the object that is vibrating, and sound energy is generated as those waves move. The way the vibration sounds depends on characteristics of the wave. Machines such as alarm clocks or radios include parts that are designed to produce sound waves.

Examples of Energy Conversions

The **law of conservation of energy** states that energy cannot be created nor destroyed; it can only be **converted,** or transformed from one form to another. In fact, many everyday actions require energy conversions. For example, batteries contain **chemical energy** in the form of charged materials. When you switch on a flashlight, it completes an electrical circuit, which converts the chemical energy from the battery into **electrical energy.** Then, the bulb on the flashlight converts this electrical energy into **light,** a form of **electromagnetic energy.** The human body also uses chemical energy by processing food to produce **mechanical energy** that can be used to move the muscles. Plugging in a space heater converts **electrical energy** into **thermal energy** or heat. Another example of energy conversion is a falling object. At its peak, an object has **gravitational potential energy**, or the potential to fall and gain speed. When an object is dropped, gravitational potential energy is converted into **kinetic energy**, the energy of motion. In some cases, it may seem like energy is being lost or destroyed, such as when a skateboarder slows down to a stop. However, in this case, the kinetic energy is instead being converted into thermal energy as a result of **friction**.

Types of Waves and their Characteristics

Transverse and Longitudinal Waves

Transverse waves have oscillations that are **perpendicular** to the direction of motion. A light wave is an example of a transverse wave. A group of light waves traveling in the same direction will be oscillating in several different planes. Light waves are said to be polarized when they are filtered such that only waves oscillating in a particular plane are allowed to pass, with the remainder being absorbed by the filter. If two such polarizing filters are employed successively and aligned to allow different planes of oscillation, they will block all light waves.

Longitudinal waves are waves that oscillate in the **same direction** as their primary motion. Their motion is restricted to a single axis, so they may not be polarized. A sound wave is an example of a longitudinal wave.

Velocity, Amplitude, Wavelength, and Frequency

The **velocity of a wave**, v, is the rate at which it travels in a given medium. It is defined in the same way that velocity of physical objects is defined, a change in position divided by a change in time. A single wave may have a different velocity for every medium in which it travels. Some types of waves, such as light waves, do not require a medium.

Amplitude, A, is one measure of a wave's strength. It is half the verticle distance between the highest and lowest points on the wave, the crest and trough, respectively. The vertical midpoint, halfway between the crest and trough, is sometimes called an equilibrium point, or a node.

The **wavelength**, λ, is the horizontal distance between successive crests or troughs, or the distance between the first and third of three successive nodes.

Frequency, f, is the number of crests or troughs that pass a particular point in a given period of time. It is the inverse of the period, the time required for the wave to cycle from one crest or trough to the next. Frequency is generally measured in hertz, or cycles per second.

Velocity, wavelength, and frequency are not independent quantities. They are related by the expression $v = \lambda f$. Note that amplitude, however, is independent from these quantities.

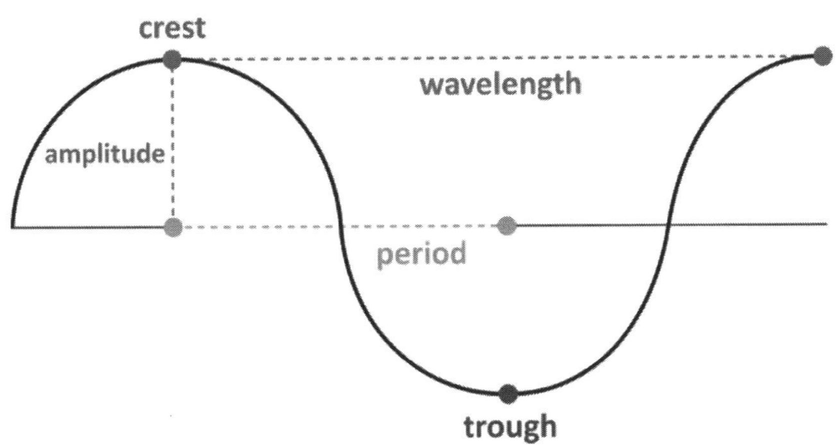

Electromagnetic Spectrum

Electromagnetic radiation is a form of energy that travels in waves. The **electromagnetic spectrum** is the range of all wavelengths and frequencies of known electromagnetic waves. Visible light occupies only a small portion of the electromagnetic spectrum. Some of the common classifications of electromagnetic waves are listed in the table below with their approximate frequency ranges.

Classification	Freq. (Hz)
Gamma Rays	$\sim 10^{19}$
X-Rays	$\sim 10^{17} - 10^{18}$
Ultraviolet	$\sim 10^{15} - 10^{16}$
Visible Light	$\sim 10^{14}$
Infra-red	$\sim 10^{11} - 10^{14}$
Microwaves	$\sim 10^{10} - 10^{11}$
Radio/TV	$\sim 10^{6} - 10^{9}$

Types of Electromagnetic Waves

- **Gamma rays** have the smallest wavelength, highest frequency, and highest energy of any type of electromagnetic radiation. Because of their small size, they can easily penetrate human skin, bones, and organs and alter DNA, making them more dangerous than other types of electromagnetic radiation. Gamma rays are produced by supernova explosions and anything traditionally known as "radioactive," such as uranium.
- **X-rays** have the second smallest wavelength, second highest frequency, and second highest amount of energy. They are used for medical imaging such as taking pictures to look at a broken bone, and they naturally occur when electrons move within an atom. X-rays can be dangerous in large amounts.
- **Ultraviolet radiation** is characterized by wavelengths larger than those of x-rays and gamma rays but smaller than those of visible light and all the other categories of electromagnetic radiation. This means that it has the third highest frequency and third highest amount of energy. Its frequency and energy can be categorized as moderate. Some species can see certain frequencies of ultraviolet light. Ultraviolet radiation most often comes from sunlight and can cause skin damage.
- **Visible light** possesses a range of moderate wavelengths, frequency, and energy levels. It falls right in the middle of the six other types of radiation. The visible light spectrum comprises approximately seven colors, with violet light having the shortest wavelength and highest frequency and red light having the longest wavelength and lowest frequency of the seven colors.
- **Infrared** waves have a larger wavelength and lower frequency than visible light and cannot be detected by human eyes. Infrared radiation is naturally produced by the Sun and by fire and causes objects it interacts with to heat up. Infrared radiation is used in thermal imaging and night vision technology.

- **Microwaves** have the second largest wavelength and the second lowest frequency and amount of energy. They are too large and lacking in energy to cause damage to human cells and have many uses, including microwave cooking.
- **Radio waves** have the largest wavelength on the spectrum along with the lowest frequency and energy. They are useful for transmitting information over large distances.

Review Video: Light
Visit mometrix.com/academy and enter code: 900556

Using Electromagnetic Waves to Learn About the Universe

While the naked eye can only detect electromagnetic waves in the visible light spectrum, scientists can use equipment such as various types of **telescopes** to detect other frequencies of radiation and gain new information about the universe. For example, **radio telescopes** detect radio waves emitted from objects in space. They are especially useful because they can be used during the day and cloudy weather, unlike telescopes that rely on visible light. **Infrared telescopes** detect infrared radiation and are useful in detecting objects that cannot be seen by the human eye, such as those with low luminosity. **Ultraviolet telescopes** observe the universe from outside Earth's atmosphere and are useful for determining what planets and other celestial bodies are made of. **X-ray telescopes** have a unique structure and have been used to estimate the mass of some stars and detect other bodies in space. **Gamma ray telescopes** are similar to x-ray telescopes and detect unique objects like black holes.

Other Applications of Electromagnetic Waves

Radiation therapy uses high-energy waves, like gamma rays and X-rays, to treat cancer patients. A machine targets the areas of the body where cancer is present, using these waves to shrink tumors and kill cancer cells by damaging the DNA in the cells. Wireless technology is technology that enables communication without the use of wires, like Wi-Fi and Bluetooth. Both Wi-Fi and Bluetooth technologies involve transferring data and communicating between devices using radio waves. Fiber optics are thin plastic or glass fibers that transmit signals from computers, televisions, and machines by converting them into infrared light pulses. This kind of data transfer includes sound, picture, or codes and is very reliable even over long distances. Ultraviolet (UV) light is on the ultraviolet end of the electromagnetic wave spectrum, meaning that humans cannot see it. Ultraviolet light is used in the sterilization of water, air, medical supplies, and surfaces because DNA absorbs it. After exposure to UV light, any microorganisms, like bacteria, fungi, and viruses, are inactive.

Chapter Quiz

1. According to Newton's Second Law of Motion, the amount of acceleration is determined by the amount of:

a. Work performed and energy within the object being moved
b. Energy and the time/duration of applied energy
c. Pressure and the distance that the object moves
d. Force and the mass of the object being moved

2. All of the following are vector quantities and will therefore have both magnitude and direction, EXCEPT for:

a. Position
b. Acceleration
c. Velocity
d. Speed

3. Which of the following is NOT true of potential energy?

a. Potential energy is the energy of motion.
b. Potential energy is based on position.
c. Potential energy is energy that is stored in matter.
d. Potential energy can be gravitational or elastic.

4. What type of electromagnetic wave has the smallest wavelength, highest frequency, and highest energy?

a. Microwaves
b. Infrared
c. Ultraviolet light
d. Gamma rays

Chapter Quiz Answer Key

1. D: See section **Motion and Force**

2. D: See section **Speed and Velocity**

3. A: See section **Energy**

4. D: See section **Types of Electromagnetic Waves**

Earth and Space

Sun

The **Sun** is the vital force of life on Earth. It is also the central component of our solar system. It is basically a sphere of extremely hot gases (close to 15 million degrees at the core) held together by gravity. Some of these gaseous molecules are ionized due to the high temperatures. The balance between its gravitational force and the pressure produced by the hot gases is called **hydrostatic equilibrium**. The source of the solar energy that keeps the Sun alive and plays a key role in the perpetuation of life on Earth is located in the Sun's core, where nucleosynthesis produces heat energy and photons. The Sun's atmosphere consists of the photosphere, the surface visible from Earth, the chromosphere, a layer outside of and hotter than the photosphere, the transition zone (the region where temperatures rise between the chromosphere and the corona), and the corona, which is best viewed at x-ray wavelengths. A solar flare is an explosive emission of ionized particles from the Sun's surface.

Position of the Sun

The Sun, which is at the center of our solar system and is the closest star to Earth, is a medium-sized, main sequence star orbited by eight main planets along with several dwarf planets. The solar system is positioned within the spiral-shaped Milky Way galaxy and located on one of the outer arms of the galaxy's spiral shape. Earth is the third planet from the Sun and is approximately 93 million miles away from it. In comparison, the second closest star to Earth is Proxima Centauri, at about 25 trillion miles or 40 trillion kilometers away from Earth. It is over 250,000 times farther away from Earth than the Sun is.

Review Video: The Sun
Visit mometrix.com/academy and enter code: 699233

Earth's Rotation

The **Earth rotates** west to east about its axis, an imaginary straight line that runs nearly vertically through the center of the planet. This rotation (which takes 23 hours, 56 minutes, and 5 seconds) places each section of the Earth's surface in a position facing the Sun for a period of time, thus creating the alternating periods of light and darkness we experience as **day and night**. This rotation constitutes a sidereal day; it is measured as the amount of time required for a reference star to cross the meridian (an imaginary north-south line above an observer). Each star crosses the meridian once every (sidereal) day. Since the speed at which Earth rotates is not exactly constant, we use the mean solar day (a 24-hour period) in timekeeping rather than the slightly variable sidereal day.

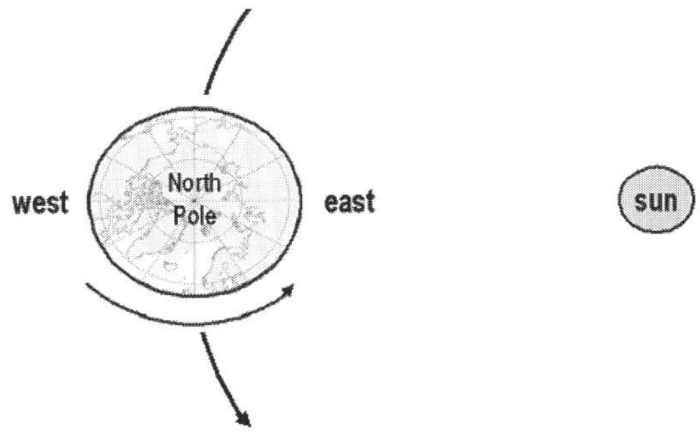

Earth's Revolution Around the Sun

Like all celestial objects in our solar system, planet **Earth** revolves around the **Sun**. This process takes approximately 365 1/4 days, the period of time that constitutes a calendar year. The path of the orbit of Earth around the Sun is not circular but **elliptical**. Therefore, the distances between the Earth and the Sun at points on either extreme of this counterclockwise orbit are not equal. In other words, the distance between the two objects varies over the course of a year. At **perihelion**, the minimum heliocentric distance, Earth is 147 million kilometers from the Sun. At **aphelion**, the maximum heliocentric distance, Earth is 152 million kilometers from the Sun. This movement of the Earth is responsible for the apparent annual motions of the Sun (in a path referred to as the ecliptic) and other celestial objects visible from Earth's surface.

Earth's Tilt and Seasons

The orbital path the Earth follows around the Sun helps create the **seasons**: winter, spring, summer, and fall. Earth is closest to the Sun in January and farthest in July. However, there is also a tilt to the Earth's axis. During July, the Northern Hemisphere is tilted towards the Sun. This causes the light and heat the Sun gives off to reach the Northern Hemisphere at a more direct angle. This is why July has hotter temperatures than January in the Northern Hemisphere, even though Earth is farthest away from the Sun during that time. These conditions are the opposite in the Southern Hemisphere, as the region's hottest temperatures occur in January. The Earth's tilt and orbit also affect the number of daylight hours a region experiences at different times, as people in the Northern Hemisphere experience longer days and summertime in July, and people in the Southern Hemisphere experience shorter days and winter in July.

Review Video: Earth's Tilt and Seasons
Visit mometrix.com/academy and enter code: 602892

Example

A disappointed traveler from the United States visits Australia in July, only to discover that it is wintertime. Which of the following correctly explains this phenomenon?

a. As Earth rotates, part of the Earth is facing away from the Sun.
b. Earth's orbit is not a perfect circle, causing it to be farther away from the Sun at certain times of the year.
c. Earth is tilted on its axis, resulting in part of the Earth getting more direct sunlight.
d. The Earth's magnetic field causes the Northern and Southern Hemispheres to have opposite seasons.

Choice A has to do with the rotation of the Earth. Earth rotates on its axis once every 24 hours, resulting in day and night, not seasons.

The part of the Earth facing away from the Sun is experiencing nighttime, not necessarily winter. Choice A is incorrect.

Choice B has to do with Earth's elliptical orbit, which resembles a squished circle in which the Sun is slightly offset. While it is true that the Earth is farther away from the Sun at certain times of the year, the effects on temperature are relatively minuscule and do not explain seasons. Choice B is not the answer.

Choice C has to do with Earth's tilt on its axis. Because Earth is tilted at 23.5°, one hemisphere is tilted more toward the Sun and receives more direct sunlight, resulting in summer. When the Earth reaches the other side of its orbit, the opposite hemisphere experiences summer and the hemisphere tilted away from the Sun experiences winter.

This explains seasons as well as the fact that the Southern Hemisphere, where Australia is located, experiences opposite seasons to the Northern Hemisphere. Choice C is the correct answer.

Choice D has to do with the Earth's magnetic field, which protects the Earth from cosmic rays and solar winds by deflecting them away from the planet. The Earth's magnetic poles have nothing to do with seasons. Choice D is incorrect.

Choice C is the correct answer because Earth's seasons are a result of the 23.5° axis tilt, which also explains the differences in seasons between the Northern and Southern Hemispheres that caused the traveler's disappointment.

Moon

Earth's Moon is historically one of the most studied celestial bodies. Its mass is approximately 1.2% of the Earth's mass, and its radius is just over one-fourth of the size of the Earth's radius. Measurements of the Moon's density suggest that its characteristics are similar to those of the rocks that make up Earth's crust. The **landscape** of the Moon consists mostly of mountains and craters formed by collisions of this surface with meteors and other interplanetary materials. The Moon's crust (estimated to be 50 to 100 kilometers in thickness) is made up of a layer of regolith (lunar soil) supported by a layer of loose rocks and gravel. Beneath the crust is a mantle made up of a solid lithosphere and a semiliquid asthenosphere. The Moon's **core** (the innermost 500 kilometers of the body) is not as dense as that of the Earth. The Moon is made up mostly of refractory elements with high melting and boiling points with low levels of heavy elements such as iron.

Phases of the Moon

The light of the Moon is a reflection of sunlight that reaches the Moon. As the moon revolves around Earth approximately every 27.3 days, light from the Sun hits it from different angles. The Moon is always orbiting Earth, and as Earth and the Moon both move throughout their orbits, sunlight reaches different areas of the Moon. A **moon phase** describes the appearance of the Moon. Moon phases depend on the position of the Moon, Earth, and Sun.

A **new moon** occurs when the Moon is between the Sun and Earth. During this phase, the Moon is not visible because the Sun is illuminating the side of the Moon that is facing away from Earth. When any sunlight reaches the side of the Moon that is facing Earth, the appearance of the Moon will depend on its phase. For example, following a new moon, the right edge of the visible side of the Moon will look like a crescent. This phase is called a **waxing crescent**. During the next phase, the **first quarter**, the right half of the visible side of the moon will be lit up in a half-circle shape. Following that phase, the moon will then appear to be in an oval shape during its **waxing gibbous** phase. After that phase is the **full moon**, where the moon appears as a bright, white circle. Then, the Moon returns to a new moon as it goes through these phases in the opposite order and direction. These phases are known as the **waning gibbous**, **third quarter**, and **waning crescent** phases.

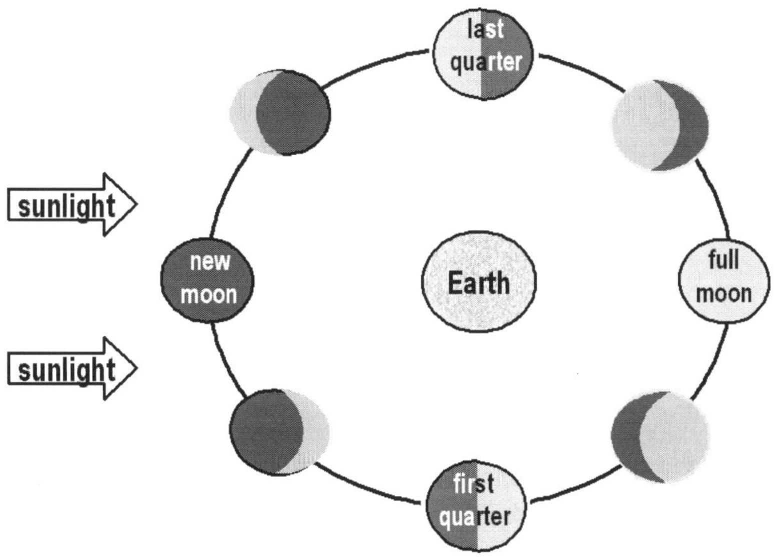

EXAMPLE

A group of students uses a calendar to keep track of the Moon's phase each night for a month. Their moon calendar so far shows the following sequence: new moon, waxing crescent, first quarter. Which moon phase can they expect to come next in the sequence?

a. Full moon
b. New moon
c. Waning gibbous
d. Waxing gibbous

Choice A: full moon. The most recent phase in the sequence is a first quarter moon, meaning the Moon appears half-illuminated in the sky. Therefore, the next phase should be more than half-illuminated but less than fully illuminated. Choice A can be eliminated.

Choice B: new moon. The first phase in the sequence is a new moon. Since the Moon has not completed a whole lunar cycle, there will not be another new moon until it does. Choice B is not the correct answer.

Choice C: waning gibbous. A gibbous is between half-illuminated and fully illuminated. A waning gibbous happens after a full moon as the illuminated portion of the moon gets smaller, so choice C is not the correct answer.

Choice D: waxing gibbous. A waxing gibbous means the illuminated moon is growing, which happens between a first quarter moon and a full moon. Choice D is the correct answer.

Choice D, waxing gibbous, is the correct answer because it follows a first quarter in the lunar sequence.

Eclipse

An **eclipse** occurs when either the Moon or Earth blocks the light from the Sun. Types of eclipses include solar eclipses and lunar eclipses. A **solar eclipse** is when the Moon is directly in between the Sun and Earth in a straight or nearly straight line. This is very similar to a new moon, but what makes it different is that the Moon is at a specific location between Earth and the Sun. In addition, instead of the Moon appearing to be gone, the moon is outlined with sunlight. A **lunar eclipse** is when Earth is directly in between the Sun and the Moon, in a straight or nearly straight line. Just as a solar eclipse is similar to a new moon, a lunar eclipse is similar to a full moon and occurs when the Moon is at a specific location on the opposite side of Earth as the Sun. During a lunar eclipse, the Moon will still appear as a full circle, but it will appear dim and red instead of bright and white.

Review Video: Moon
Visit mometrix.com/academy and enter code: 880415

Influence of the Sun and Moon on Tides

The relative positions of the Sun, Moon, and Earth influence the large-scale motions of Earth's oceans, and these motions make up **tides**. While the Sun has a much larger mass than the Moon, and therefore a larger gravitational pull, the Moon has a stronger impact on tides because it is closer to Earth than the Sun. As the Moon orbits around the Earth, it is always exerting a gravitational pull on the Earth's surface. This gravitational pull is strongest on the side of Earth that is closest to the Moon, and it pulls the oceans upward, creating a **high tide**. On the opposite side of Earth, this effect is also occurring, so there is a high tide there as well. The oceans on both sides are bulging upward. Between these areas, the ocean water levels are lower, and at their lowest, they create the **low tides**.

Earth rotates on its axis every 24 hours, so as it rotates, the areas experiencing high and low tides will change. The Sun's gravitational pull also influences the tides. When the Moon aligns with the Sun in its orbit, the gravitational forces of the Sun and the Moon have an additive effect, resulting in even higher high tides. Thus, full moon and new moon positions result in the highest high tides. Conversely, when the Moon is in first quarter and last quarter positions, the gravitational pulls of the Sun and Moon partially cancel out, causing lower high tides than other positions.

Solar System

The solar system consists of the Sun and eight **planets**. In order from the Sun, the planets are Mercury, Venus, Earth, Mars, Jupiter, Saturn, Uranus and Neptune. Six of the planets have one or more **moons**. The solar system also contains countless **meteoroids**, **asteroids,** and **comets.**

THE EFFECT OF GRAVITY IN OUR SOLAR SYSTEM

Gravity is an attractive force that impacts the motion of the bodies in our solar system. The Sun at the center of our solar system has a mass that is more than 300,000 times the mass of Earth. Due to the Sun's large mass, it exerts a strong gravitational field on nearby planets, causing them to orbit around the Sun. In order to stay in orbit, a planet must have enough **speed** to keep moving. As it moves, the Sun's gravity pulls the planet inward like an invisible leash, resulting in a circular or elliptical orbit. Gravity is also responsible for the orbit of a planet's moons, including Earth's Moon. Although Earth's mass is much smaller than the Sun, the gravitational force from the Earth holds the Moon in orbit. This happens because gravity depends on both distance and mass, and the Moon is close enough to Earth to be affected more strongly by Earth's gravity than that of the Sun.

Review Video: Astronomy
Visit mometrix.com/academy and enter code: 640556

Review Video: The Solar System
Visit mometrix.com/academy and enter code: 273231

Milky Way

On a clear dark moonless night far from city lights a broad white band of stars that stretches across the sky can be seen. This is the Milky Way galaxy, and our sun and the solar system are part of it. The Milky Way is a huge flat disk containing between 200 billion and 400 billion stars. Because Earth is in that disk, we see it edge on, which is why it appears to us as a broad band of light.

The Milky Way is a flat, disk-shaped spiral galaxy with a central bar-like bulge of stars. It is huge—between 100,000 and 120,000 light-years in diameter. A light-year is a unit of distance, not time. It is the distance light travels in one year, about 6 trillion miles. The Milky Way is between 600 thousand trillion and 700 thousand trillion miles across. Our solar system lies about two thirds of the way out on one of the spiral arms.

Components of the Universe

The universe is made up of many types of celestial objects, including stars, planets, nebulae, and galaxies, among others.

- **Stars** are giant balls of plasma that are mostly composed of helium and hydrogen. Stars have very large masses and extremely high temperatures, ranging from approximately 2,000 to 50,000 °C. There are different types of stars, and a star's type is based upon its mass, age, size, color, luminosity, and temperature.
- **Planets** are self-contained, spherical bodies that are shaped by their own gravitational force. Most planets rotate on their own axis and orbit a star. Planets can be made up of rocky material, gases, or different types of ice. They have much smaller masses and lower temperatures than stars.
- **Nebulae** are gigantic clouds of gas and dust where new stars are often born. They come in a range of shapes and sizes and are bigger than stars but smaller than galaxies. They are more diffuse and much less dense than stars and planets.

- **Galaxies** are vast systems of stars, planets, and nebulae held together by gravity. Planetary systems, consisting of planets orbiting stars, are positioned within larger galaxies such as the Milky Way, which is where our planetary system, the solar system, resides. Many galaxies have a spiral shape, but there are other shapes, such as elliptical and irregular.

Structures of Galaxies

Elliptical galaxies are roughly spherical. Within this category, subgroups based on the degree of flattening exhibited in the galaxy's shape range from E0 (spherical) to E7 (flat). A dwarf elliptical galaxy has a spheroidal shape, with low mass and low luminosity. An S0 galaxy is similar in shape to a spiral galaxy, but lacks spiral arms. **Spiral galaxies** such as the Milky Way are characterized by disk-like nuclei with spiral arms. Subtypes of this category are determined by the tightness of the spiral arms and the size of the nucleus; a spiral galaxy of Sa type has a large nucleus and tightly wound arms, and an Sc-type galaxy consists of a small nucleus with open spiral arms. A barred spiral galaxy exhibits an elongated nucleus. The subtypes of barred spiral galaxies are determined like those of spiral galaxies. Some **irregular galaxies** (type I) display a loose spiral structure with high levels of disorganization. Other irregular galaxies (type II) can be of any shape.

Review Video: Galaxies
Visit mometrix.com/academy and enter code: 226539

Example

Which of the following best explains the relationship between stars and nebulae?

a. Nebulae are clouds of dust and gas where new stars are formed.
b. Nebulae are the remnants of dying stars that eventually become galaxies.
c. Nebulae are the outer cloud of young stars where planets are formed.
d. Nebulae are the remnants of stars that have collided with one another.

Choice A states that nebulae are giant clouds of dust and gas in space where new stars can be formed. Nebulae are sometimes referred to as stellar nurseries because the density of dust and gas can lead to the formation of the new stars. Choice A could be the answer.

Choice B states that nebulae form from dying stars and eventually become galaxies. While the dust and gas that make up nebulae sometimes come from dying stars, they do not turn into galaxies, which are ginormous and complex structures. Choice B is incorrect.

Choice C states that a nebula is the outer cloud of a young star where planets are formed. While it is true that planets are formed in the outer part of young stars, this outer disk is part of the forming star and not a nebula. Choice C is incorrect.

Choice D states that nebulae are the remnants of stars that have collided with one another. While stars do occasionally collide with one another, this does not result in a nebula. Choice D is not the answer.

Choice B is the correct answer because it accurately describes the relationship between nebulae and stars: nebulae are clouds of dust and gas where new stars are formed.

Theories Relating to the Origin of the Universe

Model of the Inflationary Universe

Hubble's law states that the speed at which a galaxy appears to be moving away from the Earth is proportional to its distance from Earth. This relatively simple formula ($v = Hr$, where v is the **velocity of a receding galaxy**, r is its distance from Earth, and H is the Hubble constant) had an important implication at the time that it was developed—the universe is expanding. This fact, in turn, implies that the universe began at a **specific point** in the past. This model suggests that a random conglomeration of quarks and leptons, along with the strong force (all the forces in the universe unified as one), existed in the very dense, very hot, early universe. When the universe was a certain age (about 10–35 seconds old), the strong force separated out from the mass. This enabled the rapid expansion of the particles that formed the universe.

Big Bang Theory

The **theory of the big bang** expands upon the model of the **inflationary universe**. This theory hypothesizes that the early universe consisted of elementary particles, high energy density and high levels of pressure and heat. This single mass experienced a **phase change** (similar to that of freezing water) when it cooled and expanded. This transition caused the early universe to expand exponentially; this period of growth is called **cosmic inflation**. As it continued to grow, the temperature continued to fall. At some point, **baryogenesis** (an unknown process in which quarks and gluons become baryons, such as protons and neutrons) occurred, somehow creating the distinction between matter and antimatter. As the universe continued to cool, the **elementary forces** reached their present form, and **elementary particles** engaged in big bang **nucleosynthesis** (a process that produced helium and deuterium nuclei). **Gravity** became the predominant force governing interactions between particles; this enabled increasing accretion of particles of matter, which eventually formed the universal constituents as we recognize them today.

Stars

Sizes of Stars

Stars come in a large variety of sizes. They can be the size of a large town or larger than the Sun. The largest stars are called **supergiant** stars, and can be 1,500 times larger than the Sun. The smallest stars are called **red dwarf** stars. The Sun is considered a medium-sized star. The size of a star can be affected by the gravitational pull acting on the star and the star's radiation. As energy is released from the center of the star, the star will grow. However, gravity from the center of the star pulls against that growth and can shrink or limit the star's size. The mass and density of the star will also generally influence its size. From Earth, scientists can determine the size of a star by the star's **luminosity**, which is the total energy a star can radiate in one second, and its **temperature**. The **Hertzsprung-Russell Diagram** was created to compare stars based on these characteristics. Stars with higher temperature and luminosity are larger in size, while stars with lower temperature and lower luminosity are smaller in size.

Brightness of Stars

The brightness of a star when viewed from Earth is its **apparent brightness**. The difference in apparent brightness among stars can be affected by two factors: the distance from the star to Earth and the amount of light put out by the star. Two stars can put out the same amount of light, but from Earth, one may appear to be dimmer than the other. That is because the one that looks dimmer is further away from Earth. The closest star to the Earth is the Sun, which is why it appears to be the brightest of all the stars from Earth. Some stars are so far away that they cannot be seen from Earth, and they may only be discovered and identified by studying the motion of other stars or planets around them. The brightness of a star will vary throughout its life cycle. The more energy a star produces, the more light it will give off. Sometimes the energy produced by a star becomes greater than the gravitational pull on the star. This causes the star to explode and create a supernova, which will shine very brightly for many days.

Hertzsprung-Russell Diagram

The **Hertzsprung-Russell (H-R) diagram** was developed to explore the relationships between the luminosities and spectral qualities of stars. This diagram involves plotting these qualities on a graph, with absolute magnitude (luminosity) on the vertical and spectral class on the horizontal. Plotting a number of stars on the H-R diagram demonstrates that stars fall into narrowly defined regions, which correspond to stages in stellar evolution. Most stars are situated in a diagonal strip that runs from the top-left (high temperature, high luminosity) to the lower-right (low temperature, low luminosity). This diagonal line shows stars in the **main sequence** of star evolution. Stars that fall above this line on the diagram (low temperature, high luminosity) are believed to be much larger than the stars on the main sequence (because their high luminosities are not due to higher temperatures than main sequence stars). They are termed **giants** and **supergiants**. Stars below the main sequence (high temperature, low luminosity) are called **white dwarfs**. The H-R diagram is useful in calculating distances to stars.

Types of Stars

Stars are categorized by several characteristics, including temperature, mass, age, size, and **luminosity**, or brightness. Different types of stars form due to processes that depend on the mass and age of a star.

- **Main sequence stars** are the most abundant type in the galaxy and are characterized by the fusion of hydrogen atoms into helium atoms that occurs in their cores. They range in size, temperature, and luminosity. The Sun at the center of our solar system sits in the middle of the range, possessing average characteristics for a main sequence star.
- **Giant stars** form when main sequence stars run out of fusible hydrogen in their core. They are characterized by their larger size and higher luminosity. On average, giant stars have lower temperatures than main sequence stars.
- **White dwarf** stars are later life-cycle stars that form after giant stars run out of energy. Giant stars shed their outer layers, which become planetary nebulae, and the small, dense core that remains is the white dwarf, with high temperatures and low luminosity.
- **Supergiant stars** have similar characteristics to giant stars, but even larger masses and higher luminosity. They are formed when larger-than-average main sequence stars run out of hydrogen in their core. They tend to become supernovas, followed by neutron stars or black holes.

Stellar Evolution

The life cycle of a star is closely related to its **mass**—low-mass stars become white dwarfs, while high-mass stars become **supernovae**. A star is born when a **protostar** is formed from a **collapsing interstellar cloud**. The temperature at the center of the protostar rises, allowing nucleosynthesis to begin. **Nucleosynthesis**, or hydrogen-burning through fusion, entails a release of energy. Eventually, the star runs out of fuel (hydrogen). If the star is relatively low mass, the disruption of hydrostatic equilibrium allows the star to contract due to gravity. This raises the temperature just outside the core to a point at which nucleosynthesis and a different kind of fusion (with helium as fuel) that produces a carbon nucleus can occur. The star swells with greater energy, becoming a red giant. Once this phase is over, gravity becomes active again, shrinking the star until the degeneracy pressure of electrons begins to operate, creating a white dwarf that will eventually burn out. If the star has a high mass, the depletion of hydrogen creates a supernova.

Supernova

When a star on the main sequence runs out of hydrogen fuel, it begins to burn helium (the by-product of nucleosynthesis). Once helium-burning is complete in a massive star, the mass causes the core temperature to rise, enabling the fusion of carbon, then silicon, and a succession of other atomic nuclei, each of which takes place in a new shell further out of the core. When the fusion cycle reaches iron (which cannot serve as fuel for a nuclear reaction), an iron core begins to form, which accumulates over time. Eventually, the temperature and pressure in the core become high enough for electrons to interact with protons in the iron nuclei to produce neutrons. In a matter of moments, this reaction is complete. The core falls and collides with the star's outer envelope, causing a massive explosion (a supernova). This continues until the neutrons exert degeneracy pressure; this creates a pulsar. In more massive stars, nothing can stop the collapse, which ends in the creation of a black hole.

Plate Tectonics

Main Concepts

Plate tectonics is a geological theory that was developed to explain the process of continental drift. The theoretical separation of the Earth's lithosphere and asthenosphere is based upon the mechanical properties of the materials in the two respective layers and is distinct from the chemical separation of Earth's crust, mantle, and core. According to the theory of plate tectonics, the Earth's lithosphere is divided into **ten major plates**: African, Antarctic, Australian, Eurasian, North American, South American, Pacific, Cocos, Nazca, and Indian; it floats atop the asthenosphere. The plates of the lithosphere abut one another at plate boundaries (divergent, convergent, or transform fault), where the formation of topological features of Earth's surface begins.

Seafloor Spreading

Seafloor spreading was originally put forth as an explanation for the existence of midocean ridges such as the Mid-Atlantic Ridge. These ridges were identified as features of a vast undersea mountain system that spans the globe. Seafloor spreading postulates that the ocean floor expands outward from these ridges. The process occurs when the upper mantle layer of the Earth (the asthenosphere), just beneath the planet's crust, is heated through convection. The heat causes the asthenosphere to become more elastic and less dense. This heated material causes the crust to bow outward and eventually separate. The lighter material then flows out through the resultant rift and hardens, forming new oceanic crust. If a rift opens completely into an ocean, the basin will be flooded with seawater and create a new sea. Often, the process results in failed rifts, rifts that stopped opening before complete separation is achieved.

Continental Drift

Continental drift is a theory that explains the separation and movement of the continents based on shifts in a plastic layer of Earth's interior caused by the planet's rotation (seafloor spreading). Continental drift is part of the larger theory of plate tectonics. In the early twentieth century, many scientists and scholars noted that the edges of certain continents seemed to look like connecting pieces of a puzzle. Due to this observation, as well as the fact that similar geologic features, fossils, fauna, and flora existed on the Atlantic coasts of continents like South America and Africa, these observers theorized the previous existence of a supercontinent (referred to as Pangaea), in which all of the discrete continents identifiable today were joined together.

Theory

This theory of plate tectonics arose from the fusion of **continental drift** (first proposed in 1915 by Alfred Wegener) and **seafloor spreading** (first observed by Icelandic fishermen in the 1800s and later refined by Harry Hess and Robert Dietz in the early 1960s) in the late 1960s and early 1970s. Prior to this time, the generally accepted explanation for continental drift was that the continents were floating on the Earth's oceans. The discovery that mountains have "roots" (proved by George Airy in the early 1950s) did not categorically disprove the concept of floating continents; scientists were still uncertain as to where those mountainous roots were attached. It was not until the identification and study of the Mid-Atlantic Ridge and magnetic striping in the 1960s that plate tectonics became accepted as a scientific theory. Its conception was a landmark event in the field of Earth sciences—it provided an explanation for the empirical observations of continental drift and seafloor spreading.

Tectonic Plate Motion

The two main sources of **tectonic plate motion** are **gravity** and **friction**. The energy driving tectonic plate motion comes from the dissipation of heat from the mantle in the relatively weak asthenosphere. This energy is converted into gravity or friction to incite the motion of plates. Gravity is subdivided by geologists into ridge-push and slab-pull. In the phenomenon of **ridge-push**, the motion of plates is instigated by the energy that causes low-density material from the mantle to rise at an oceanic ridge. This leads to the situation of certain plates at higher elevations; gravity causes material to slide downhill. In **slab-pull**, plate motion is thought to be caused by cold, heavy plates at oceanic trenches sinking back into the mantle, providing fuel for future convection. Friction is subdivided into mantle drag and trench suction. Mantle drag suggests that plates move due to the friction between the lithosphere and the asthenosphere. Trench suction involves a downward frictional pull on oceanic plates in subduction zones due to convection currents.

Review Video: Plate Tectonic Theory
Visit mometrix.com/academy and enter code: 535013

Results of Tectonic Plate Motion

Earthquakes result from the movement of a dozen or so major lithospheric (crustal) plates that float upon Earth's mantle (asthenosphere). These **plates** move about each other, at **transform boundaries**, in response to complex convection cells set in motion by Earth's interior heat. Two plates move apart from each other at **divergent boundaries**, or spreading centers, and come together at **convergent boundaries**. When thin, denser, iron- and magnesium- rich oceanic crust collides with thicker, lighter, silica-rich continental crust, the former is **subducted** beneath the latter. The subducted material carries scraped-off continental crust and seawater down with it. As this material melts, it rises as a mixture of magma and steam to produce explosive **volcanic mountain ranges** such as those surrounding the Pacific Ocean Basin. A **hot spot** is an area of the Earth's surface that experiences high levels of volcanic activity, created by hypothetical phenomena called mantle plumes. Mantle plumes are exceptionally hot portions of the Earth's mantle that rise (through convection) to the crust. Hot spots are responsible for the formation of volcanic chains such as the Hawaiian Islands. **Supervolcanoes** are the most explosive volcanoes, as rated on the volcanic explosivity index. They form when magma is unable to break through the crust, resulting in even more pressure building up. When two continental plates collide at convergent boundaries, the crust buckles and thrusts up massive mountain ranges such as the Alps and Himalayas. When plates diverge, magma rises up from the mantle, cools on the seafloor, and creates new crust under the ocean. This process is called seafloor spreading, and it forms **ocean basins**.

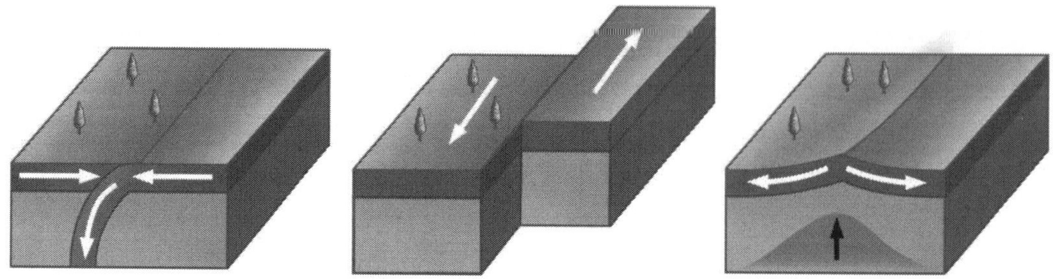

Convergent Transform Divergent

EXAMPLE

The Andes volcanic mountain range on the western coast of South America is the longest mountain range in the world, consisting of hundreds of volcanoes. Which of the following processes is most likely responsible for the formation of these volcanoes?

a. Convergence of a continental plate and oceanic plate
b. Two tectonic plates moving side-by-side
c. Divergence of two tectonic plates
d. Existence of a hotspot

Choice A describes a continental plate, also referred to as a land plate, colliding with an oceanic plate. When this happens, the oceanic plate slides underneath the continental plate, which is called subduction. This results in long chains of volcanoes, such as the Cascades in the United States, along with earthquakes and sometimes tsunamis. The Andes are a long chain of volcanoes, so Choice A could be correct.

Choice B describes two tectonic plates moving side-by-side. When this happens, it causes earthquakes and rolling hills, not volcanoes. Choice B is not the answer.

Choice C describes the divergence, or separation, of two continental plates. This results in large troughs in the land called rift valleys, not volcanoes. Choice C is not the answer.

Choice D describes the existence of a hotspot, which is a high-temperature spot below Earth's crust that causes magma to rise up through the crust. Hotspots form individual volcanoes or small volcanic groups, such as those in Hawaii and Yellowstone. However, the Andes are a long chain of volcanic mountains, which are not associated with hotspots. Choice D is incorrect.

Choice A is the correct answer. Chains of volcanic mountains like the Andes are formed through subduction when an oceanic plate slides underneath a continental plate.

DETERMINING THE ORDER IN WHICH GEOLOGIC EVENTS OCCURRED USING THE ROCK RECORD

The **Law of Superposition** logically assumes that the bottom layer of a series of sedimentary layers is the oldest, unless it has been overturned or older rock has been pushed over it. In addition, igneous intrusions can cut through or flow above already present rocks (e.g., lava flows). This is a further indication that the lower rock layers are older. Another guideline for the rock record is that **rock layers** are older than the folds and faults in them because the rocks must exist before they can be folded or faulted. If a rock contains **atomic nuclei**, reference tables of the half-lives of commonly used radio isotopes can be used to match the decay rate of known substances to the nuclei in a rock, and thereby determine its age. Ages of rocks can also be determined from **contact metamorphism**, the re-crystallization of pre-existing rocks due to changes in physical and chemical conditions, such as heat, pressure, and chemically active fluids that might be present in lava or polluted waters.

Matching Rocks and Geologic Events in One Place with Those of Another

Geologists physically follow rock layers from one location to another by a process called "walking the outcrop." Geologists walk along the outcropping to see where it goes and what the differences and similarities of the neighboring locations they cross are. Similar rock **types** or **patterns** of rock layers that are similar in terms of thickness, color, composition, and fossil remains tell geologists that two locations have a similar geologic history. Fossils are found all over the Earth, but are from a relatively **small time period** in Earth's history. Therefore, fossil evidence helps date a rock layer, regardless of where it occurs. **Volcanic ash** is a good time indicator since ash is deposited quickly over a widespread area. Matching the date of an eruption to the ash allows for a precise identification of time. Similarly, the **meteor impact** at the intersection of the Cretaceous and Tertiary Periods left a time marker. Wherever the meteor's iridium content is found, geologists are able to date rock layers.

Sequencing the Earth's Geologic History from the Fossil and Rock Record

Reference tables are used to match specimens and time periods. For example, the fossil record has been divided into time units of the Earth's history. Rocks can therefore be dated by the fossils found with them. There are also reference tables for dating plate motions and mountain building events in geologic history. Since humans have been around for a relatively short period of time, **fossilized human remains** help to affix a date to a location. Some areas have missing **geologic layers** because of erosion or other factors, but reference tables specific to a region will list what is complete or missing. The theory of **uniformitarianism** assumes that geologic processes have been the same throughout history. Therefore, the way erosion or volcanic eruptions happen today is the same as the way these events happened millions of years ago because there is no reason for them to have changed. Therefore, knowledge about current events can be applied to the past to make judgments about events in the rock record.

Revealing Changes in Earth's History by the Fossil and Rock Records

Fossils can show how animal and plant life have changed or remained the same over time. For example, fossils have provided evidence of the existence of dinosaurs even though they no longer roam the Earth, and have also been used to prove that certain insects have been around for hundreds of millions of years. Fossils have been used to identify four basic eras: **Proterozoic**, the age of primitive life; **Paleozoic**, the age of fishes; **Mesozoic**, the age of dinosaurs; and **Cenozoic**, the age of mammals. Most ancient forms of life have disappeared, and there are reference tables that list when this occurred. Fossil records also show the evolution of certain life forms, such as the horse from the eohippus. However, the majority of changes do not involve evolution from simple to complex forms, but rather an increase in the variety of forms.

Paleontology

Paleontology is the study of prehistoric plant and animal life through the analysis of **fossil remains**. These fossils reveal the ecologies of the past and the path of evolution for both extinct and living organisms. A historical science, paleontology seeks information about the identity, origin, environment, and evolution of past organisms and what they can reveal about the past of the Earth as a whole. Paleontologists seek to explain causes rather than conduct experiments to observe effects. It is related to the fields of biology, geology, and archaeology, and is divided into several sub-disciplines concerned with the types of fossils studied, the process of fossilization, and the ecology and climate of the past. Paleontologists also help identify the composition of the Earth's rock layers by the fossils that are found, thus identifying potential sites for oil, mineral, and water extraction.

Weather and Climate

Weather describes conditions or changes in sunshine, temperature, cloud coverage, precipitation, warm and cold fronts, and more during a specific time in a specific area. These components can change throughout a day, week, or month. Meteorologists track and report what is happening in the atmosphere to help predict how the weather will change in the near future. Weather data is collected and studied over long periods of time, often multiple decades, to evaluate the climate of a particular area. **Climate** refers to patterns in weather conditions, such as temperature, precipitation, and any extremes related to them, in a specific area over a very long period of time. A large factor that influences climate is latitude, which is the distance of an area from the equator.

Weather

Heat energy from the Sun warms different parts of the planet in different ways at different times. As warm air rises it expands and cools. This causes moisture to condense as liquid drops or freeze as ice crystals to form clouds. When the water drops or ice crystals become too large to stay aloft, they fall as precipitation. As warm air rises it also leaves a low-pressure zone behind. This causes air from high surrounding high-pressure zones to rush in as wind.

Climate

Climate is usually defined as the "**average weather**" in a particular area on Earth. The timespan over which climate is measured is variable, but it is generally accepted that the climate of an area does not vary during a human life span (though climate is extremely various in geologic time). This may change, however, due to the increasing greenhouse effect. Meteorologists measure climate by averaging certain quantifiable elements such as rainfall or temperature. Climate may be studied on several different scales:

- **Local climate** refers to the climate of small geographic areas (generally up to tens of miles wide). The local climate of an area is affected by things such as its location relative to an ocean and the presence of mountains near the location.
- A **regional climate** is the climate of a larger geographic area, such as a country. A regional climate may also be delineated due to climate features that are distinctive from the surrounding climate.
- **Global climate** refers to the average weather experienced across the Earth.

Clouds

Clouds form when water vapor in the atmosphere cools to the point where it **condenses** and becomes water droplets or small particles of frozen ice crystals. Clouds form when moisture is added to the air through evaporation until the air becomes **saturated** and cannot hold any more water. Then, the water vapor can condense into visible droplets.

Precipitation

Precipitation is water that falls back to the surface of the Earth from the atmosphere. This water may be in the form of **rain**, which is water in liquid form. Raindrops are formed in clouds due to **condensation**. When the drops become too large to remain in the clouds, gravity causes them to fall toward the surface of the Earth. Extremely small raindrops are called **drizzle**. If the temperature of a layer of air through which rain passes is below the freezing point of water, the rain may take the form of **sleet**, which is partially frozen water. Precipitation may also fall in the form of **snow**, which is made of ice crystals. When clumps of snowflakes melt and refreeze, **hail** is formed. Hail may also be formed when liquid water gathers on the surface of a snowflake and then freezes.

Temperature

Temperature describes the amount of **heat** in an area. The Earth's tilt and shape impact the average temperatures in each region. The Sun shines on the areas closest to the equator most directly, causing those areas to have warmer average temperatures. All other areas receive energy from the Sun at different angles, causing lower average temperatures. The farther North or South an area is from the equator, the less directly the Sun will shine on them. Since temperature is an important part of the water cycle, it also has an effect on the humidity, precipitation, and air pressure in an area. Since weather processes are like cycles, these factors can also impact the temperature in an area. Temperature can be predicted based on an area's location, the time of year, the moisture in an area, and the air pressure in an area.

Wind

When the Sun shines, it heats the surface of Earth, including Earth's atmosphere. This heating does not occur evenly because some places on Earth, such as the equator, receive more direct sunlight than others. When air is heated and becomes warmer, it rises due to decreased density, causing more dense air from colder parts of the planet to rush in under it. As the warm air moves in the atmosphere, it cools and begins to sink again. This creates a cycle of heat movement within Earth's atmosphere called **convection**. This circular motion of air in the atmosphere is responsible for winds.

Air Pressure

Pressure describes the amount of force applied to an object over a certain area. For example, a person standing on a bed sinks deeper into the bed than a person laying on it. This occurs because the same amount of force is applied to a smaller area, which means the pressure is higher. Pressure applies to all forces that are applied to other objects, including air. The pressure applied by air in a given place is called **air pressure**, or **barometric pressure**. Because air has mass, and gravity is pulling it toward the Earth, air applies force on everything beneath it. Air pressure changes with **altitude**, which is the height of an object above sea level. The lower the altitude, the higher the air pressure. This is because the air at higher altitudes is weighing on the air underneath it. Similarly, air pressure is lower at higher altitudes.

Pressure Systems

The atoms in warm air are less densely packed, causing them to exert less pressure. In contrast, cold air is characterized by closely packed atoms, which means it has high density and exerts much pressure. A **low-pressure system** attracts air from surrounding areas, causing it to rise and condense higher in the atmosphere, leading to clouds and precipitation such as rain. A **high-pressure system** blows air away from itself and is associated with fewer clouds and calmer weather. The boundary where two systems interact is called a **front** and is associated with turbulent, stormy weather. Scientists like **meteorologists** use **pressure maps** to predict the weather, usually for a specific area that is local to them. By mapping out the location of high- and low-pressure systems and examining the boundaries between them, meteorologists can predict future weather based on the weather patterns associated with each system and type of boundary.

Impact of Temperature and Humidity on Air Pressure

Humidity and temperature also affect air pressure. **Humidity** refers to how much moisture is in the air. Air that contains more water molecules contains more mass than drier air. Therefore, gravity pulls more on air that has higher humidity, which causes increased air pressure. Similarly, **temperature** can affect the density of air. Gases do not have a constant volume, but the space between the molecules in a gas grows and shrinks with changes in temperature, causing changes in air pressure.

Impact of Air Pressure on Climate and Weather

Weather systems are often described based on air pressure. A **high-pressure system** means that an area has higher air pressure, while a **low-pressure system** has a lower pressure. Pressure will move toward **equilibrium**, or a state of **balance**. Therefore, high- and low-pressure systems naturally interact with each other. Low pressure systems try to **pull air** toward them to reach equilibrium. This causes condensation to form and can eventually produce storms. High pressure systems **push air** away from them and are usually associated with sunny or clear weather.

Lightning Bolt

Lightning is a huge electric spark that can occur inside a cloud, go from one cloud to another, or go from a cloud to the ground. The turbulent rising air and rising and falling raindrops or ice crystals in a thunderstorm cause differences in electric charge in different parts of the cloud and between the bottom of the cloud and the ground. When the difference in charge is large enough, a lightning bolt will discharge which neutralizes the difference.

Thunder

As a lightning bolt travels through the air, it pushes the air aside faster than the speed of sound. This produces a shock wave of very hot air that creates a loud sonic boom, which we hear as thunder. If a person can hear thunder, he needs to get indoors quickly as possible since he could be struck by lightning.

We hear thunder later because sound travels much slower than light. Light travels so fast that it is almost instantaneous from one point to another anywhere on Earth. Sound travels much more slowly—about one mile every five seconds or so. Light would travel one mile in only about 5 millionths of a second. Therefore, the distance from a lightning flash can be determined by counting the number of seconds until the thunder it made is heard.

Tornado

A tornado is a violent rotating column of air that is in contact with both the ground and a cloud. The column is visible because the very low pressure causes water vapor to condense out as visible water droplets. Where the tornado touches the ground it usually stirs up a cloud of dirt and debris like the one in this photo. Tornadoes are the most violent storms on Earth, and the strongest spin at 300 miles per hour.

Review Video: Tornadoes
Visit mometrix.com/academy and enter code: 540439

Tropical Cyclones

A tropical cyclone is potentially the most destructive and dangerous type of cyclone. Such a formation is referred to as a **hurricane** when it occurs over the Atlantic Ocean or as a **typhoon** when it occurs over the Pacific or Indian Oceans. **Tropical cyclones** develop at low latitudes (specifically, between 8 and 15 degrees North or South latitude) when the surface waters below reach temperatures of 81 degrees Fahrenheit or above. From their zone of origination, tropical cyclones often travel westward through the trade-wind belt; westerly winds may push the storm northward as well. This type of cyclone is associated with high wind speeds and high levels of rainfall. A tropical cyclone also displays extremely low pressure in its center, or eye, where weather conditions are fair (in contrast to the rest of the storm). These weather systems occur seasonally: in the Northern Hemisphere, cyclonic activity is highest from May to November; in the Southern Hemisphere, the cyclone season is roughly the opposite.

Hurricane

A **hurricane** is a very large tropical storm that forms over the open ocean and produces very strong winds and heavy rains. A **tropical storm** forms when warm water evaporates and the saturated air rises and forms a column of condensed water vapor. As the wind speed increases the pressure falls even more and a hurricane can be born. Sinking air in the center of the storm produces an **eye** (arrow) where the weather is quite calm and free of clouds.

Measuring Weather

Weather can be measured by a variety of methods. The simplest include measurement of rainfall, sunshine, pressure, humidity, temperature, and cloudiness with basic instruments such as thermometers, barometers, and rain gauges. However, the use of **radar** (which involves analysis of microwaves reflecting off of raindrops) and satellite imagery grants meteorologists a look at the big picture of weather across, for example, an entire continent. This helps them understand and make predictions about current and developing weather systems. Infrared (heat-sensing) imaging allows meteorologists to measure the temperature of clouds above ground. Using weather reports gathered from different weather stations spread over an area, meteorologists create synoptic charts. The locations and weather reports of several stations are plotted on a chart; analysis of the pressures reported from each location, as well as rainfall, cloud cover, and so on, can reveal basic weather patterns.

Effects of Natural Processes on Climate Change

Natural Processes That Impact the Climate

Many natural processes have extreme effects on Earth systems. **Volcanic eruptions** have largely short-term effects on global temperature due to the emissions of ash and CO_2, which affect how sunlight is absorbed and reflected in the atmosphere. **Asteroids** usually burn up in the atmosphere, but impacts of significant sizes can cause similar effects to that of volcanos, such as introducing chemicals into the atmosphere or severely damaging ecosystems. **Meteoroids** are fragments of asteroids of various sizes. If they come through Earth's atmosphere, they are called meteors or shooting stars. If they land on Earth, they are called meteorites, and create craters on impact (the Barringer Crater in Arizona). **Ocean currents** and **subsurface processes** within the earth also can change how temperature variation is distributed across the Earth. **Magmatic cycles** of temperature change cause surface level heating and cooling, referred to as **El Nino** (heating) and **La Nina** (cooling). **Solar variations** usually come in cycles which also have powerful effects on the temperature of the planet. These temperature changes affect temperature of the climate directly, but also influence systems such as weather, oceanic currents, and ecological systems.

Global Warming

The **natural greenhouse effect** of the atmosphere is beneficial to life on Earth; it keeps temperatures on the planet 33 degrees higher than they would be without this phenomenon. Originally, this helped sustain life. However, it has been discovered in the last 20 years that this effect is being intensified by the actions of humans. In the twentieth century, certain activities of mankind, including the burning of fossils fuels like coal and oil, have resulted in an **increase in the levels of greenhouse gases** (such as methane and carbon dioxide) being released into the atmosphere. Also, increasing deforestation has affected the number of photosynthesis-practicing plants. The combined effect of these trends is a higher-than-normal concentration of greenhouse gases in the atmosphere. This, in turn, produces the effect of global warming. The average temperature at the Earth's surface has gone up 0.6 degrees Celsius in the last 100 years. Continuation of this trend is likely to have a detrimental effect on many of the planet's ecosystems, including that of human beings.

Biogeochemical Cycle

The term biogeochemical cycle refers to one of several chemical processes in which chemical elements are (re)cycled among **biotic** (living) and **abiotic** (nonliving) constituents of an ecosystem. The theory of relativity necessitates the presence of such cycles in nature by virtue of its supposition that energy and matter are not created or destroyed in a closed system such as Earth's ecosystem. Generally, a **biogeochemical cycle** operates as follows: inorganic compounds, such as carbon, are converted from water, air, and soil to organic molecules by organisms called **autotrophs**. **Heterotrophs** (organisms that cannot independently produce their own food) consume the autotrophs; some of the newly formed organic molecules are transferred. Finally, the organic molecules are broken down and processed once again into inorganic compounds by secondary and tertiary consumers and replaced within water, air, and soil. Carbon, nitrogen, and phosphorus provide examples of nutrients that are recycled in the Earth's ecosystem.

CARBON CYCLE

The **carbon cycle** is a biogeochemical cycle that describes the continuous movement of the Earth's carbon. Carbon is in the atmosphere, the soil, living organisms, fossil fuels, oceans, and freshwater systems. These areas are referred to as **carbon reservoirs**. Carbon flows between these reservoirs in an exchange called the carbon cycle. In the atmosphere, carbon is in the form of carbon dioxide. Carbon moves from the atmosphere to plants through the process of photosynthesis. Carbon moves from plants to animals through food chains, and then moves from living organisms to the soil when these organisms die. Carbon moves from living organisms to the atmosphere through cellular respiration. Carbon moves from fossil fuels to the atmosphere when fossil fuels are burned. Carbon moves from the atmosphere to the oceans and freshwater systems through absorption.

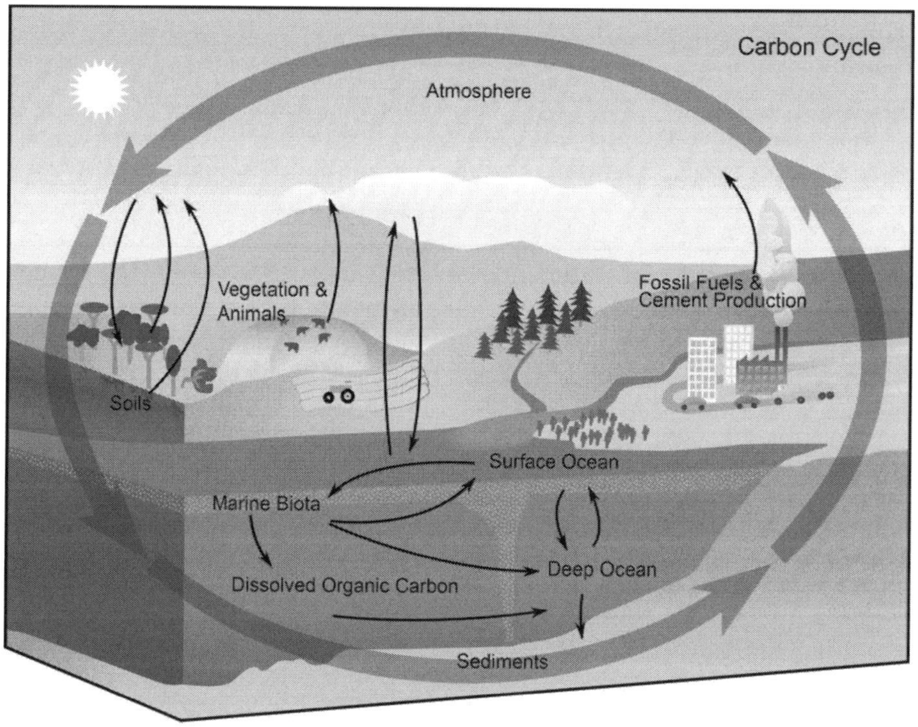

Watersheds

A **watershed** is a defined area where all the water from one place or multiple nearby places drains into a common location such as a river or ocean. A watershed is made up of two main types of water: surface water and ground water. **Surface water** is any water visible above ground, such as lakes and rivers, and **groundwater** is freshwater contained underneath the soil and fills the space between rocks and soil particles. Human activities can impact surface water through contamination, pollution, and the construction of dams. Human activities can also contaminate groundwater through the dumping of waste and the use of chemicals near the soil. Groundwater can also be depleted when people use wells to acquire drinking water. One of the most significant impacts on watersheds is **agricultural runoff**, which the result of fertilizers and pesticides from farms leaking into surface water and groundwater sources. Because all the water in a watershed drains into the same location, pollution present in any of the water sources can impact the entire watershed. This can potentially reduce the amount of freshwater available to humans and wildlife in an area.

Environmental Impacts

Greenhouse Effect

The **greenhouse effect** refers to a naturally occurring and necessary process. **Greenhouse gases**, which are ozone, carbon dioxide, water vapor, and methane, trap infrared radiation that is reflected toward the atmosphere. Without the greenhouse effect, it is estimated that the temperature on Earth would be 30 degrees less on average. The problem occurs because human activity generates more greenhouse gases than necessary. Practices that increase the amount of greenhouse gases include the burning of natural gas and oil, farming practices that result in the release of methane and nitrous oxide, factory operations that produce gases, and deforestation practices that decrease the amount of oxygen available to offset greenhouse gases. Population growth also increases the volume of gases released. Excess greenhouse gases cause more infrared radiation to become trapped, which increases the temperature at the Earth's surface.

Ozone Depletion

Ultraviolet light breaks O_2 into two very reactive oxygen atoms with unpaired electrons, which are known as **free radicals**. A free radical of oxygen pairs with another oxygen molecule to form **ozone** (O_3). Ultraviolet light also breaks ozone (O_3) into O_2 and a free radical of oxygen. This process usually acts as an ultraviolet light filter for the planet. Other free radical catalysts are produced by natural phenomena such as volcanic eruptions and by human activities. When these enter the atmosphere, they disrupt the normal cycle by breaking down ozone so it cannot absorb more ultraviolet radiation. One such catalyst is the chlorine in chlorofluorocarbons (CFCs). CFCs were used as aerosols and refrigerants. When a CFC like CF_2Cl_2 is broken down in the atmosphere, chlorine free radicals are produced. These act as catalysts to break down ozone. Whether a chlorine free radical reacts with an ozone or oxygen molecule, it is able to react again.

Human Impacts on Ecosystems

Human impacts on **ecosystems** take many forms and have many causes. They include widespread disruptions and specific niche disturbances. Humans practice many forms of **environmental manipulation** that affect plants and animals in many biomes and ecosystems. Many human practices involve the consumption of natural resources for food and energy production, the changing of the environment to produce food and energy, and the intrusion on ecosystems to provide shelter. These general behaviors include a multitude of specific behaviors, including the use and overuse of pesticides, the encroachment upon habitat, over hunting and over fishing, the introduction of plant and animal species into non-native ecosystems, and the introduction of hazardous wastes and chemical byproducts into the environment. These behaviors have led to a number of consequences, such as acid rain, ozone depletion, deforestation, urbanization, accelerated species loss, genetic abnormalities, endocrine disruption in populations, and harm to individual animals.

Global Warming

Global warming may cause the permanent loss of glaciers and permafrost. There might also be increases in air pollution and acid rain. Rising temperatures may lead to an increase in sea levels as polar ice melts, lower amounts of available fresh water as coastal areas flood, species extinction because of changes in habitat, increases in certain diseases, and a decreased standard of living for humans. Less fresh water and losses of habitat for humans and other species can also lead to decreased agricultural production and food supply shortages. Increased desertification leads to habitat loss for humans and other species. There may be more moisture in the atmosphere due to evaporation.

Acid Rain and Eutrophication

Acid rain is made up water droplets for which the pH has been lowered due atmospheric pollution. The common sources of this pollution are **sulfur** and **nitrogen** that have been released through the burning of fossil fuels. This can lead to a lowering of the pH of lakes and ponds, thereby destroying aquatic life, or damaging the leaves and bark of trees. It can also destroy buildings, monuments, and statues made of rock.

Eutrophication is the depletion of oxygen in a body of water. It may be caused by an increase in the amount of nutrients, particularly **phosphates**, which leads to an increase in plant and algae life that use up the oxygen. The result is a decrease in water quality and death of aquatic life. Sources of excess phosphates may be detergents, industrial run-off, or fertilizers that are washed into lakes or streams.

Waste Disposal Methods

- Landfills – **Methane** (CH_4) is a greenhouse gas emitted from landfills. Some is used to generate electricity and some gets into the atmosphere. CO_2 is also emitted, and landfill gas can contain nitrogen, oxygen, water vapor, sulfur, mercury, and radioactive contaminants such as tritium. **Landfill leachate** contains acids from car batteries, solvents, heavy metals, pesticides, motor oil, paint, household cleaning supplies, plastics, and many other potentially harmful substances. Some of these are dangerous when they get into the ecosystem.
- Incinerators – These contribute to air pollution in that they can release nitric and sulfuric oxides, which cause **acid rain**.
- Sewage – When dumped in raw form into oceans, sewage can introduce **fecal contaminants** and **pathogenic organisms**, which can harm ocean life and cause disease in humans.

Effects of Consumerism

Economic growth and quality of living are associated with a wasteful cycle of production. Goods are produced as cheaply as possible with little or no regard for the **ecological effects**. The ultimate goal is profitability. The production process is wasteful, and often introduces **hazardous byproducts** into the environment. Furthermore, byproducts may be dumped into a landfill instead of recycled. When consumer products get dumped in landfills, they can leach **contamination** into groundwater. Landfills can also leach gases. These are or have been dumping grounds for illegal substances, business and government waste, construction industry waste, and medical waste. These items also get dumped at illegal dump sites in urban and remote areas.

Energy Production

- **Coal-fired power plants**: These generate electricity fairly cheaply, but are the largest source of **greenhouse gases**.
- **Gasoline**: Gasoline is cheap, generates less CO_2 than coal, and requires less water than coal. But it nevertheless releases a substantial amount of CO_2 in the aggregate and is a limited resource. The burning of gas and other fossil fuels releases carbon dioxide (a greenhouse gas) into the atmosphere.
- **Nuclear power plants**: A small nuclear power plant can cheaply produce a large amount of electricity. But the waste is potentially harmful and a substantial amount of **water** is required to generate electricity. The cost of storing and transporting the **radioactive waste** is also very large.
- **Hydropower**: Hydropower is sustainable and environmentally benign once established. A disadvantage is that the building of a dam and the re-routing of a river can be very **environmentally disruptive**.
- **Wind power**: Wind power is sustainable, non-polluting, and requires little to no cooling water. But it will not produce power in the absence of **wind** and requires a large area over which the turbines can be laid out.
- **Solar power**: Solar power is sustainable, can be used for a single house or building, and generates peak energy during times of peak usage. But production is limited to when the sun is shining, the panels themselves are expensive to make, and making the panels generates harmful **toxins**.
- **Geothermal power:** Geothermal power is sustainable, relatively cheap, and non-polluting. Disadvantages are that it can only be utilized in areas with specific **volcanic activity**.

Chapter Quiz

1. What part of the Sun's atmosphere is the surface that we can see from Earth?

a. The photosphere
b. The chromosphere
c. The corona
d. The transition zone

2. Which of the following is NOT true of Earth?

a. Earth is closest to the Sun in July and farthest in January.
b. The path of the orbit of Earth around the Sun is not circular but elliptical.
c. The speed at which Earth rotates is not exactly constant.
d. Earth's northern and southern hemispheres have opposite seasons.

3. Which of the following is a true statement concerning the Moon?

a. The Moon emits light because of radiation.
b. The Moon's phase depends on the position of the Moon, Earth, and Sun.
c. The Moon has a weaker impact on tides than the Sun because it is so much smaller.
d. The Moon's radius is just over one-third of the size of the Earth's radius.

4. What type of star is the most abundant in the galaxy, and is characterized by the fusion of hydrogen atoms into helium atoms in its core?

a. White dwarf star
b. Main sequence star
c. Giant star
d. Supergiant star

5. What type of gravitational tectonic plate motion is thought to be caused by cold, heavy plates at oceanic trenches sinking back into the mantle, providing fuel for future convection?

a. Ridge-push
b. Slab-pull
c. Mantle drag
d. Trench suction

6. High-pressure systems are associated with what type of weather?

a. Fronts
b. Clouds
c. Clear skies
d. Precipitation

7. Which of the following is NOT true about stars?

a. The largest stars are called red dwarf stars, and can be 3,000 times larger than the Sun.
b. The Sun is considered a medium-sized star.
c. From Earth, scientists can determine the size of a star by its luminosity and temperature.
d. The brightness of a star will change throughout its life cycle.

Chapter Quiz Answer Key

1. A: See section **Sun**

2. A: See section **Earth's Tilt and Seasons**

3. B: See section **Phases of the Moon**

4. B: See section **Types of Stars**

5. B: See section **Tectonic Plate Motion**

6. C: See section **Pressure Systems**

7. A: See section **Stars**

Organisms and Environments

Populations of Animals or Plants

A **population** consists of all of the **organisms** of a **certain kind** in a **defined area**, **region**, or **habitat**. It may be all the red foxes in a given national park, all the loblolly pines in Virginia (very hard to count), all the bullfrogs in a certain pond, or even all of the boxelder bugs on a single box elder tree. In the case of rare or endangered species it may be all of the individuals still living in the wild.

Several factors operate to keep animal and plant populations under control. Predation, grazing, disease, competition for limiting resources such as food or nutrients, water, habitat and living space, hunting and breeding territory, and sunlight for plants all play important roles. Even the size of the population can influence factors such as birth rate and severity of disease outbreaks or force individuals to migrate to other less crowded areas.

Abiotic and Biotic Factors

An ecosystem is a connected community of organisms that interact with one another as well as with their physical environment. Nonliving aspects of an organism's physical environment are called **abiotic factors**. Abiotic factors include things like water, air, soil, minerals, and sunlight. Animals drink water from sources such as streams and breathe in oxygen (O_2) from fresh air. Plants use their roots to obtain water and minerals from the soil. In addition, plants require sunlight and carbon dioxide (CO_2) from the air in order to carry out photosynthesis to live and grow. The living aspects of the ecosystem are called **biotic factors**. They include other organisms in that community, such as plants, animals, bacteria, fungi and protists.

Relationships Between Organisms

Organisms can interact with one another in many ways. For example, **herbivores** eat plants, and **predators**, or **carnivores**, eat other animals. Organisms can also **compete** for biotic or abiotic resources in an ecosystem. In addition, organisms can rely on each other through **mutualism**, which is a relationship between at least two organisms in which both organisms benefit from each other. One organism can also rely on another through **commensalism**, which is a relationship between at least two organisms in which one organism benefits while the other is not harmed or benefitted.

Competition

In order to survive, organisms must **compete** for resources. Competition can occur either between individuals of the same species **(intraspecific competition)** or individuals of different species **(interspecific competition)**. Each species in an ecosystem occupies a specific **niche** or role due to its unique interactions with the resources and other organisms in the ecosystem. Two species with the exact same niche cannot coexist in the same habitat because one species will **outcompete** the other, driving the other to extinction. However, niches of two species in the same habitat may partly overlap due to similar behavior, such as hunting the same prey. These species will compete more for resources, but, since they don't have exactly the same niche, they may be able to coexist. While this type of competition occurs naturally in ecosystems, competition also occurs when new species are introduced to an ecosystem. **Invasive species** are non-native, introduced species that threaten the balance of the ecosystem they have joined. Because they evolved in a different environment, invasive species can outcompete the native species in an ecosystem, leading to reductions in population numbers or extinction and other harmful outcomes in the ecosystem.

Plant Species Competing with Each Other

Creosote bush is the most widespread shrub in the deserts of the American Southwest where water can be very scarce for long periods. The roots of mature creosote bushes are extremely efficient and absorb all the water in the sandy soil around them. This creates very dry zones around each plant. The seeds of other plants cannot survive long enough to germinate. Therefore, the plants tend to be spaced far apart from each other.

Animals of the Same Species Competing with Each Other

Male elk known as bulls have large antlers, which they shed and regrow each year. Like their smaller deer cousins, bull elk engage in bugling contests and ritual combat (like the photo below) to dominate other males and win all the female (cow) elk in a harem.

Different species of animals often compete for food. The spotted hyena and the African lion shown here compete for prey like zebras and wildebeest. Both hyenas and lions run in groups. A larger pack of hyenas can drive a smaller pride of lions away from prey the lions have killed. However, one lion can easily kill one or more hyenas. They rarely tolerate each other as they seem to be doing below.

EXAMPLE

Two lizard species live in the same desert and require similar resources. They both hunt insects, rely on limited water sources, and seek shade to regulate their body temperature. Which of these relationships is most likely to occur between the two lizard species?

a. The two species will form a mutualistic relationship and hunt together.
b. The two species will not affect one another.
c. The two species will compete for limited resources such as water.
d. One species will become a predator to the other.

Choice A proposes a mutualistic relationship, where two species help one another, in this case by hunting together. Two species with similar niches are unlikely to develop a mutualistic relationship, and hunting together would not be very beneficial for either species. Choice A is probably incorrect.

Choice B proposes that the two species will not affect one another at all. This is unlikely because the two lizards occupy similar niches and require similar resources, meaning they might have to compete for limited resources. Choice B is probably incorrect.

Choice C proposes that the two species will have to compete for limited resources such as water. Species that require similar resources such as these lizard species are very likely to compete, particularly if resources ar e scarce. Choice C could be the correct answer.

Choice D proposes that one species will become a predator to the other. While some lizards do eat smaller lizard species, there is no evidence to suggest this adaptation will happen. Based on the lizard's similar diet and ecological requirements, it is more likely that they would compete for limited resources. Choice D is not the answer.

Choice C is the correct answer. Species that occupy similar niches or require the same resources, such as these two lizard species, are very likely to compete with one another.

Organisms and Environmental Changes

Sudden environmental changes can include **natural disasters**, **diseases**, and **habitat destruction**. Examples of more **gradual** changes include **climate change** or **gradual habitat loss** due to population growth, agriculture, or the harvesting of natural resources. Both sudden and gradual environmental changes have the potential to significantly disrupt the balance of an ecosystem. When organisms die due to natural disasters, disease, or environmental changes, the number of individuals in a population changes. In more sudden environmental changes, these shifts in population numbers are more dramatic. Additionally, these changes in population numbers can have a **domino effect** on the ecosystem. For example, when a predator population decreases, the prey populations increase because of the reduced risk of being hunted. However, another predator population could increase because there is now reduced **competition** for resources. Environmental changes can also affect populations by influencing the presence of certain physical traits. Because individuals with certain traits are more likely to survive specific environmental changes, those traits will become more common in a population through the process of **natural selection.**

EXAMPLE

A remote island consisting of rainforest habitats has experienced consistently rising temperatures over the course of a decade. Scientists have made several observations of changes to local populations. Which of the following observations is most likely a beneficial change to a trait that will affect subsequent generations?

a. The population of frogs has declined.
b. Old-growth trees are producing fewer leaves.
c. Birds spend less time in the canopy.
d. A small mammal species produces a thinner coat of fur.

Choice A describes a decline in the population of frogs. Rising temperatures are likely to cause certain populations to decline, particularly amphibians. However, the question asks for an example of a beneficial change to a trait that will be inherited by subsequent populations. In this case, population decline is not a change to a trait, and population decline is rarely beneficial. Choice A is not the answer.

Choice B describes trees producing fewer leaves. This answer specifies that the trees are old-growth trees, meaning they have been around for a long time. In this case, producing fewer leaves is likely to be an individual response to limited resources and environmental changes. This is unlikely to be a beneficial change because fewer leaves mean the trees cannot photosynthesize as much. In addition, this describes an immediate survival response rather than an inherited change to a trait. Choice B is probably not the answer.

Choice C describes a change in birds' behavior, who begin to spend less time in the canopy, likely to avoid the sun. Because this is a change in behavior, it is unclear whether it would be passed on to subsequent generations. Choice C is probably not the answer.

Choice D describes a change to a physical trait, specifically fur thickness in small mammal species. With rising temperatures, having thinner fur is likely to be beneficial in keeping the animal from overheating. Additionally, a physical trait is more likely to be passed on to subsequent generations than a behavioral change. Choice D is the correct answer.

Choice D is the correct answer because it describes a change to a trait that is most likely to be beneficial and to be inherited by subsequent generations.

HUMAN IMPACT ON MARINE ENVIRONMENTS

Humans can impact ecosystems directly and indirectly. For example, humans can **directly** impact an ecosystem through deforestation and overfishing, while humans can **indirectly** impact ecosystems through the burning of fossil fuels, which can contribute to climate change and pollution. Marine ecosystems are some of the most vulnerable to these impacts. For example, the ocean absorbs some of the carbon dioxide (CO_2) that goes into the atmosphere, and so as more CO_2 goes into the atmosphere due to human activity, more CO_2 goes into the ocean. This absorption has caused chemical reactions that have led the oceans to become more acidic. This **ocean acidification** poses a threat to shell-building organisms and coral. Because coral reefs provide food and habitats for a significant portion of marine life, ocean acidification poses intense danger for marine ecosystems. Human agricultural activity also contributes to ocean pollution, as **runoff** from fertilizers and other chemicals leaks into the ocean.

Overfishing and Artificial Reefs

Reliance on oceans for food has led to **overfishing**, which is when fish are caught and removed from a body of water at a higher rate than the fish can reproduce and replenish. This threatens fish populations as well as entire marine ecosystems. To increase fish populations in a certain area, humans have used **artificial reefs**, which are created by submerging materials into the water to replicate a coral reef habitat. Although artificial reefs can quickly increase the populations of fish and other marine life, they can have negative impacts, such as contributing to ocean pollution. Ironically, they can increase the fish population so much that many people will fish there and repeat the process of overfishing. Because of this, overfishing is a cyclical process that must constantly be kept in check.

Food Web in a Meadow

Sunlight allows grass and other plants to grow. These plants are eaten by a variety of *herbivores* like insects, rodents, and rabbits. Their seeds are consumed by various birds such as sparrows and quail. The insects are eaten by *carnivores*, including other kinds of birds, shrews, and bats. The rodents, rabbits, and some of the birds are then eaten by larger carnivores like weasels and foxes. Also, the quail, mice, rabbits and shrews are eaten by owls at night and by hawks during the day. This whole food web could be altered or destroyed simply through farming. Grass and other plants are removed to grow specific crops. Pesticides and fertilizers are also typically used. All of these alter the ecosystem, and the food web is impacted.

Ecological Succession

Environmental changes such as natural disasters can affect whole ecosystems and individual populations. Some examples of natural disasters include forest fires, droughts, floods, earthquakes, or volcanic eruptions. When a natural disaster occurs, it threatens the balance of an ecosystem. For example, a forest fire will reduce edible vegetation and available shade from trees. A drought reduces access to water sources and affects food availability. The short-term effects of a natural disaster include a reduction in the number of individuals in a population. These population changes can lead to an effect called **ecological succession**. As some populations die or weaken due to the disaster, they leave room for other populations to thrive. These populations are called **early successional species**. Gradually, the ecosystem continues to change, eventually returning to its original state as populations increase and overtake early successional species.

Biodiversity

Biodiversity refers to the variability and variety of living things on Earth. While there are many ways to measure diversity, the most common types are species diversity and genetic variability. **Species diversity** refers to the number of species within an ecosystem or community, while **genetic variability** describes the presence of different genetic traits within a population or species. Biodiversity helps an ecosystem adapt to environmental changes and prevent collapse. When an event such as a natural disaster or human disturbance occurs, the balance of an ecosystem is affected. For example, food or water resources could become scarce, which will make it difficult for many organisms to survive. Populations with high genetic diversity will have a range of different physical traits, such as beak size or fur thickness. Some of these traits can help an organism survive by leading it to eat a more varied diet or survive cold winters, for example. These adaptive traits make it more likely that some individuals within a population will survive. Similarly, species diversity in an ecosystem increases the likelihood that some populations in an ecosystem will withstand an environmental change. In this way, biodiversity contributes to a functioning ecosystem by making ecosystems more resilient to environmental changes and threats.

Adaptation to Environment

Organisms must be able to adapt to their environment in order to thrive or survive. Individuals must be able to recognize stimuli in their surroundings and adapt quickly. For example, an individual euglena can sense light and respond by moving toward the light. Individual organisms must also be able to adapt to changes in the environment on a larger scale. For example, plants must be able to respond to the change in the length of the day to flower at the correct time. Populations must also be able to adapt to a changing environment. Evolution by **natural selection** is the process by which populations change over many generations to become better adapted to their environment, thus surviving longer and reproducing more successfully.

Natural and Artificial Selection

Natural selection and artificial selection are both mechanisms of evolution. **Natural selection** is a process of nature in which a population can change over generations. Every population has variations in individual heritable traits and organisms best suited for survival typically reproduce and pass on those genetic traits to offspring to increase the likelihood of them surviving. Typically, the more advantageous a trait is, the more common that trait becomes in a population. Natural selection brings about evolutionary **adaptations** and is responsible for biological diversity. Artificial selection is another mechanism of evolution. **Artificial selection** is a process brought about by humans. Artificial selection is the **selective breeding** of domesticated animals and plants such as when farmers choose animals or plants with desirable traits to reproduce. Artificial selection has led to the evolution of farm stock and crops. For example, cauliflower, broccoli, and cabbage all evolved due to artificial selection of the wild mustard plant.

Example of Natural Selection

Historical biologist Charles Darwin observed finches in the Galápagos islands for evidence of these changes. In more recent history, a drought occurred in the Galápagos, making food resources scarce. Scientists observed that individual finches with larger beaks were more able to adapt to this environmental change because they could eat different types of seeds, while birds with smaller beaks had difficulty finding food. Because the birds with larger beaks were more likely to find food, they were more likely to survive and produce offspring. Since beak size is a genetic or **inheritable** trait, more birds in the next generation were born with larger beaks, while the number of birds born with smaller beaks decreased over time. When environmental pressures favor a certain trait because it helps a species survive, it causes a change in the frequency of that trait within the population, and this process is called **natural selection**.

Innate Behaviors

Similar to genetics, there are some behaviors that are innate, or instinctual. Many animals do not nurture their young, but instead, the newborn creatures are capable of fending for themselves. Below are some examples of innate behaviors that are not learned or taught.

- Birds migrate from North to South for the winter to protect themselves from the cold.
- Salmon swim upstream to nesting grounds.
- Some insects migrate and form cocoons to metamorphose.
- Rattlesnakes shake their rattles to warn other animals.

Learned Behaviors

Some behaviors and traits may be inherited, but many behaviors must be taught by the parents or pack to the young. Below are some examples of learned or taught behaviors.

- A wolf pack teaches the young wolves how to hunt effectively as a group.
- Some primates use sticks as tools to gather food.
- Dogs learn tricks and commands from their owners.
- Pelicans learn to hunt for fish in groups.
- Humans teach their children words and how to read.

Genetics and Heredity

Genetics is the study of biological inheritance in organisms. Animals generally reproduce with a mother and a father, which both contribute their **genetic** information to offspring. The passing along of genetic traits is also known as **heredity**. The offspring of a mother with red hair and blue eyes with a father who has brown hair and brown eyes may receive any combination of those traits. Another example may be a red fox mating with a brown fox; the offspring may have either brown fur or red fur, and a pack of siblings may have a mixture of inherited traits. This type of inheritance can also be seen in plant life, as pink and white flowered plants may breed together to produce either pink or white flowered offspring, or even special hybrids with blended colors.

Modes of Reproduction

Animals can reproduce sexually or asexually. Most animals reproduce sexually. In **sexual reproduction**, males and females have different reproductive organs that produce **gametes**. Males have testes that produce sperm, and females have ovaries that produce eggs. During fertilization, a sperm cell unites with an egg cell, forming a **zygote**. Fertilization can occur internally such as in most mammals and birds or externally such as aquatic animals such as fish and frogs. The zygote undergoes cell division, which develops into an embryo and eventually develops into an adult organism. Some embryos develop in eggs such as in fish, amphibians, reptiles, and birds. Some mammals are **oviparous** meaning that they lay eggs, but most are **viviparous** meaning they have a uterus in which the embryo develops. One particular type of mammal called **marsupials** give birth to an immature fetus that finishes development in a pouch. However, there are some animals reproduce **asexually**. For example, hydras reproduce by budding, and starfish and planarians can reproduce by fragmentation and regeneration. Some fish, frogs, and insects can even reproduce by parthenogenesis, which is a type of self-reproduction without fertilization.

Effects of the Modes of Reproduction on Offspring

With **asexual reproduction**, an organism provides all of the **genes** to its offspring, making it like a **clone**, or exactly like the parent in its genetic makeup. This means that the offspring will be very similar to the parent unless there is a random mutation that causes a change. This means that the offspring will be very uniform to each other. In **sexual reproduction**, both parents provide genetic information that can be inherited, causing much more variety in the offspring from generation to generation. This more aggressive variation means that natural selection and adaptation is more likely to make a difference for the species in the long-term.

Review Video: Asexual Reproduction
Visit mometrix.com/academy and enter code: 565616

Due to mutations over long periods, genes come in alternate forms, called **alleles**, that determine how a **trait** will be represented in the offspring. Different alleles govern many different traits. Sexual reproduction makes new combinations of existing alleles. These new combinations lead to variations in physical and behavioral traits that lead to adaptation and selection, which are key components of evolution.

Domain Classification System

In 1990, Carl Woese introduced his domain classification system. **Domains** are broader groupings above the kingdom level. This system consists of three domains- *Archaea*, *Bacteria*, and *Eukarya*. All eukaryotes such as plants, animals, fungi, and protists are classified in the *Eukarya* domain. The *Bacteria* and *Archaea* domains consist of prokaryotes. Organisms previously classified in the *Monera* kingdom are now classified into either the *Bacteria* or *Archaea* domain based on their ribosomal RNA structure. Members of the *Archaea* domain often live in extremely harsh environments.

Review Video: Biological Classification Systems
Visit mometrix.com/academy and enter code: 736052

Taxonomies

A **taxonomy** is a classification system that helps sort out different groups of something. A strong example of a taxonomy is the classification system for animals. The animal kingdom is often depicted as a pyramid showing different levels of the taxonomy. The lower down the pyramid, the more specific the definition. For instance, an animal's Class identifies whether it is a fish, reptile, amphibian, bird, or mammal.

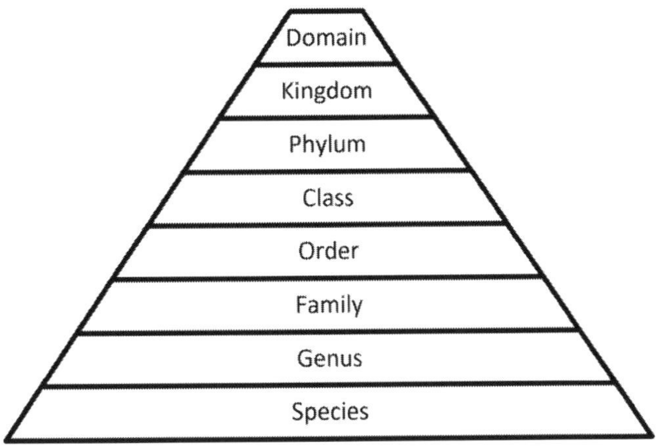

Viruses

Viruses are nonliving, infectious particles that act as parasites in living organisms. Viruses are acellular, which means that they lack cell structure. Viruses cannot reproduce outside of living cells. The structure of a virus is a nucleic acid genome, which may be either DNA or RNA, surrounded by a protective protein coat or **capsid**. In some viruses, the capsid may be surrounded by a lipid membrane or envelope. Viruses can contain up to 500 genes and have various shapes. They usually are too small to be seen without the aid of an electron microscope. Viruses can infect plants, animals, fungi, protists, and bacteria. Viruses can attack only specific types of cells that have specific receptors on their surfaces. Viruses do not divide or reproduce like living cells. Instead, they use the host cell they infect by "reprogramming" it, using the nucleic acid genome, to make more copies of the virus. The host cell usually bursts to release these copies.

Bacteria

Bacteria are small, prokaryotic, single-celled organisms. Bacteria have a circular loop of DNA (plasmid) that is not contained within a nuclear membrane. Bacterial ribosomes are not bound to the endoplasmic reticulum, as in eukaryotes. A cell wall containing peptidoglycan surrounds the bacterial plasma membrane. Some bacteria such as pathogens are further encased in a gel-like, sticky layer called the **capsule**, which enhances their ability to cause disease. Bacteria can be autotrophs or heterotrophs. Some bacterial heterotrophs are saprophytes that function as decomposers in ecosystems. Many types of bacteria share commensal or mutualistic relationships with other organisms. Most bacteria reproduce asexually by binary fission. Two identical daughter cells are produced from one parent cell. Some bacteria can transfer genetic material to other bacteria through a process called conjugation, while some bacteria can incorporate DNA from the environment in a process called transformation.

Protists

Protists are small, eukaryotic, single-celled organisms. Although protists are small, they are much larger than prokaryotic bacteria. Protists have three general forms, which include plantlike protists, animal-like protists, and fungus-like protists. **Plantlike protists** are algae that contain chlorophyll and perform photosynthesis. Animal-like protists are **protozoa** with no cell walls that typically lack chlorophyll and are grouped by their method of locomotion, which may use flagella, cilia, or a different structure. **Fungus-like protists**, which do not have chitin in their cell walls, are generally grouped as either slime molds or water molds. Protists may be autotrophic or heterotrophic. Autotrophic protists include many species of algae, while heterotrophic protists include parasitic, commensal, and mutualistic protozoa. Slime molds are heterotrophic fungus-like protists, which consume microorganisms. Some protists reproduce sexually, but most reproduce asexually by binary fission. Some reproduce asexually by spores while others reproduce by alternation of generations and require two hosts in their life cycle.

Fungi

Fungi are nonmotile organisms with eukaryotic cells and contain chitin in their cell walls. Most fungi are multicellular, but a few including yeast are unicellular. Fungi have multicellular filaments called **hyphae** that are grouped together into the mycelium. Fungi do not perform photosynthesis and are considered heterotrophs. Fungi can be parasitic, mutualistic or free living. Free-living fungi include mushrooms and toadstools. Parasitic fungi include fungi responsible for ringworm and athlete's foot. Mycorrhizae are mutualistic fungi that live in or near plant roots increasing the roots' surface area of absorption. Almost all fungi reproduce asexually by spores, but most fungi also have a sexual phase in the production of spores. Some fungi reproduce by budding or fragmentation.

Review Video: Feeding Among Heterotrophs
Visit mometrix.com/academy and enter code: 836017

Plants

Plants are multicellular organisms with eukaryotic cells containing cellulose in their cell walls. Plant cells have chlorophyll and perform photosynthesis. Plants can be vascular or nonvascular. **Vascular plants** have true leaves, stems, and roots that contain xylem and phloem. **Nonvascular plants** lack true leaves, stems and roots and do not have any true vascular tissue but instead rely on diffusion and osmosis to transport most of materials or resources needed to survive. Almost all plants are autotrophic, relying on photosynthesis for food. A small number do not have chlorophyll and are parasitic, but these are extremely rare. Plants can reproduce sexually or asexually. Many plants reproduce by seeds produced in the fruits of the plants, while some plants reproduce by seeds on cones. One type of plant, ferns, reproduce by a different system that utilizes spores. Some plants can even reproduce asexually by vegetative reproduction.

Prokaryotes and Eukaryotes

Sizes and Metabolism

Cells of the domains of Bacteria and Archaea are **prokaryotes**. Bacteria cells and Archaea cells are much smaller than cells of eukaryotes. Prokaryote cells are usually only 1 to 2 micrometers in diameter, but eukaryotic cells are usually at least 10 times and possibly 100 times larger than prokaryotic cells. Eukaryotic cells are usually 10 to 100 micrometers in diameter. Most prokaryotes are unicellular organisms, although some prokaryotes live in colonies. Because of their large surface-area-to-volume ratios, prokaryotes have a very high metabolic rate. **Eukaryotic cells** are much larger than prokaryotic cells. Due to their larger sizes, they have a much smaller surface-area-to-volume ratio and consequently have much lower metabolic rates.

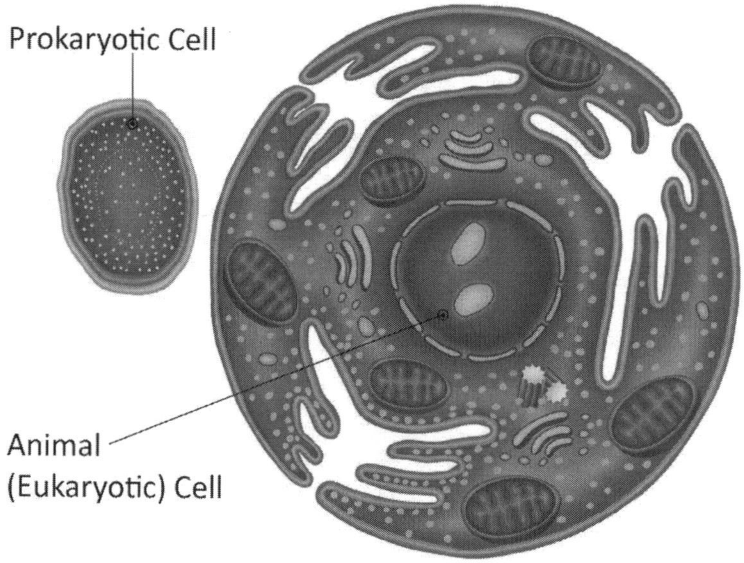

Review Video: Eukaryotic and Prokaryotic Cells
Visit mometrix.com/academy and enter code: 231438

Review Video: Cell Structure
Visit mometrix.com/academy and enter code: 591293

Organizational Hierarchy within Multicellular Organisms

Cell theory states that all organisms are made of cells, that cells are the basic unit of biological life, and that all cells arise from other cells. In **multicellular** organisms, cells combine to create different physiological structures with specific functions. There are four levels of organization in the human body: cells, tissues, organs, and organ systems. Different types of **cells** make up **tissues**. For example, muscle cells make up muscular tissue. Tissues make up **organs** with specific functions, such as the brain, heart, or liver. Organs work together as **organ systems**, such as the digestive system or the cardiovascular system. Organ systems are complex networks that achieve processes necessary to sustain life, such as breathing, moving, or eating.

CELLS

Cells are the basic structural units of all living things. Cells are composed of various molecules including proteins, carbohydrates, lipids, and nucleic acids. All animal cells are eukaryotic and have a nucleus, cytoplasm, and a cell membrane. Organelles include mitochondria, ribosomes, endoplasmic reticulum, Golgi apparatuses, and vacuoles. Specialized cells are numerous, including but not limited to, various muscle cells, nerve cells, epithelial cells, bone cells, blood cells, and cartilage cells. Cells are grouped to together in tissues to perform specific functions.

MEMBRANE-BOUND ORGANELLES

Prokaryotic cells are much simpler than eukaryotic cells. Prokaryote cells do not have a nucleus due to their small size and their DNA is located in the center of the cell in a region referred to as a **nucleoid**. Eukaryote cells have a **nucleus** bound by a double membrane. Eukaryotic cells typically have hundreds or thousands of additional **membrane-bound organelles** that are independent of the cell membrane. Prokaryotic cells do not have any membrane-bound organelles that are independent of the cell membrane. Once again, this is probably due to the much larger size of the eukaryotic cells. The organelles of eukaryotes give them much higher levels of intracellular division than is possible in prokaryotic cells.

Review Video: Cell Structure
Visit mometrix.com/academy and enter code: 591293

CELL WALLS

Not all cells have cell walls, but most prokaryotes have cell walls. The cell walls of organisms from the domain Bacteria differ from the cell walls of the organisms from the domain Archaea. Some eukaryotes, such as some fungi, some algae, and plants, have cell walls that differ from the cell walls of the Bacteria and Archaea domains. The main difference between the cell walls of different domains or kingdoms is the composition of the cell walls. For example, most bacteria have cell walls outside of the plasma membrane that contains the molecule peptidoglycan. **Peptidoglycan** is a large polymer of amino acids and sugars. The peptidoglycan helps maintain the strength of the cell wall. Some of the Archaea cells have cell walls containing the molecule pseudopeptidoglycan, which differs in chemical structure from the peptidoglycan but basically provides the same strength to the cell wall. Some fungi cell walls contain **chitin**. The cell walls of diatoms, a type of yellow algae, contain silica. Plant cell walls contain cellulose, and woody plants are further strengthened by lignin. Some algae also contain lignin. Animal cells do not have cell walls.

CHROMOSOME STRUCTURE

Prokaryote cells have DNA arranged in a **circular structure** that should not be referred to as a chromosome. Due to the small size of a prokaryote cell, the DNA material is simply located near the center of the cell in a region called the nucleoid. A prokaryotic cell may also contain tiny rings of DNA called plasmids. Prokaryote cells lack histone proteins, and therefore the DNA is not actually packaged into chromosomes. Prokaryotes reproduce by binary fission, while eukaryotes reproduce by mitosis with the help of **linear chromosomes** and histone proteins. During mitosis, the chromatin is tightly wound on the histone proteins and packaged as a chromosome. The DNA in a eukaryotic cell is located in the membrane-bound nucleus.

CELLS AND ORGANELLES OF PLANT CELLS AND ANIMAL CELLS

Plant cells and animal cells both have a nucleus, cytoplasm, cell membrane, ribosomes, mitochondria, endoplasmic reticulum, Golgi apparatus, and vacuoles. Plant cells have only one or two extremely large vacuoles. Animal cells typically have several small vacuoles. Plant cells have chloroplasts for photosynthesis and use this process to produce their own food, distinguishing plants as **autotrophs**. Animal cells do not have chloroplasts and therefore cannot use photosynthesis to produce their own food. Instead animal cells rely on other sources for food, which classifies them as **heterotrophs**. Animal cells have centrioles, which are used to help organize microtubules and in in cell division, but only some plant cells have centrioles. Additionally, plant cells have a rectangular and more rigid shape due to the cell wall, while animal cells have more of a circular shape because they lack a cell wall.

Review Video: Difference Between Plant and Animal Cells
Visit mometrix.com/academy and enter code: 115568

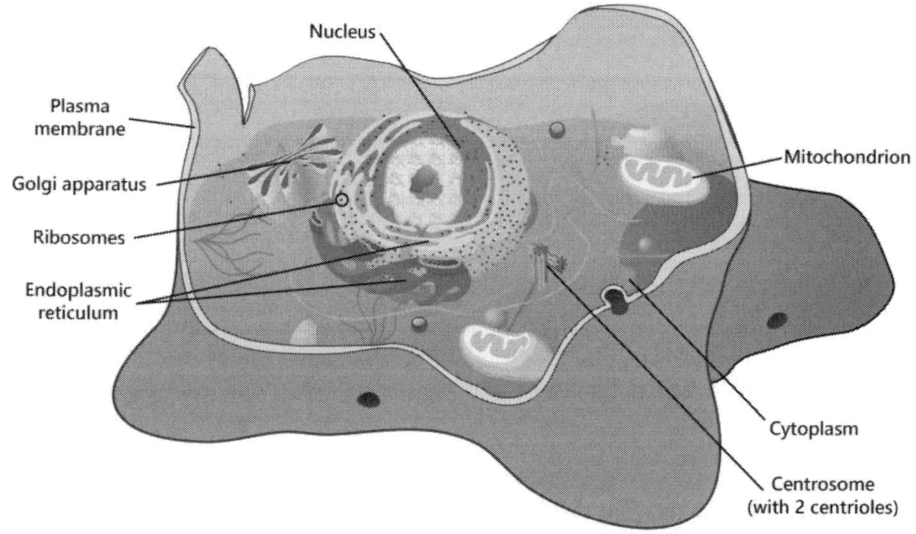

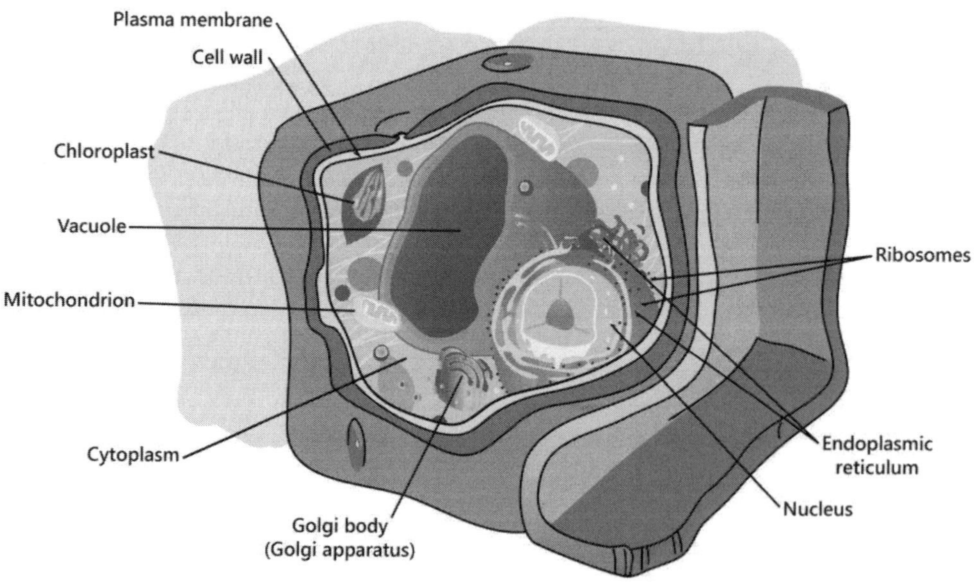

CELL MEMBRANES

The **cell membrane**, also referred to as the plasma membrane, is a thin semipermeable membrane of lipids and proteins. The cell membrane isolates the cell from its external environment while still enabling the cell to communicate with that outside environment. It consists of a phospholipid bilayer, or double layer, with the hydrophilic ("water-loving") ends of the outer layer facing the external environment, the inner layer facing the inside of the cell, and the hydrophobic ("water-fearing") ends facing each other. Cholesterol in the cell membrane adds stiffness and flexibility. Glycolipids help the cell to recognize other cells of the organisms. The proteins in the cell membrane help give the cells shape. Special proteins help the cell communicate with its external environment, while other proteins transport molecules across the cell membrane.

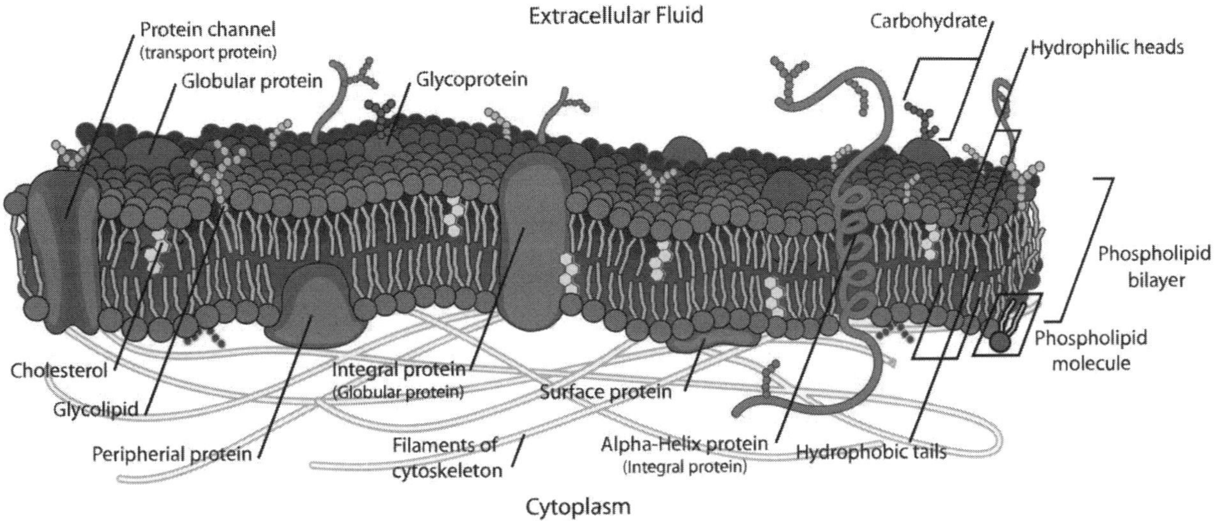

Review Video: Function of the Plasma Membrane
Visit mometrix.com/academy and enter code: 943095

NUCLEUS

Typically, a eukaryote has only one nucleus that takes up approximately 10% of the volume of the cell. Components of the nucleus include the nuclear envelope, nucleoplasm, chromatin, and nucleolus. The **nuclear envelope** is a double-layered membrane with the outer layer connected to the endoplasmic reticulum. The nucleus can communicate with the rest of the cell through several nuclear pores. The chromatin consists of deoxyribonucleic acid (DNA) and histones that are packaged into chromosomes during mitosis. The **nucleolus**, which is the dense central portion of the nucleus, produced and assembles ribosomes with the help of ribosomal RNA and proteins.

Functions of the nucleus include the storage of genetic material, production of ribosomes, and transcription of ribonucleic acid (RNA).

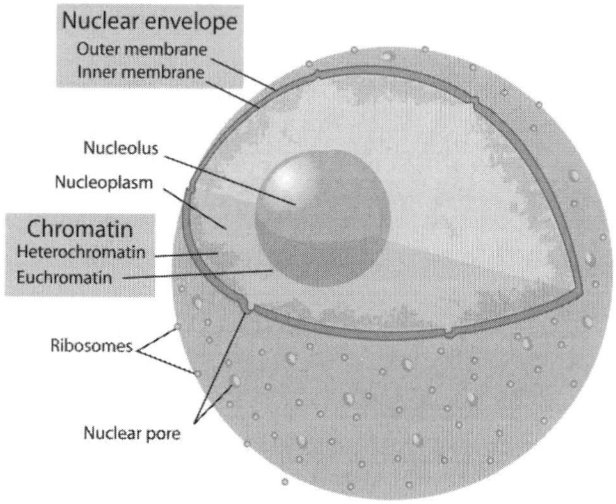

Chloroplasts

Chloroplasts are large organelles that are enclosed in a double membrane. Just as cells contain a fluid called cytoplasm, chloroplasts contain a fluid called the **stroma**. Within the stroma, there are discs called **thylakoids**, which are arranged in stacks called **grana** (singular: granum). The thylakoids have chlorophyll molecules on their surfaces. **Stromal lamellae** separate the thylakoid stacks. Chloroplasts perform photosynthesis and make food (in the form of sugars) for the plant. The light reaction stage of photosynthesis occurs in the grana, and the dark reaction stage of photosynthesis occurs in the stroma. Sugars are formed in the stroma. Chloroplasts have their own DNA and can reproduce by fission independently.

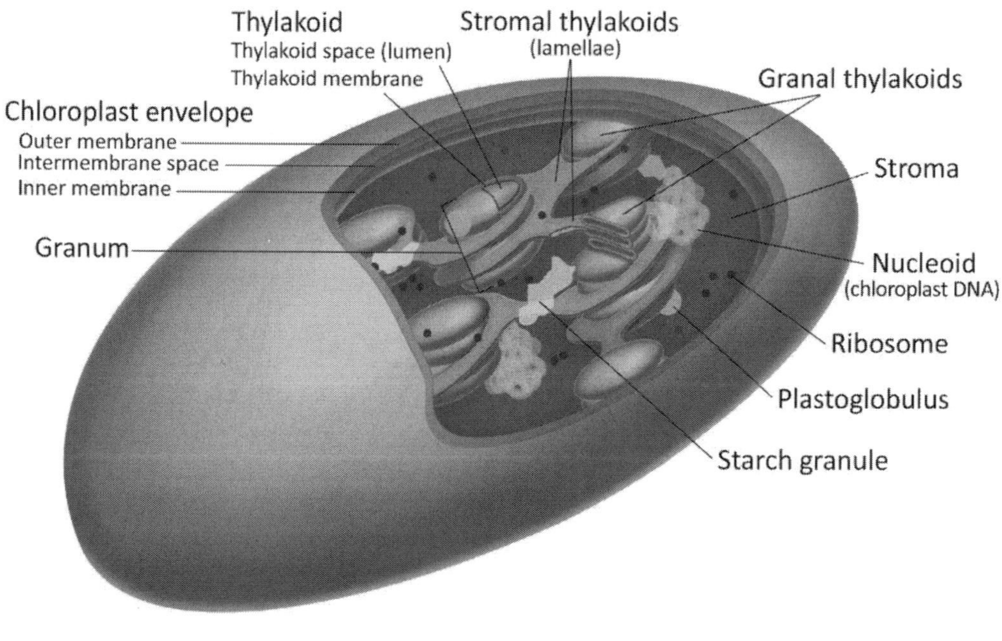

MITOCHONDRIA

Mitochondria break down sugar molecules and produce energy in the form of molecules of adenosine triphosphate (ATP). Both plant and animal cells contain mitochondria. Mitochondria are enclosed in a bilayer semi-membrane of phospholipids and proteins. The intermembrane space is the space between the two layers. The **outer membrane** has proteins called porins, which allow small molecules through. The **inner membrane** contains proteins that aid in the synthesis of ATP. The matrix consists of enzymes that help synthesize ATP. Mitochondria have their own DNA and can reproduce by fission independently. Mitochondria also help to maintain calcium concentrations, form blood components and hormones, and are involved in activating cell death pathways.

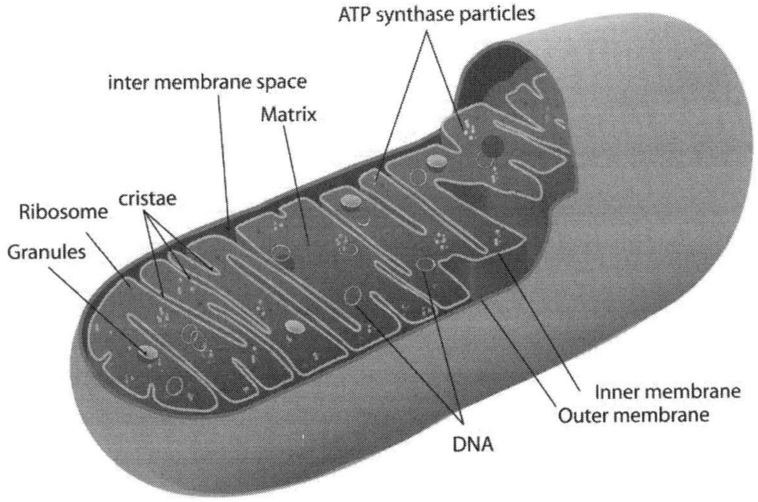

Review Video: Mitochondria
Visit mometrix.com/academy and enter code: 444287

RIBOSOMES

A **ribosome** consists of RNA and proteins. The RNA component of the ribosome is known as ribosomal RNA (rRNA). Ribosomes consist of two subunits, a large subunit and a small subunit. Few ribosomes are free in the cell. Most of the ribosomes in the cell are embedded in the rough endoplasmic reticulum located near the nucleus. Ribosomes are protein factories and translate the code of DNA into proteins by assembling long chains of amino acids. **Messenger RNA** (mRNA) is used by the ribosome to generate a specific protein sequence, while **transfer RNA** (tRNA) collects the needed amino acids and delivers them to the ribosome.

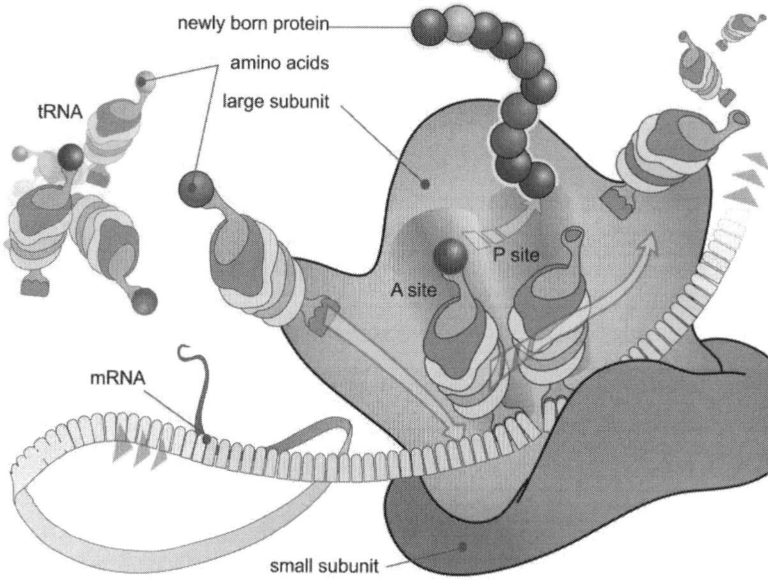

Golgi Apparatus

The **Golgi apparatus**, also called the Golgi body or Golgi complex, is a stack of flattened membranes called **cisternae** that package, ship, and distribute macromolecules such as carbohydrates, proteins, and lipids in shipping containers called **vesicles**. It also helps modify proteins and lipids before they are shipped. Most Golgi apparatuses have six to eight cisternae. Each Golgi apparatus has four regions: the cis region, the endo region, the medial region, and the trans region. Transfer vesicles from the rough endoplasmic reticulum (ER) enter at the cis region, and secretory vesicles leave the Golgi apparatus from the trans region.

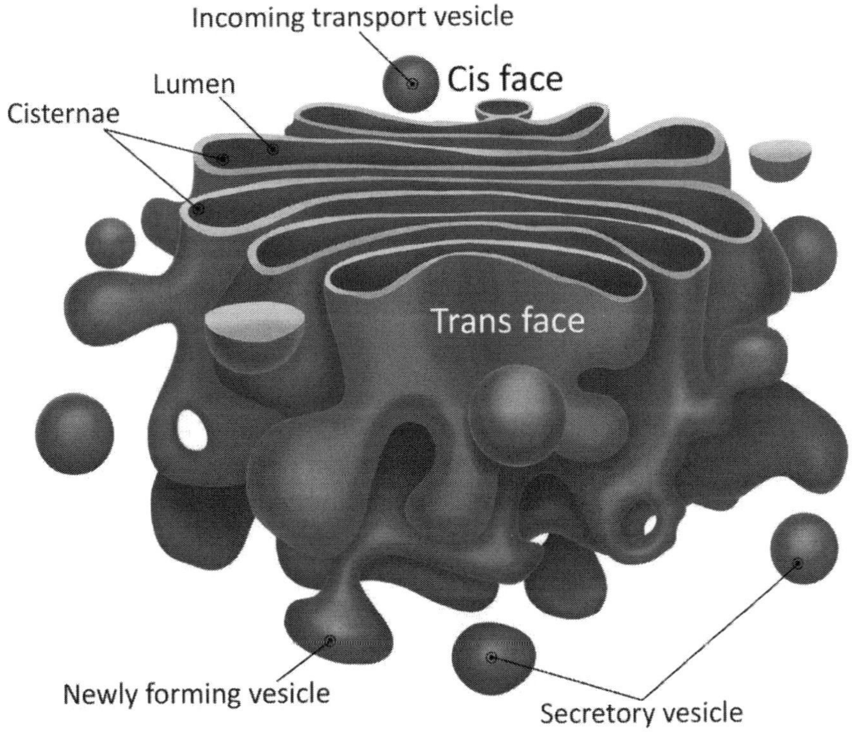

CYTOSKELETON

The **cytoskeleton** is a scaffolding system located in the cytoplasm. The cytoskeleton consists of elongated organelles made of proteins called microtubules, microfilaments, and intermediate filaments. These organelles provide shape, support, and the ability to move. These structures also assist in moving the chromosomes during mitosis. Microtubules and microfilaments help transport materials throughout the cell and are the major components in cilia and flagella.

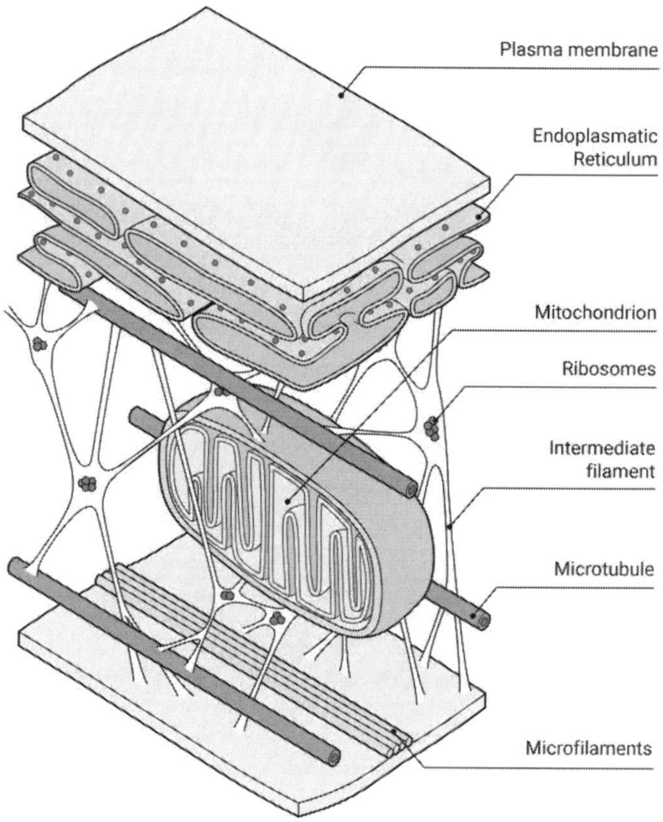

TISSUES

Tissues are groups of cells that work together to perform a specific function. Tissues can be grouped into four broad categories: muscle tissue, connective tissue, nerve tissue, and epithelial tissue. Muscle tissue is involved in body movement. **Muscle tissues** can be composed of skeletal muscle cells, cardiac muscle cells, or smooth muscle cells. Skeletal muscles include the muscles commonly called biceps, triceps, hamstrings, and quadriceps. Cardiac muscle tissue is found only in the heart. Smooth muscle tissue provides tension in the blood vessels, controls pupil dilation, and aids in peristalsis. **Connective tissues** include bone tissue, cartilage, tendons, ligaments, fat, blood, and lymph. **Nerve tissue** is located in the brain, spinal cord, and nerves. **Epithelial tissue** makes up the layers of the skin and various membranes. Tissues are grouped together as organs to perform specific functions.

ORGANS AND ORGAN SYSTEMS

Organs are groups of tissues that work together to perform specific functions. **Organ systems** are groups of organs that work together to perform specific functions. Complex animals have several organs that are grouped together in multiple systems. In mammals, there are 11 major organ systems: integumentary system, respiratory system, circulatory system, endocrine system, nervous system, digestive system, excretory system, muscular system, skeletal system, reproductive system, and immune system.

1. **Integumentary system:** the protective barrier of the body, including skin, hair, and nails.
2. **Respiratory system:** responsible for allowing air to enter and exit the lungs to obtain oxygen and release carbon dioxide. The respiratory system consists of the nasal passages, pharynx, larynx, trachea, bronchial tubes, lungs, and diaphragm.
3. **Circulatory system:** includes the heart, blood, and blood vessels that carry blood through the body, delivering oxygen to tissues.
4. **Endocrine system:** manages and releases hormones responsible for bodily functions and behavior, including hunger, stress, sleep, and many others. The endocrine system consists of several ductless glands, which secrete hormones directly into the bloodstream.
5. **Nervous system:** includes your brain, spinal cord, sense organs, and nerves. The nervous system allows you to sense, process, and respond to external stimuli. It also helps regulate physiological and behavioral processes.
6. **Digestive system:** processes and extracts nutrients from food. The excretory system is responsible for removing waste following digestion. The digestive system includes the stomach, intestines, liver, gallbladder, pancreas, and anus.
7. **Excretory system:** metabolizes food, filters blood, and excretes waste. It includes the kidneys and bladder.
8. **Muscular system:** includes muscles that allow the body to move. The muscles work in combination with the skeletal system.
9. **Skeletal system:** includes the bones, joints, and cartilage that make up your skeleton.
10. **Reproductive system:** enables humans to produce offspring. It includes the external and internal reproductive organs.
11. **Immune System:** keeps a record of microbes to recognize and destroy the microbes that enter your body and make you feel sick. It includes white blood cells, antibodies, complement system, lymphatic system, spleen, bone marrow, and thymus.

Dichotomous Keys

Species change and evolve over time to adapt to their environment. For example, mutations to a trait that cause beneficial changes can arise and become common in a population through natural selection. When two populations become so different that they are unable to reproduce with one another, they are considered separate species, and this process is called **speciation**. In speciation, while many of the original traits remain the same, the descendant species possesses unique traits. These unique traits make it possible to identify similar species from one another. A **dichotomous key** helps scientists tell two similar or related species apart. To use a dichotomous key, you must choose between two traits, such as "long wings" or "short wings" for a specimen. Depending on the answer, the key directs you to another set of traits to choose from, and you keep doing this until the specimen is narrowed down to one species.

Chapter Quiz

1. Which of the following is a relationship between at least two organisms in which both organisms benefit from each other?

a. Amensalism
b. Parasitism
c. Mutualism
d. Commensalism

2. What ecosystem is one of the most vulnerable to the direct and indirect impact of humans, and has become more acidic with the absorption of CO_2?

a. Taiga
b. Dessert
c. Tunda
d. Marine

3. In 1990, Carl Woese introduced his domain classification system, which consists of three domains. Which of the following is NOT one of the three domains?

a. *Archaea*
b. *Bacteria*
c. *Monera*
d. *Eukarya*

4. In the sexual reproduction process, during fertilization, a sperm cell unites with an egg cell to form a:

a. Gamete
b. Zygote
c. Vivipar
d. Embryo

5. Which of the following are acellular, nonliving, infectious particles that act as parasites in living organisms?

a. Viruses
b. Bacteria
c. Protists
d. Fungi

6. Which of the following is NOT true of eukaryotic and prokaryotic cells?

a. Eukaryotic cells are much larger than prokaryotic cells.
b. Plants, protists, and fungi all have eukaryotic cells.
c. Most prokaryotes are multicellular organisms.
d. Cells of the domains of Bacteria and Archaea are prokaryotes.

7. What category of tissue includes bone tissue, cartilage, tendons, ligaments, fat, blood, and lymph?

a. Nerve tissue
b. Muscle tissue
c. Epithelial tissue
d. Connective tissue

8. What major mammalian organ system constitutes the protective barrier of the body, including skin, hair, and nails?

a. Endocrine system
b. Excretory system
c. Respiratory system
d. Integumentary system

9. What type of cells do NOT have cell walls?

a. Animal cells
b. Plant cells
c. Bacteria cells
d. Archaea cells

10. Plant cells and animal cells both have all of the following, EXCEPT animal cells are missing:

a. Chloroplasts
b. Cell membrane
c. Cytoplasm
d. Vacuoles

11. Which of the following is a stack of flattened membranes called cisternae that package, ship, and distribute macromolecules?

a. Nucleus
b. Mitochondria
c. Ribosomes
d. Golgi Apparatus

Chapter Quiz Answer Key

1. **C:** See section **Relationships Between Organisms**

2. **D:** See section **Human Impact on Marine Environment**

3. **C:** See section **Domain Classification System**

4. **B:** See section **Modes of Reproduction**

5. **A:** See section **Viruses**

6. **C:** See section **Prokaryotes and Eukaryotes**

7. **D:** See section **Tissues**

8. **D:** See section **Organs and Organ Systems**

9. **A:** See section **Cell Walls**

10. **A:** See section **Cells and Organelles of Plant Cells and Animal Cells**

11. **D:** See section **Golgi Apparatus**

Scientific and Engineering Practices

Safety

Safety Procedures

Everyone working in a lab setting should be careful to follow these rules to protect themselves and others from injury or accidents.

- Students should wear a **lab apron** and **safety goggles**.
- **Loose** or **dangling** clothing and jewelry, necklaces, and earrings should not be worn.
- Those with **long hair** should tie it back.
- Care should always be taken not to **splash chemicals**.
- **Open-toed shoes** such as sandals and flip-flops should not be worn, nor should wrist watches.
- **Glasses** are preferable to contact lenses since the latter carries a risk of chemicals getting caught between the lens and the eye.
- Students should always be **supervised** during an experiment.
- The area where the experiment is taking place and the surrounding floor should be **free of clutter**.
- **Food** and **drink** should also not be allowed in a lab setting.
- **Cords** should not be allowed to **dangle** from work stations.
- There should be no **rough-housing** in the lab.
- **Wash hands** before and after the lab is complete.

Safety Gloves

There are many types of **gloves** available to help protect the skin from cuts, burns, and chemical splashes. There are many considerations to take into account when choosing a glove. For example, gloves that are highly protective may limit grip or accuracy. Some gloves may not offer appropriate protection against a specific chemical. Disposable latex, vinyl, or nitrile gloves are usually appropriate for most circumstances, and offer protection from incidental splashes and contact.

Other Safety Equipment

Equipment	Description
Chemical Splash Goggles	Protect the eyes from chemical splashes, can usually be worn over glasses
Lab Apron	Protects clothes from chemical splashes and other hazards in the lab
Eyewash Station	Helps flush chemicals from the eyes and face using clean water
Fire Blanket	Puts out fires by smothering the flames
Fire Extinguisher	Puts out fires by spraying a chemical that cools an area and smothers the flames

Laboratory Accidents

Accidents happen in labs, so it is important to know how to clean up, stay safe, and report the accident to the teacher. Any spills or accidents should be **reported** to the teacher so that the teacher can determine the safest clean-up method. The student should start to wash off a **chemical** spilled on the skin while reporting the incident. Some spills may require removal of contaminated clothing and use of the **safety shower**. Broken glass should be disposed of in a designated container. If someone's clothing catches fire they should walk to the safety shower and use it to extinguish the flames. A fire blanket may be used to smother a **lab fire**. A fire extinguisher, phone, spill neutralizers, and a first aid box are other types of **safety equipment** found in the lab. Students should be familiar with **routes** out of the room and the building in case of fire.

Reusing and Disposing of Materials

When conducting an investigation, scientists try to **conserve** materials by making sure they are not overused or wasted. To prevent overuse, it is important for scientists to consider potential ways to **limit** the use of certain materials. For example, consider glass and plastic. In a lab, plastic is not the most durable material, so it is not often reusable. Because of this, a scientist would try to limit its use by using something more durable, like glass. By using a more durable material that can be reused, the scientist would reduce the amount of waste produced by the experiment. Next, scientists consider whether it is possible to **reuse** the material in another investigation.

Disposal

Materials made of glass or plastic may be reusable, depending on how they have been used. However, in some cases, the dangers of reusing equipment outweigh the benefits of conservation. For example, plastic containers can be degraded by harsh chemicals, and glass microscope slides used to look at harmful microbes can be difficult to sterilize. In these cases, scientists follow a set of procedures for the proper **disposal** of materials. **Plastics** should be rinsed thoroughly and recycled or disposed of according to local regulations. Contaminated or broken **glass** should be placed in a container separate from regular waste, such as a cardboard box or dedicated glass bin. Guidelines for **chemical** disposal vary widely based on the properties of the chemical, and some chemicals are unsafe to dispose of down the drain or in the trash. Therefore, it is important that scientists research and consider the proper disposal method of any chemicals prior to using them in an investigation.

Science Knowledge and Scientific Process

Scientific knowledge is knowledge about the world that we understand by observing and testing. The **scientific process** is how we try to gain scientific knowledge. The steps are to make an initial observation, make a hypothesis, test the hypothesis with an experiment, draw conclusions from the experiment, then start over with new observations.

Scientific Knowledge

Scientific knowledge refers to any topic that is studied **empirically**, meaning that it is based on observation of a **phenomenon** in an objective way. The body of **scientific knowledge** is often broken down into several domains including biology, ecology, Earth science, space science, physics, and chemistry. These each have further subdomains and are overlapping in many ways. For instance, ecology is the study of ecosystems, which are made up of biological factors and geological factors, so it contains elements of both biology and Earth science. Each of these domains is subject to the concepts of scientific inquiry, such as the scientific method, scientific facts, hypotheses, and scientific laws.

Important Terminology

- A **phenomenon** is an event or effect that is observed.
- A **scientific fact** is considered an objective and verifiable observation. Usually, a fact can be repeated or demonstrated to others.
- A **scientific theory** is a proposition explaining why or how something happens and is built on scientific facts and laws. Scientific theories can be tested, but are not fully proven. If new evidence is found that disproves the theory, it is no longer considered true.
- A **hypothesis** is an educated guess that is not yet proven. It is used to predict the outcome of an experiment in an attempt to solve a problem or answer a question.
- A **law** is an explanation of events that always leads to the same outcome. It is a fact that an object falls. The law of gravity explains why an object falls. The theory of relativity, although generally accepted, has been neither proven nor disproved.
- A **model** is used to explain something on a smaller scale or in simpler terms to provide an example. It is a representation of an idea that can be used to explain events or applied to new situations to predict outcomes or determine results.

History of Scientific Knowledge

When one examines the history of **scientific knowledge**, it is clear that it is constantly **evolving**. The body of facts, models, theories, and laws grows and changes over time. In other words, one scientific discovery leads to the next. Some advances in science and technology have important and long-lasting effects on science and society. Some discoveries were so alien to the accepted beliefs of the time that not only were they rejected as wrong, but were also considered outright blasphemy. Today, however, many beliefs once considered incorrect have become an ingrained part of scientific knowledge, and have also been the basis of new advances. Examples of advances include: Copernicus's heliocentric view of the universe, Newton's laws of motion and planetary orbits, relativity, geologic time scale, plate tectonics, atomic theory, nuclear physics, biological evolution, germ theory, industrial revolution, molecular biology, information and communication, quantum theory, galactic universe, and medical and health technology.

Scientific Inquiry and Scientific Method

Scientists use a number of generally accepted techniques collectively known as the **scientific method**. The scientific method generally involves carrying out the following steps:

- Identifying a problem or posing a question
- Formulating a hypothesis or an educated guess
- Conducting experiments or tests that will provide a basis to solve the problem or answer the question
- Observing the results of the test
- Drawing conclusions

An important part of the scientific method is using acceptable experimental techniques. Objectivity is also important if valid results are to be obtained. Another important part of the scientific method is peer review. It is essential that experiments be performed and data be recorded in such a way that experiments can be reproduced to verify results. Historically, the scientific method has been taught with a more linear approach, but it is important to recognize that the scientific method should be a cyclical or **recursive process**. This means that as hypotheses are tested and more is learned, the questions should continue to change to reflect the changing body of knowledge. One cycle of experimentation is not enough.

Review Video: The Scientific Method
Visit mometrix.com/academy and enter code: 191386

Observations

An **observation** is something specific you notice about the world or an event. For instance, a very obvious event that takes place is if we leave milk out on the counter overnight, the milk will go bad. We observe this event by using our five senses: sight, taste, smell, touch, and sound. When milk goes bad, there are several ways it changes.

Asking Questions

Observations may inspire new questions. These questions can be used to form a hypothesis, which can be used to design an experiment. When trying to gain scientific knowledge, it is best to ask questions that are clear and specific, or well defined. This can make answering the question easier. When a question is not clear or is not specific, it may have several possible answers. It also may have an answer that only leads to more questions. For example, the question "what will happen if you drop an egg" is not a well-defined question. The result of dropping an egg depends on many factors, and there are many possible answers to the question. However, the question "what will happen if you drop an uncooked egg on concrete" is a well-defined question. The question is specific and clear, and it can be tested using a simple experiment.

Hypothesis

The next step of the scientific process is to make a hypothesis. A **hypothesis** is a proposed explanation for the expected results of an experiment. A testable hypothesis is one that is written prior to an investigation and can be easily supported or opposed using evidence from an experiment. A hypothesis about milk might be that if I keep milk above a certain temperature for a long time, it will go bad. Hypotheses need to be specific and testable so we can decide if it is true or false.

Experiment

The step after making a hypothesis is to check if it is true by testing it with an **experiment**. An experiment should be a controlled, specific situation that shows whether or not a hypothesis is correct. Experiments need to ask questions about **facts**, rather than **opinions**. Usually, the more specific the experiment, the clearer the answer will be. For instance, if I test my hypothesis by putting milk outside overnight, but do not set a timer, then I can get an answer, but I will not be able to record how time affected the experiment. Similarly, if the milk is outside and the temperature changes overnight, I will not be able to learn much about what effect the temperature had on the milk.

Variables

These two aspects of the experiment are examples of variables. **Variables** are parts of the experiment that can change. An **independent variable** is a variable that the experimenter will change during the experiment, so it is **controlled**. A **dependent variable** is a variable that changes in response to changes to an independent variable, and it is **observed**. For instance, we cannot control time, but we can observe the milk over time by checking it every half hour. Temperature, on the other hand, can be controlled with technology. We can keep the milk inside the house, where the temperature will always be around 70 degrees, or we can keep it in the refrigerator, where the milk will stay close to 40 degrees. These variables need to be controlled as best as possible to get the most specific results.

EXPERIMENTS TESTING ONE VARIABLE

Experiments should be designed to only test the effects of one variable. This helps experimenters make sure that the cause of the experiment's results is clear and certain. To make sure that the experiment only tests one variable, the experiment should only have one independent variable. For example, the height that sunflowers would grow in different circumstances depends on many factors that could be changed by the experimenter. Sunflowers are affected by the amount of water and sunlight they receive, the soil in which they are planted, the amount of space they have to grow, and the temperature of the air around them. If more than one of these factors are independent variables, then the experimenter may not be able to tell which factor affected growth of the sunflower. If only one of these factors is an independent variable, then the experimenter will know which factor affected the sunflower, since it will be the only thing that was changed by the experimenter.

CONSTANTS AND CONTROLS

To ensure that there is only one independent variable, other factors cannot be changed by the experimenter. These factors are called **constants**. Another aspect of an experiment is the control. A **control** is an example where the independent variable is not manipulated. The group in which the independent variable was manipulated can then be compared to the control group.

COLLECTING INFORMATION DURING AN EXPERIMENT

An experimenter makes observations during an experiment, writes them down, and then uses those observations to **draw conclusions**. Observations made during an experiment become **data**. Accurately **measuring** and **recording** data is necessary for an effective scientific investigation. **Accuracy** describes how close a measurement is to the true value. Not accurately measuring during an experiment may cause an experimenter to misunderstand the results of the experiment. For example, investigating how much plants grow when given different amounts of water would require the experimenter to accurately measure and record how much water each plant received and how much each plant grew daily. When an experimenter is writing and sharing the conclusion of a scientific investigation, accurate information and specific observations are needed so the experiment can be repeated and considered to be reliable.

OBSERVED AND MEASURED DATA

Data can be either measurable or observable. **Observable data** is often referred to as **qualitative data**, because it describes specific **qualities** of something being observed. An example of this is color or smell. It is very difficult to find numbers to describe a color or smell, but it is not hard to describe that a liquid changed from red to blue. **Measurable data** is also known as **quantitative data** because it refers to the quantity or amount of something. A good example of quantitative data is weight. Any time someone steps on a scale to know how much they weigh, they are looking at quantitative data. Both types of data are important to keep track of and record.

REPEATING EXPERIMENTS

Experiments should be **repeated** to see if the same result happens every time. For example, if you can get the same result in only three out of ten attempts, then the result is not reliable, and the experiment should be changed and tried again.

The results of an investigation that is only run once are not completely reliable. When an investigation is run the exact same way again and again and the result is the same every time, then the result is more likely to be considered reliable. If the investigation has only been completed once, or even just a few times, the results may be a result of chance or an error. When an investigation can be repeated, there is an opportunity for other discoveries to occur. An investigation may be repeated and produce different results. While those results may not be reliable, they can still lead to a new discovery or idea that can be investigated. The results of a repeated investigation may become a scientific theory, which is an explanation of an event that has become widely accepted by the science community.

Reflect

After an experiment is complete, the scientist needs to **reflect** on what happened by asking questions:

- Did the experiment answer the question?
- Was the hypothesis true or false?
- Did repeated attempts produce the same results?
- Is there anything I should change for future attempts?
- What did I learn?
- What questions can I ask now that I have learned something?

Making Observations After an Experiment

Once an investigation is complete, scientists will make more observations and try to interpret the data, which can be done in multiple ways. One way is by looking for **patterns**. For example, a scientist might notice a pattern in the data that shows when one variable is increased, another variable increases as well. Alternatively, increasing one variable could result in a decrease in another. These patterns help scientists to develop explanations for phenomena by determining how two variables are related.

Repeat the Process

After the experiment and reflection is over, the scientist hopefully learned something and can ask new questions. These questions should be more specific, or the experiment should be improved to get better answers.

Sharing Results

The result of a scientific investigation is valuable information that others may want to know. These results may help other scientists learn new information that is related to their own research and investigations. They may also help others if the information changes the way people may look at an everyday product or activity. However, results can be communicated in different ways, depending on whether the data is qualitative or quantitative. **Qualitative data** is valuable for understanding changes that cannot be represented by numbers, such as color changes in a chemical reaction. Meanwhile, **quantitative data** provides measurements that helps scientists to understand how two variables are connected. Qualitative data is best suited to a drawing, diagram, or a list of written descriptions, while quantitative data is typically represented in the form of a table or graph.

Lab Reports

A **lab report** should begin with a statement describing the problem or question being investigated. It should also include the hypothesis and list the variables in the experiment. Both a list of all materials used and the detailed procedure that was followed during the investigation are important to include. These will allow other scientists to replicate the investigation. A lab report should also list the results of an investigation. Any data tables or observations that are part of the results need to be labeled correctly and include accurate measurements and calculations. Finally, a lab report should conclude with an explanation that uses the evidence that was found during the investigation to state whether the hypothesis was supported or not supported. Also, the conclusion should include a detailed summary of the data collected during the investigation, and it should describe any errors that might have occurred during the investigation.

Venn Diagrams

One helpful way of sorting out information when comparing two things is a **venn diagram.** This tool is essentially just two circles that overlap, and it is used to display what aspects of one thing are similar or different from another thing. In the following diagram, notice how fish and frogs are similar in some ways, but different in others.

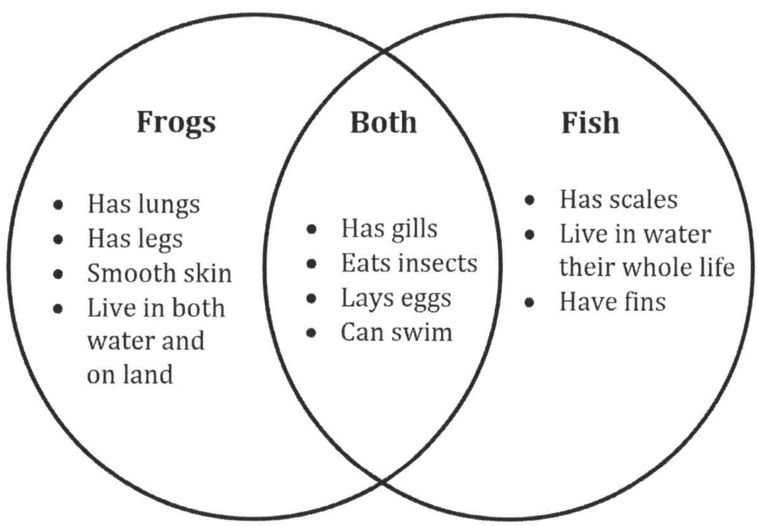

Frequency Tables

Frequency tables show how frequently each unique value appears in a set. A **relative frequency table** is one that shows the proportions of each unique value compared to the entire set. Relative frequencies are given as percentages; however, the total percent for a relative frequency table will not necessarily equal 100 percent due to rounding. An example of a frequency table with relative frequencies is below.

Favorite Color	Frequency	Relative Frequency
Blue	4	13%
Red	7	22%
Green	3	9%
Purple	6	19%
Cyan	12	38%

Circle Graphs

Circle graphs, also known as *pie charts*, provide a visual depiction of the relationship of each type of data compared to the whole set of data. The circle graph is divided into sections by drawing radii to create central angles whose percentage of the circle is equal to the individual data's percentage of the whole set. Each 1% of data is equal to 3.6° in the circle graph. Therefore, data represented by a 90° section of the circle graph makes up 25% of the whole. When complete, a circle graph often looks like a pie cut into uneven wedges. The pie chart below shows the data from the frequency table referenced earlier where people were asked their favorite color.

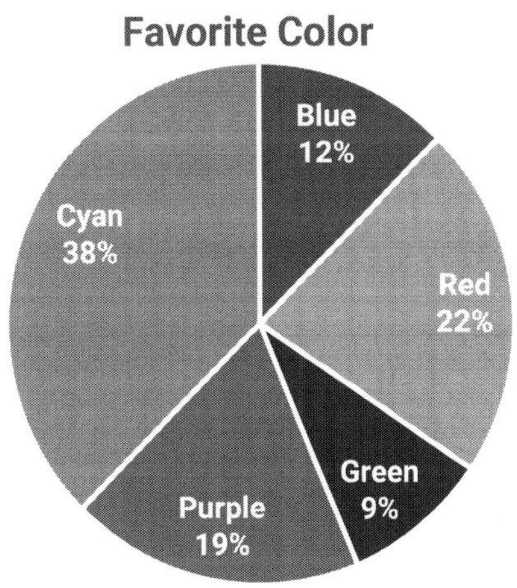

Pictographs

A **pictograph** is a graph, generally in the horizontal orientation, that uses pictures or symbols to represent the data. Each pictograph must have a key that defines the picture or symbol and gives the quantity each picture or symbol represents. Pictures or symbols on a pictograph are not always shown as whole elements. In this case, the fraction of the picture or symbol shown represents the same fraction of the quantity a whole picture or symbol stands for. For example, a row with $3\frac{1}{2}$ ears of corn, where each ear of corn represents 100 stalks of corn in a field, would equal $3\frac{1}{2} \times 100 = 350$ stalks of corn in the field.

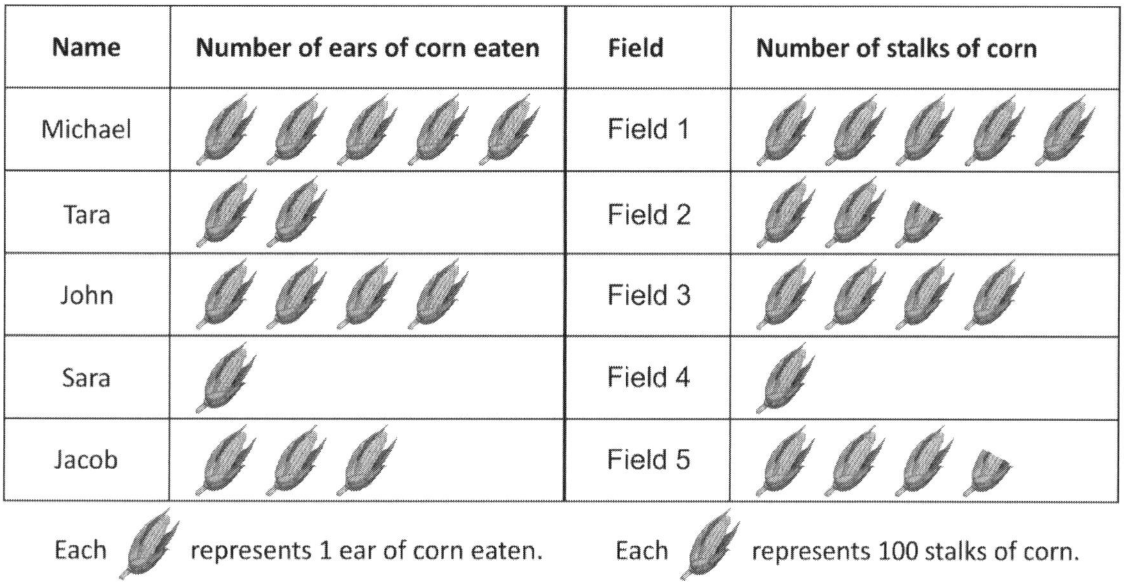

Review Video: Pictographs
Visit mometrix.com/academy and enter code: 147860

Line Graphs

Line graphs have one or more lines of varying styles (solid or broken) to show the different values for a set of data. The individual data are represented as ordered pairs, much like on a Cartesian plane. In this case, the *x*- and *y*-axes are defined in terms of their units, such as dollars or time. The individual plotted points are joined by line segments to show whether the value of the data is increasing (line sloping upward), decreasing (line sloping downward), or staying the same (horizontal line). Multiple sets of data can be graphed on the same line graph to give an easy visual comparison. An example of this would be graphing achievement test scores for different groups of students over the same time period to see which group had the greatest increase or decrease in performance from year to year (as shown below).

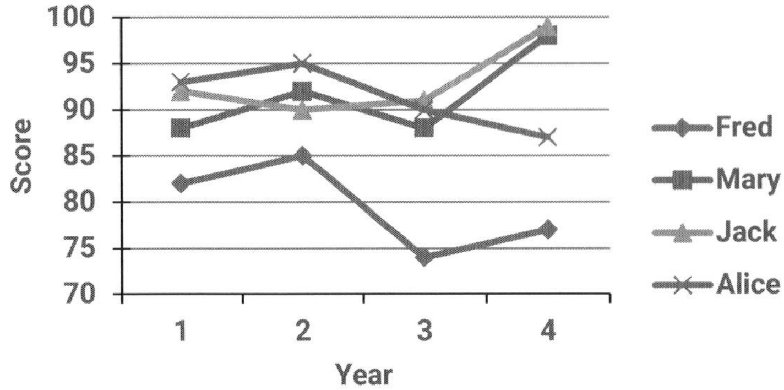

Review Video: How to Create a Line Graph
Visit mometrix.com/academy and enter code: 480147

Line Plots

A **line plot**, also known as a *dot plot*, has plotted points that are not connected by line segments. In this graph, the horizontal axis lists the different possible values for the data, and the vertical axis lists the number of times the individual value occurs. A single dot is graphed for each value to show the number of times it occurs. This graph is more closely related to a bar graph than a line graph. Do not connect the dots in a line plot or it will misrepresent the data.

Review Video: Line Plot
Visit mometrix.com/academy and enter code: 754610

Stem and Leaf Plots

A **stem and leaf plot** is useful for depicting groups of data that fall into a range of values. Each piece of data is separated into two parts: the first, or left, part is called the stem; the second, or right, part is called the leaf. Each stem is listed in a column from smallest to largest. Each leaf that has the common stem is listed in that stem's row from smallest to largest. For example, in a set of two-digit numbers, the digit in the tens place is the stem, and the digit in the ones place is the leaf. With a stem and leaf plot, you can easily see which subset of numbers (10s, 20s, 30s, etc.) is the largest. This information is also readily available by looking at a histogram, but a stem and leaf plot also allows you to look closer and see exactly which values fall in that range. Using a sample set of test scores (82, 88, 92, 93, 85, 90, 92, 95, 74, 88, 90, 91, 78, 87, 98, 99), we can assemble a stem and leaf plot like the one below.

Test Scores

7	4	8							
8	2	5	7	8	8				
9	0	0	1	2	2	3	5	8	9

Review Video: Stem-and-Leaf Plots
Visit mometrix.com/academy and enter code: 302339

Bar Graphs

A **bar graph** is one of the few graphs that can be drawn correctly in two different configurations – both horizontally and vertically. A bar graph is similar to a line plot in the way the data is organized on the graph. Both axes must have their categories defined for the graph to be useful. Rather than placing a single dot to mark the point of the data's value, a bar, or thick line, is drawn from zero to the exact value of the data, whether it is a number, percentage, or other numerical value. Longer bar lengths correspond to greater data values. To read a bar graph, read the labels for the axes to find the units being reported. Then, look where the bars end in relation to the scale given on the corresponding axis and determine the associated value.

The bar chart below represents the responses from our favorite-color survey.

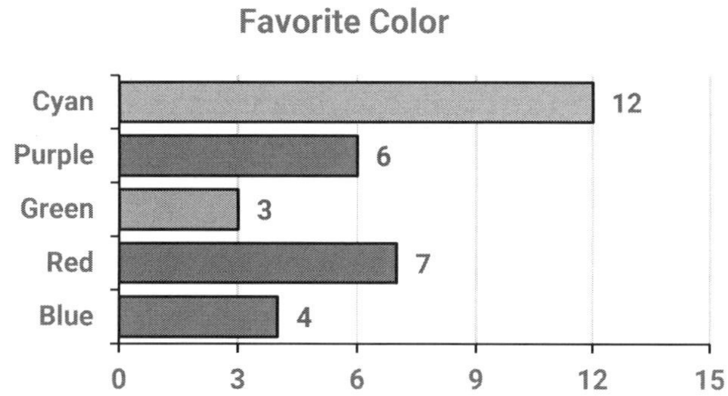

Constructing Explanations

In science, an explanation is only considered credible if it is based upon and supported by **empirical** evidence, which includes data from an experiment and unbiased observations. Scientists construct credible explanations by analyzing data. The first step of constructing an explanation is deciding whether the data **supports** or **opposes** the hypothesis. When the data supports a scientist's hypothesis, the scientist can make a **conclusion** about the relationship he or she studied. This conclusion is combined with scientific reasoning and existing information to form a well-rounded explanation. When the data does not support a scientist's initial hypothesis, the scientist can make a conclusion about what is not true and suggest potential explanations that could be tested in future experiments. When a scientific idea is consistently supported by evidence and data from many experiments, it may be referred to as a **theory**, which is a well-tested and widely accepted explanation for a phenomenon.

Predicting Trends and Patterns

When analyzing scientific data, scientists look for **patterns** or associations, which can be used to make predictions or generalizations about the natural world. One method for making predictions is to identify the relationship between two factors. For example, a data set may show that cities with more buildings have higher amounts of light pollution. This connection is called a **correlation**. When two variables are correlated, it is usually possible to predict an effect. For example, when given the number of buildings in a certain city, a scientist could make a reasonable prediction about the amount of light pollution in that city. In addition, scientists can use previous research and scientific explanations to predict **trends**. Trends show the relationship of two factors over a certain period of time.

Evaluating Scientific Explanations

The results of an investigation and the conclusions that scientists make after studying data are used to create scientific explanations. **Explanations** seek to describe why natural events happen and provide new details about scientific discoveries. However, some explanations are not reliable. When new scientific explanations are made, it is important to evaluate them to see if they are reliable and possible. Important factors to think about and questions to ask when evaluating a scientific explanation are:

- **Logic:** Does the explanation make sense? Is the explanation reasonable? Does it seem possible?
- **Question or Problem:** Was the question or problem that the investigation studied well-defined? Did the investigation results answer that question?
- **Experimental methods:** Is the method used in the experiment reliable? Did the experimenter record their process? Was the experiment performed properly and carefully?
- **Tools:** Did the tools used take accurate measurements? Were the correct tools used?
- **Evidence:** Is the explanation based on direct or indirect evidence? Does the evidence support the explanation well?
- **Research:** Did the investigator use reliable, scientific resources when doing research related to the investigation or experiment?

Evaluating Conflicting Explanations

When a scientist is presented with two opposing explanations of a scientific phenomenon, it is important that he or she first look at the **evidence** used to support each explanation. All strong scientific explanations are supported by experimental evidence, typically in the form of data from an investigation. In addition, scientists must carefully analyze the **methods** of an experiment to make sure the experiment was well-designed. Checking that the experiment was well designed helps to determine whether the evidence itself is valid. Lastly, scientists might question the conclusion and explanation itself by asking whether the data could be explained by an **alternative explanation.** In this case, scientists can conduct **follow-up experiments** to help rule out opposing explanations.

Scientific Models

Scientists often create **models** to help express and understand scientific ideas. A model is a representation of an idea that is used to experience something that cannot be experienced directly. For instance, we cannot see and experience evaporation directly, but we can easily draw out the process of evaporation, condensation, and precipitation. Having a drawing helps us to understand the concept since we cannot experience it directly. Models can be three-dimensional, such as something you can hold, or they can be simple diagrams demonstrating a process. For instance, a planetarium is a large model that helps someone see the size of planets and stars and how they interact. More typical models in the classroom include baking soda and vinegar volcanoes, solar system mobiles, or atoms and molecules made from foam and straws. Other models can include a diagram showing the water cycle.

Limitations of Models

Models can be helpful for experiencing a scientific process that normally could not be observed directly, but they are limited. Models are usually used to display a very large thing in a small way, such as a volcano or the Earth in a way that a human can look at it and touch it. Models are also often used to express very small things or invisible things in a more observable way. Changing the size or the materials used to express something limits how similar a model can be to the real thing. For instance, if a model of the water cycle used cotton balls to show clouds, it limits our understanding of clouds. Clouds are not made of dry, solid cotton, but are made up of vapor filled with water. Volcanos made from clay that use baking soda and vinegar do not demonstrate the extreme heat or mass of volcanic materials. Similarly, a mobile of the solar system cannot express how extremely large the sun and planets are. When using a model to understand a concept, the observer needs to be aware that they are probably only getting a clear picture of a small part of the concept, not gaining full understanding from the model.

Measurement

Tools for Measuring and Observation

Purpose	Tool
Measuring Length	Rulers, meter sticks
Measuring Weight or Mass	Spring scales, pan balances
Measuring Volume	Beakers, graduated cylinders
Measuring Time	Timers, clocks
Measuring Temperature	Thermometer
Measuring Light	Spectroscope (or spectrometer)
Recording Information	Journals, notebooks
Observing Animals and Plants	Terrariums, aquariums, collecting nets
Observing Weather	Rain Gauges, wind vanes, anemometers, psychrometers
Observing effects of heat	Hot plates
Models for Understanding Concepts	Sun-Earth-Moon System Models, volcano models, water cycle models
Visual Observation	cameras, hand lenses, microscopes
Making calculations	Calculators, computers
Holding substances	Test Tubes

Metric and International System of Units

The **metric system** is the accepted standard of measurement in the scientific community. The **International System of Units (SI)** is a set of measurements (including the metric system) that is almost globally accepted. The United States, Liberia, and Myanmar have not accepted this system. **Standardization** is important because it allows the results of experiments to be compared and reproduced without the need to laboriously convert measurements. The SI is based partially on the **meter-kilogram-second (MKS) system** rather than the **centimeter-gram-second (CGS) system**. The MKS system considers meters, kilograms, and seconds to be the basic units of measurement, while the CGS system considers centimeters, grams, and seconds to be the basic units of measurement. Under the MKS system, the length of an object would be expressed as 1 meter instead of 100 centimeters, which is how it would be described under the CGS system.

Review Video: Metric System Conversions
Visit mometrix.com/academy and enter code: 163709

Metric System

The **metric system** is the accepted standard of measurement in the scientific community. **Standardization** is important because it allows the results of experiments to be compared and reproduced without the need to convert measurements. The metric system uses similar conversions between all types of measurement, including length, mass, volume, time, and temperature.

Customary and Metric (Scientific) Units of Measurement

The customary system commonly used in the United States is not based on consistent smaller units. Thus, 12 inches equal 1 foot, 3 feet equal 1 yard, and 5,280 feet equal 1 mile. The metric system used in science and in most countries is based on units of 10. Therefore, 1000 millimeters and 100 centimeters equal 1 meter, and 1,000 meters equal 1 kilometer. The same pattern is true for the other units of measurement in the two systems. The following table shows the different units.

Unit	Customary System	Metric System
length	inch, foot, mile	centimeter, meter, kilometer
mass, weight	net weight ounce, pound	gram, kilogram, newton
volume	fluid ounce, pint, quart	milliliter, liter
temperature	Fahrenheit degree	Celsius degree

Fahrenheit and Celsius Temperature Scales

In the Fahrenheit scale the point where water freezes and ice melts is set at 32°, and the point where water boils and water vapor condenses is 212°. That means a difference of 180° between the freezing and boiling points of water. In the Celsius scale, the freezing/melting point is set at 0°and the boiling/condensation point at 100°, making this scale much easier to use.

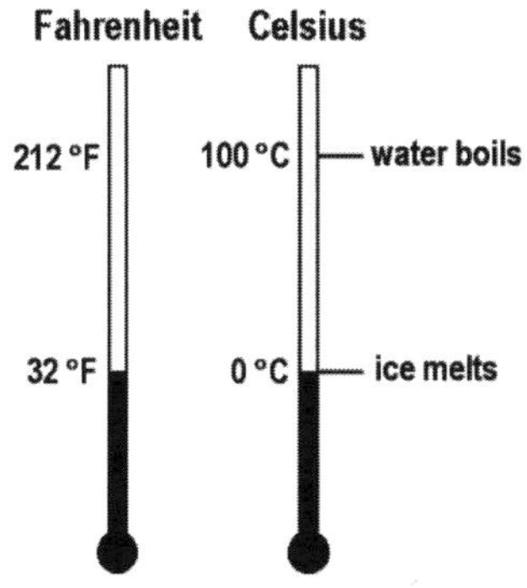

Basic Units of Measurement

The **metric system** is generally accepted as the preferred measurement system. Having a **universal standard** allows individuals to interpret measurements more easily, regardless of where they are located. The basic units of measurement are the **meter**, which measures length; the **liter**, which measures volume; and the **gram**, which measures mass. The metric system starts with a base unit and increases or decreases in units of 10. The prefix and the base unit combined are used to indicate an amount. For example, deka- is 10 times the base unit. A decameter, or dekameter, is 10 meters; a decaliter, or dekaliter, is 10 liters; and a decagram, or dekagram, is 10 grams. The prefix hecto- refers to 100 times the base amount and kilo- is 1,000 times the base amount. The prefixes that indicate a fraction of the base unit are deci-, which is 1/10 of the base unit; centi-, which is 1/100 of the base unit; and milli-, which is 1/1000 of the base unit.

Common Prefixes

The prefixes for **multiples** are as follows:

Deca or Deka	(da)	10
Hecto	(h)	100
Kilo	(k)	1,000
Mega	(M)	100,000

The prefixes for **subdivisions** are as follows:

Deci	(d)	1/10
Centi	(c)	1/100
Milli	(m)	1/1,000
Micro	(μ)	1/100,000

Contributions of Scientists

- **Sir Francis Bacon** – contributed many ideas that helped develop the modern scientific method.
- **Gallileo Galilei**– one of the first people to use a telescope and contributed ideas about how gravity works. He also contributed the idea that the Earth revolved around the Sun, and not the other way around.
- **Leonardo da Vinci** – known for his contributions to art and to science, he was an avid inventor, designing a submarine, an armored tank, and several aircraft far before any of which were actually built.
- **Sir Isaac Newton** – best known for his contributions to physics. He described the principals of inertia and friction.
- **Louis Pasteur** – discovered bacteria and invented the process of pasteurization and developed some of the first vaccines.
- **Thomas Edison** – invented many distinct devices, including the phonograph, improved upon the telephone, the lightbulb, and the kinetoscope, an early form of movie projector.
- **Albert Einstein** – studied theoretical physics with the use of mathematics and is particularly famous for his theory of relativity.

Chapter Quiz

1. All of the following are recommended for safety within a lab setting, and are the preferred procedure, EXCEPT for:

a. Close-toed shoes (instead of open-toed shoes)
b. Form fitting clothes (instead of loose clothing)
c. Contact lenses (instead of glasses)
d. Long hair tied back (instead of left down)

2. If someone's clothing catches fire while in the laboratory what should be used to extinguish the flames?

a. Safety shower
b. Fire blanket
c. Fire extinguisher
d. Eyewash station

3. In the scientific process, what step comes after forming a hypothesis?

a. Make observations
b. Experiment
c. Draw conclusions
d. Questioning

4. A change in which of the following would be considered quantitative data?

a. Smell
b. Weight
c. Color
d. Luster

5. The following graph is used to organize and display the test scores 82, 88, 92, 93, 85, 90, 92, 95, 74, 88, 90, 91, 78, 87, 98, and 99. What type of graph is being used?

Test Scores

Stem	Leaf								
7	4	8							
8	2	5	7	8	8				
9	0	0	1	2	2	3	5	8	9

a. Pictograph
b. Line plot
c. Bar graph
d. Stem and leaf plot

6. Which of the following tools is used to measure light?

a. Thermometer
b. Spectrometer
c. Anemometer
d. Psychrometer

7. Within the metric system, the gram is the basic unit used to measure:

a. Length
b. Volume
c. Mass
d. Temperature

8. Which of the following prefixes indicates multiples of 100?

a. Deca or Deka
b. Hecto
c. Kilo
d. Mega

9. What scientist contributed many ideas that helped develop the modern scientific method?

a. Gallileo Galilei
b. Sir Isaac Newton
c. Thomas Edison
d. Sir Francis Bacon

Chapter Quiz Answer Key

1. C: See section **Safety Procedures**

2. A: See section **Laboratory Accidents**

3. B: See section **Experiment**

4. B: See section **Observed and Measured Data**

5. D: See section **Stem and Leaf Plots**

6. B: See section **Tools for Measuring and Observing**

7. C: See section **Basic Units of Measurement**

8. B: See section **Common Prefixes**

9. D: See section **Contributions of Scientists**

Practice Test #1

1. Many water sports take place in the ocean. Some of these sports can negatively impact the aquatic populations in the areas where they take place. Those impacts not only hurt aquatic life, but they can also reduce human access to aquatic resources. Which of the following water sports is the most likely to have a negative impact on aquatic populations and resources?

a. Competitive surfing
b. Competitive sailing
c. Competitive fishing
d. Competitive swimming

2. The rainforest is home to thousands of different types of vegetation. There are four main levels of the rainforest as pictured below.

Which abiotic factor are the plants on the forest floor NOT competing with the other layers for?

a. Oxygen
b. Water
c. Sunlight
d. Fertile soil

3. Decide whether each of the actions below would increase or not increase the sustainability of an ecosystem in a city park. Write your answer for each action in the corresponding blank. The options are listed below.

Will increase sustainability	Will not increase sustainability

Action	Impact on Sustainability
Planting native shrubs about the perimeter of the park	
Spraying ant piles regularly to prevent bites	
Cutting shrubs regularly to prevent insect infestation	
Adding a pollinator garden	
Placing bird feeders in the trees	
Placing park benches around common areas of the playground	
Decreasing the number of trees to allow for more sunlight	

4. List the number of neutrons, protons, and electrons in ^{238}U.

a. 238, 92, 238
b. 92, 146, 146
c. 146, 92, 92
d. 92, 92, 146

5. Students were asked to match the body system to its function. Which student correctly completed this task?

a. Student 1

Body System	Functions
Nervous system	Sends signals between the brain and other parts of the body
Respiratory system	Responsible for the exchange of oxygen and carbon dioxide
Excretory system	Eliminates waste from the body
Integumentary system	Makes, sends, and regulates hormones

b. Student 2

Body System	Functions
Respiratory system	Carries blood, oxygen, nutrients, and hormones
Circulatory system	Responsible for the exchange of oxygen and carbon dioxide
Excretory system	Sends signals between the brain and other parts of the body
Integumentary system	Makes, sends, and regulates hormones

c. Student 3

Body System	Functions
Circulatory system	Carries blood, oxygen, nutrients, and hormones
Respiratory system	Responsible for the exchange of oxygen and carbon dioxide
Integumentary system	Protects body from outside harm
Endocrine system	Makes, sends, and regulates hormones

d. Student 4

Body System	Functions
Nervous system	Sends signals between the brain and other parts of the body
Respiratory system	Responsible for the exchange of oxygen and carbon dioxide
Excretory system	Makes, sends, and regulates hormones
Endocrine system	Eliminates waste from the body

6. Students are working in groups to complete an experiment their teacher assigned. The steps for the experiment are listed below.

Experiment Steps
1. Pour $\frac{1}{2}$ cup of hydrogen peroxide into an empty water bottle.
2. Add 1 teaspoon of dish soap to the water bottle.
3. Swirl the water bottle to mix the liquids.
4. In a small glass, mix 1 tablespoon of yeast and 3 tablespoons of warm water.
5. Pour the yeast mixture into the water bottle containing the hydrogen peroxide and dish soap.
6. Place your hand right above the water bottle and notice the heat coming from it.
7. Notice the foam rises in the water bottle and begins to overflow.

Which step above suggests that a chemical reaction occurred during the experiment?

a. Step 2: add 1 teaspoon of dish soap to the water bottle.
b. Step 3: swirl the water bottle to mix the liquids.
c. Step 5: pour the yeast mixture into the water bottle containing the hydrogen peroxide and dish soap.
d. Step 6: place your hand right above the water bottle and notice the heat coming from it.

7. The structure of the Milky Way galaxy is best described as:

a. Spiral
b. Starburst
c. Elliptical
d. Irregular

8. The grasshopper population in a garden was completely wiped out when a farmer used an all-natural repellent to rid the garden of the grasshoppers since they were eating the tomato plants. The main source of food for the small lizards that also lived in the garden was grasshoppers. Which statement below describes the indirect effect the farmer's action most likely had on the lizards?

a. The lizard population in the garden increased because the competition for space with the grasshoppers had been eliminated.
b. The lizard population decreased because the tomato plants no longer provided adequate shelter.
c. The lizard population in the garden decreased because the lizards were forced to relocate to a different area where the grasshoppers weren't affected by the farmer's actions.
d. The lizard population in the garden stayed the same because the lizards were forced to find a new source of food in the environment.

9. Substance A has a density of $5.0\ kg/m^3$, and substance B has a density of $4.0\ kg/m^3$. What is the ratio of volume A to volume B when the masses of the two substances are equal?

a. 1.25
b. 0.80
c. 1.12
d. 0.89

10. The Hertzsprung–Russell diagram was created to help scientists organize stars by temperature and luminosity. Fill in the bubbles to match the descriptions below with their correct placement on the Hertzsprung–Russell diagram.

a. A white dwarf star that is hotter and less bright than the Sun

b. A supergiant that is cooler than the Sun but has more luminosity

c. A main sequence star that is both brighter and hotter than the Sun

d. A main sequence star that is cooler and dimmer than the Sun

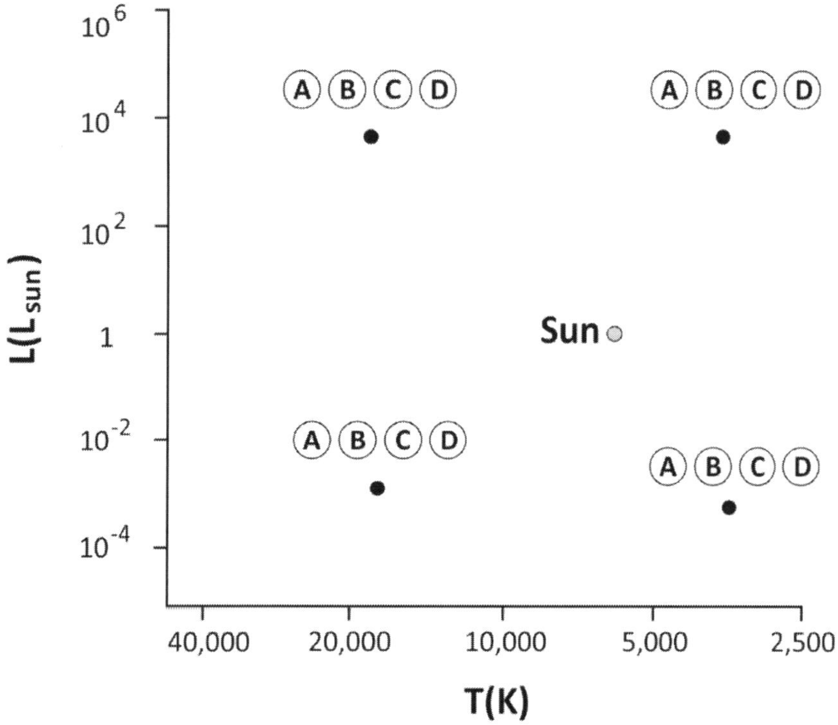

11. The photographs below show a skier on a mountain skiing down a hill. The mountain diagram shows the skier at different points on the mountain.

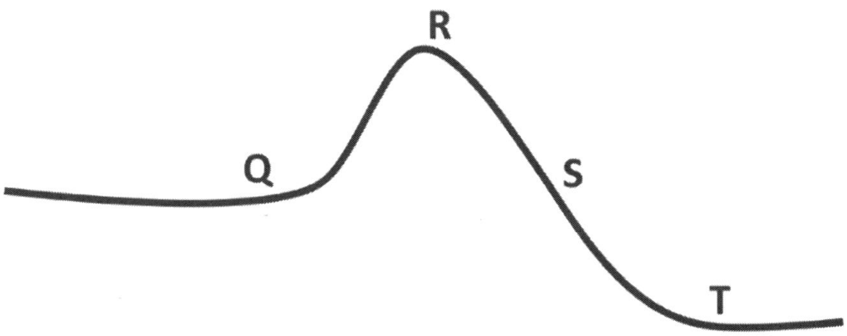

Which of the following statements correctly compares the kinetic and potential energy of the skier on different parts of the mountain?

a. The skier has more potential energy at position S than position R, and the skier has more kinetic energy at position S than position Q.
b. The skier has more potential energy at position R than position T, and the skier has less kinetic energy at position Q than position S.
c. The potential energy and kinetic energy of the skier are the same at position T.
d. The kinetic energy and potential energy of the skier increase from position R to position T.

12. Examine each circled set of elements and classify each set as metals, nonmetals, metalloids, or rare earth elements. For each set, fill in the bubble that corresponds to the correct similarity from the options below.

a. Metals
b. Metalloids
c. Nonmetals
d. Rare Earth Metals

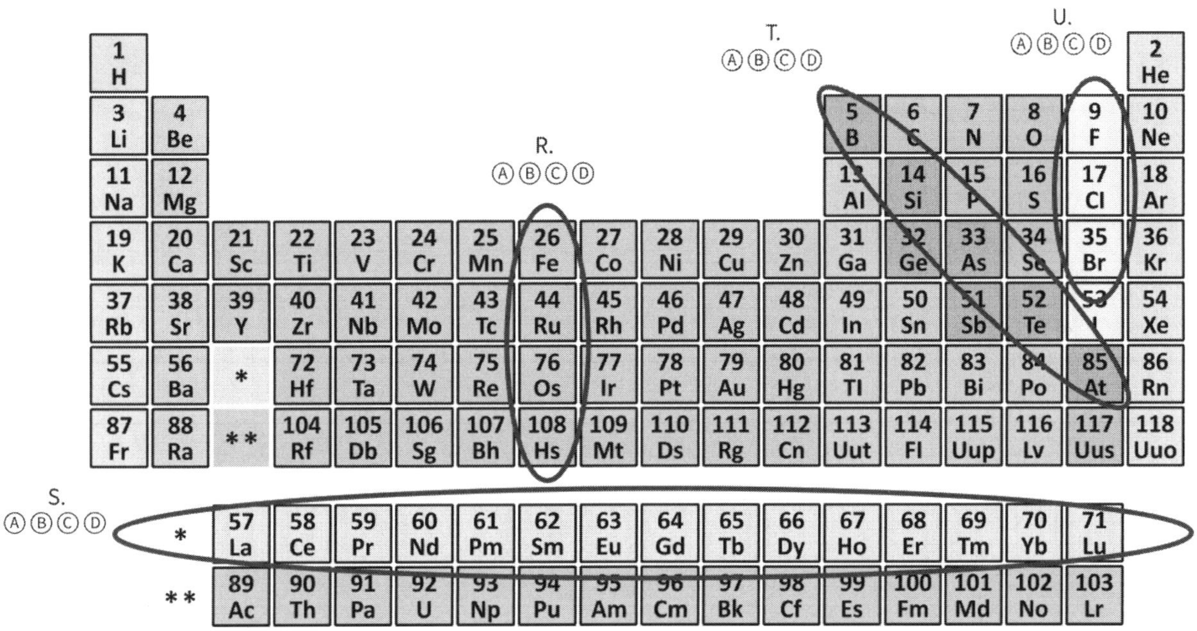

13. Which of the following describes two species that depend on a similar biotic and abiotic factor in their environment?

a. Giraffes eat the leaves of the acacia tree, while ants feed on the sap inside the same tree. Giraffes and ants both thrive in warm temperatures.
b. Grizzly bears and black bears in Yellowstone National Park feast on huckleberry plants and ants.
c. Sharks and dolphins both swim in the waters of the Pacific Ocean and prefer the water temperature to be fairly warm.
d. The yucca and the prickly pear both have root systems that thrive in sandy soil. Both plants need very little rain, making the desert an ideal environment them to live in.

14. You blow up a rubber balloon and hold the opening tight with your fingers. You then release your fingers, causing air to blow out of the balloon. This pushes the balloon forward, causing the balloon shoots across the room. Which of Newton's laws best explains the cause of this motion? Write your answer in the blank below.

Refer to the following for questions 15-16:

Mount Everest is the tallest mountain, above sea level, in the world.

15. Which image below shows how tectonic plates interact to form mountains like Mount Everest?

a. 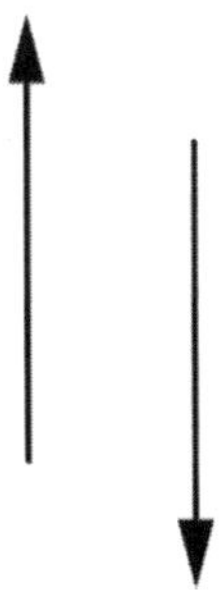

b. 

c. 

d. 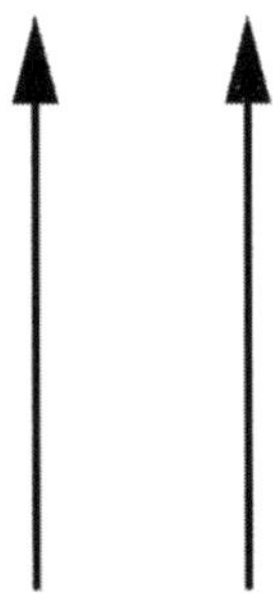

16. Which term correctly identifies the type of boundary identified in the previous question that can result in the formation of a mountain?

a. Divergent boundary
b. Transform boundary
c. Fault boundary
d. Convergent boundary

17. Three students on the football team were competing to see who could throw the football the fastest. The students were given three attempts to throw as hard as possible. The charts below show the results of the time the football was in the air and the distance the football traveled for each attempt.

Student 1		Student 2		Student 3	
Time (s)	Distance (m)	Time (s)	Distance (m)	Time (s)	Distance (m)
4	50	4	55	6	63
5	56	4	60	4	56
4	48	6	57	7	63

Based on the information in the chart, which student, on average, can throw the football the fastest, and what was that student's average speed?

a. Student 1 can throw the football the fastest with the average speed of 13.9 m/s.
b. Student 2 can throw the football the fastest with the average speed of 12.75 m/s.
c. Student 3 can throw the football the fastest with the average speed of 12.95 m/s.
d. Students 1 and 2 throw the football at the same average speed of 13.9 m/s.

18. Students living in Texas have pen pals living in the South American country of Bolivia in the Southern Hemisphere. Both Texas and Bolivia are marked on the globe.

Which statement below about the pen pals in Texas and Bolivia is INCORRECT?

a. In June it is summer in Texas, but it is winter in Bolivia.
b. When it is day in Texas, it is night in Bolivia.
c. In December it is summer in Bolivia, but it is winter in Texas.
d. The pen pal in Bolivia is sleeping at about the same time as the pen pal in Texas.

19. What is the primary driving force in the development of a hurricane?

a. High winds
b. Ocean temperatures
c. Cloud cover
d. Contact with land

20. English ivy is a vine that is native to Ireland and grows and multiplies quickly. English ivy vines wrap themselves around the trunks of trees and continue to grow over the branches and leaves. They can easily cover an entire tree from the ground up, damaging the bark, and they will compete with the tree for sun and water.

How might the growth of English ivy affect the ecosystem of a wooded area over time?

a. The ivy will provide additional shelter for animals living in the wooded area.
b. The trees overtaken by the ivy will eventually die, and the tree population will decrease.
c. The trees will benefit from the extra moisture that the ivy traps.
d. The ivy will strengthen the trees and help them grow more quickly.

21. The graph below shows the speed that an object traveled relative to time in seconds.

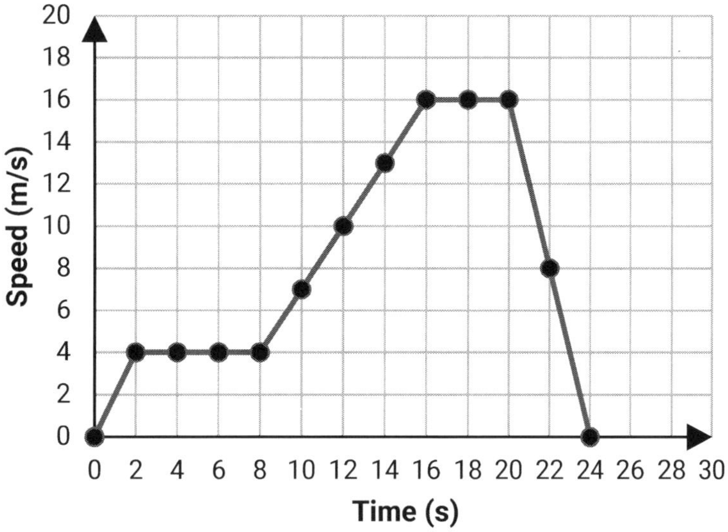

On the lines below, describe the relative speed of the object at each of the following time intervals.

- 0 to 2 seconds
- 2 to 8 seconds
- 8 to 16 seconds
- 16 to 20 seconds
- 20 to 24 seconds
- 24 seconds

22. Below is a food web of marine organisms.

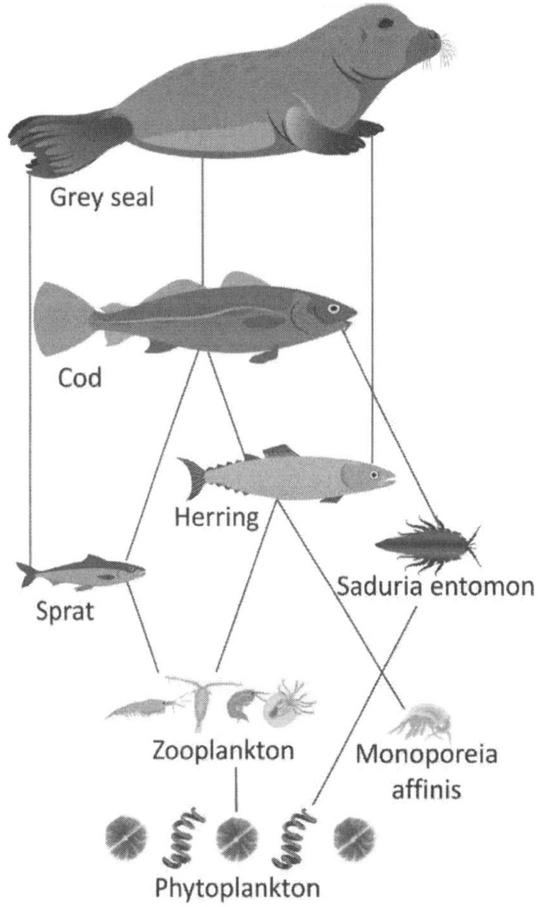

According to the food web, which correctly describes the flow of energy within these marine animals?

a. Phytoplankton → sprat → zooplankton → herring → gray seal
b. Zooplankton → sprat → cod → herring → gray seal
c. Cod → sprat → zooplankton → phytoplankton
d. Phytoplankton → *Saduria entomon* → cod → gray seal

23. Silver (Ag) is one of the best conductors of heat and electricity. What other element would be a great conductor of heat and electricity like silver?

a. Hydrogen (H)
b. Phosphorus (P)
c. Krypton (Kr)
d. Copper (Cu)

24. Fresh lemonade and fresh limeade both contain high amounts of citric acid, which is a mild acid. The chemical formula for citric acid is $C_6H_8O_7$. Caffeine is a stimulant that is found in drinks like coffee and many different sodas. The chemical formula for caffeine is $C_8H_{10}N_4O_2$. How many more atoms are present in caffeine than in citric acid? Write your answer in the blank below.

25. The students were asked to identify an unknown cell from the image below.

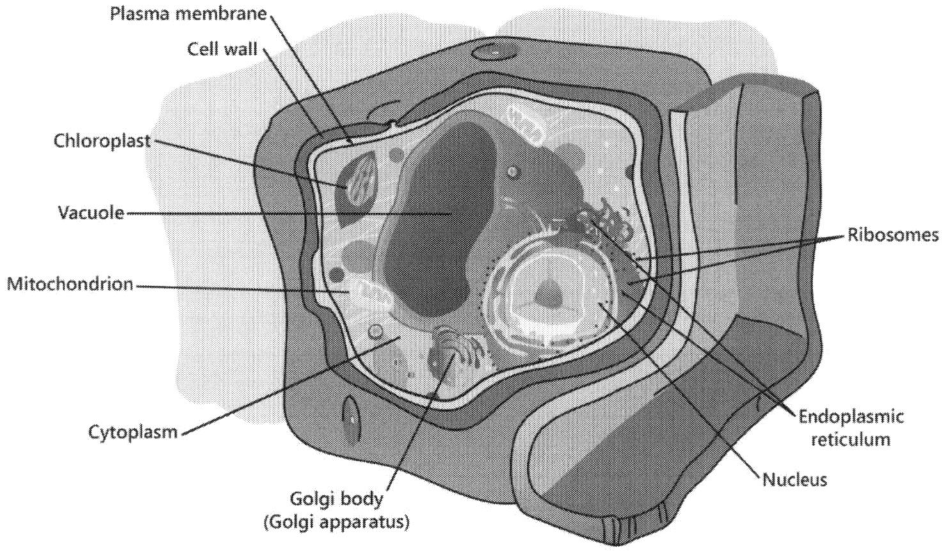

The table below shows the argument each student made about his or her determination. Which argument is correct?

Argument 1	The cell is an animal cell because it has mitochondria. The mitochondria in animal cells produce food. Plants don't have mitochondria because they make their own food.
Argument 2	The cell is a plant cell because it has a large vacuole, a cell wall, and chloroplasts.
Argument 3	The cell is an animal cell because it has a cell wall and mitochondria, which are only present in animal cells.
Argument 4	The cell is a plant cell because it has a plasma membrane, which is only present in plant cells. The nucleus is small, which is also a characteristic of plant cells.

a. Argument 1
b. Argument 2
c. Argument 3
d. Argument 4

26. A student is pushing a book at an acceleration of 12 m/s^2. The net force of this interaction was 71 N. What was the mass of the book?

a. 852 m
b. 0.17 m
c. 5.92 m
d. 7 m

27. A meteorologist displayed this weather map as she gave her forecast for the day.

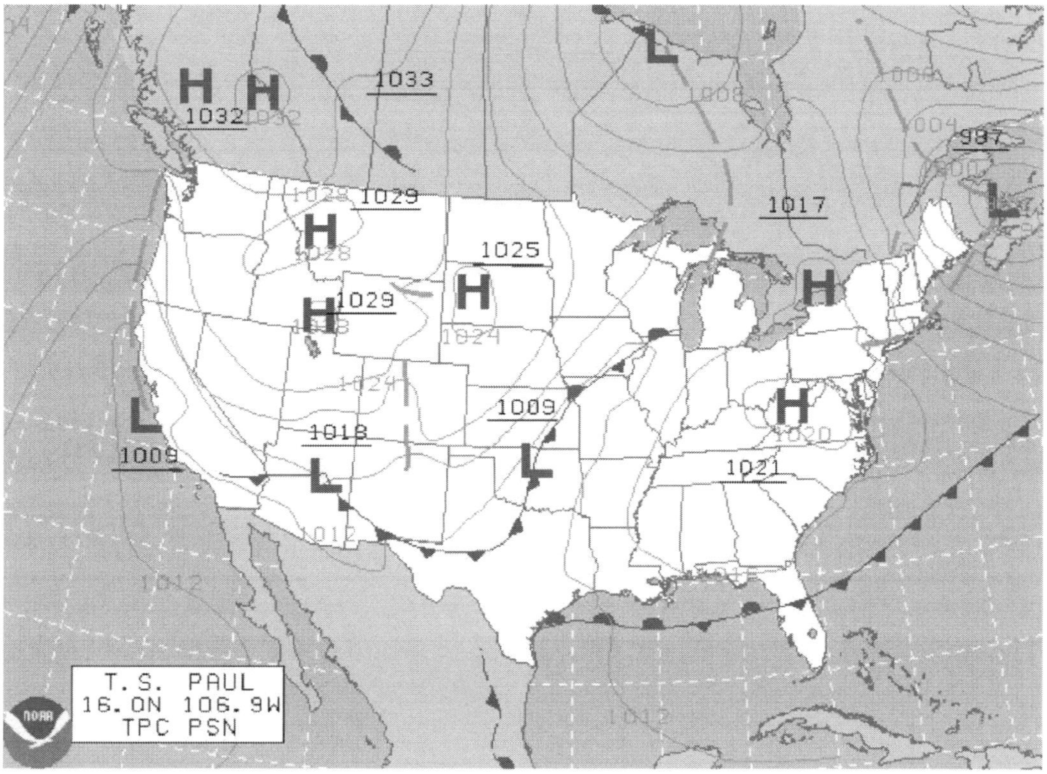

Which forecast would correctly describe the weather conditions in Montana and Oklahoma?

a. It will be overcast but warm in Montana, and it will be warm and rainy in Oklahoma.
b. It is expected to be clear and sunny in Montana, while Oklahoma will experience cold and cloudy conditions.
c. The weather in Montana will be cold and cloudy with possible storms, while in Oklahoma it will be sunny and warm.
d. Montana will have dry and warm conditions. Oklahoma will be warm, but it will be cloudy and stormy.

28. The students pictured below are playing the game of tug-of-war.

Combined Mass of Side 1	Combined Mass of Side 2
72 kg	68 kg

If side 2 wins with an acceleration rate of 1.5 m/s2, what net force did side 2 use to win the game?

a. 102 N
b. 108 N
c. 210 N
d. 48 N

29. A factory is being built next to a local watershed. The factory owners release chemical waste into the surface water. Which of the following answer choices best describes the most probable effect on the watershed?

a. The chemicals from the factory will be found in the surface water and groundwater.
b. The chemicals from the factory will be neutralized in the surface water.
c. The chemicals from the factory will be neutralized in the groundwater.
d. The chemicals from the factory will only be found in the surface water.

30. A boy and girl were racing go-carts at the amusement park. The boy suddenly swerved in front of the girl, forcing her to slam on her brakes. Her car stopped suddenly, but she continued to move forward. Her seat belt held her in the go-cart. Which statement below explains why the girl continued to move forward even after the car had stopped?

a. The girl continued to move forward because her mass was less than the mass of the go-cart, causing her to accelerate.
b. The go-cart forced the girl to move forward because the go-cart and the girl were acting in opposite directions.
c. Although the brakes forced the go-cart to stop, there was no force stopping the movement of the girl, so she continued to move forward.
d. The force of the car caused the girl to move forward.

31. The diagram below shows Earth orbiting the Sun.

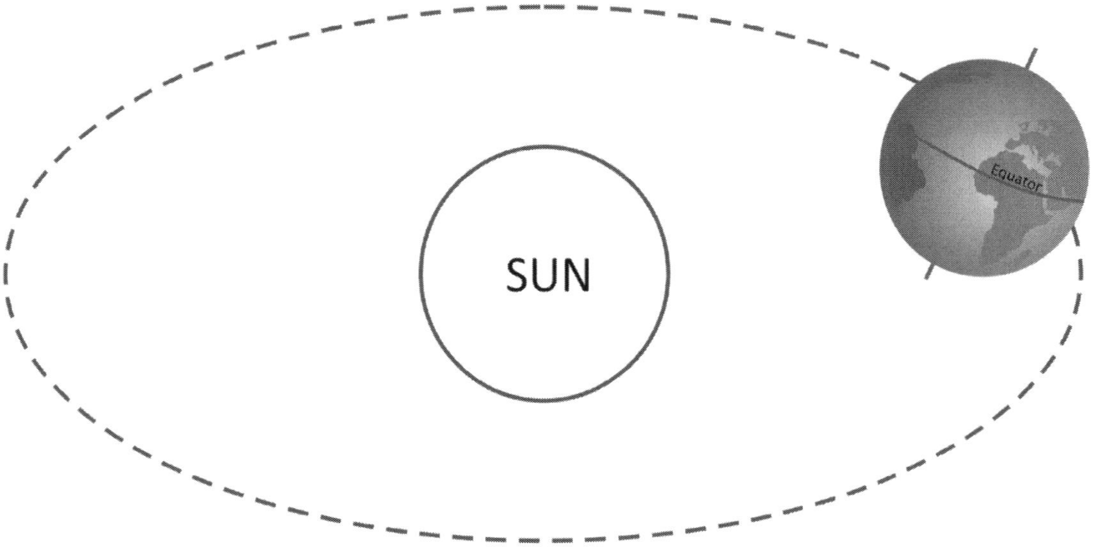

Based on the diagram, which of the following statements is true?

a. It is summer in the Northern Hemisphere because the Northern Hemisphere is tilted toward the Sun.
b. It is daytime in the Northern Hemisphere and nighttime in the Southern Hemisphere because of the way the Earth is tilted on its axis.
c. It is summer in the Western Hemisphere because the Western Hemisphere is facing the Sun.
d. It is summer in the Southern Hemisphere because the Southern Hemisphere is tilted toward the Sun.

32. Many homeowners are adding solar panels to the roofs of their homes to help lower their electricity bills. In the home below, the family uses solar panels to help provide power for appliances like their oven.

How is energy being transformed in the home of the family described above?

a. Light energy from the Sun is converted by the solar panels to mechanical energy to power the oven and then converted to thermal energy to cook the food.
b. Thermal energy from the Sun is converted by the solar panels to mechanical energy to power the oven and then converted to light energy to cook food.
c. Light energy from the Sun is converted by the solar panels to electrical energy to power the oven and then converted into thermal energy to cook the food.
d. Chemical energy from the Sun is converted by the solar panels to electrical energy to power the oven and then converted into light energy to cook food.

33. A father and son were taking turns pushing each other on a skateboard.

If the net force on the child and the skateboard is 85 N, and they are accelerating at a rate of 2.5 m/s^2, what is the total mass of the child and skateboard in kilograms? Write your answer in the blank below.

[ ] kg

34. All of the following are examples of chemical changes in the digestive system EXCEPT:

a. Converting starches in carbohydrates to simple sugars
b. Protein digestion in the stomach
c. Chewing food into smaller pieces
d. Digestion of fat in the small intestine

35. The major advantage of sexual reproduction over asexual reproduction is:

a. It requires two parents.
b. It promotes diversity.
c. It produces more offspring.
d. It involves chromosomes.

36. Which of the following below is NOT considered evidence of plate tectonics?

a. The shape of continents fits together like a puzzle
b. Fossil comparisons exist along where the continents would fit together
c. The Mid-Atlantic Ridge shows where new crust is formed
d. There is a large amount of inland seismic activity

37. Which two of the following are NOT results of a chemical reaction? Select all that apply.

a. Temperature change
b. Mass decrease
c. Melting
d. Bubbles
e. Precipitate forming

38. A student was given a solid object and made observations about it. Based on the observations provided, classify the solid as a metal or metalloid, and determine if this object conducts electricity.

Classification	Conductivity	Observation 1	Observation 2	Observation 3
______________	______________	Not malleable & broke easily when hammered	Shiny, reflective luster	High melting point

Match the correct response to the location in the table. Not all options will be used.

Metalloid	Metal
Conductor	Does not conduct electricity
Semiconductor	

Answer Key and Explanations for Test #1

1. C: TEKS Standard 7.11(B)

Competitive fishing is the most likely of these sports to cause disruptions and harm to aquatic populations and ecosystems. Fishing requires removing fish from the ocean, and though many fish caught for sport are released back into the water, many are not returned to the site where they were caught. These fish may not be able to return to their original location and may not survive if they were harmed when they were caught or during transport in the boat. Additionally, most competitive fishing is done using motorboats, which can release harmful chemicals into ocean waters and harm aquatic populations. Options A and B are incorrect because, although surfing and sailing might have some negative impacts on aquatic populations and resources, they are much less harmful than competitive fishing. Option D is incorrect because swimming is also not very disruptive to marine life.

2. A: TEKS Standard 6.12(A)

The plants on the forest floor are covered by three other layers of vegetation and are competing for water, sunlight, and fertile soil space. Since these plants are on the bottom, they must adapt the most to receive the abiotic factors they need to survive. Oxygen flows freely throughout all levels.

3. TEKS Standard 8.12(C)

Action	Impact on Sustainability
Planting native shrubs about the perimeter of the park	Will increase sustainability
Spraying ant piles regularly to prevent bites	Will not increase sustainability
Cutting shrubs regularly to prevent insect infestation	Will not increase sustainability
Adding a pollinator garden	Will increase sustainability
Placing bird feeders in the trees	Will increase sustainability
Placing park benches around common areas of the playground	Will not increase sustainability
Decreasing the number of trees to allow for more sunlight	Will not increase sustainability

The sustainability of the park ecosystem would be increased through the creation of more biodiversity. This could be done by adding living elements such as shrubs, a pollinator garden to attract bees and butterflies, and bird feeders to attract birds. The sustainability would decrease by killing ants, shrubs, and trees, since these actions would limit biodiversity. Placing park benches has no effect on sustainability.

4. C: TEKS Standard 7.6(B)

The mass number is the number of protons and the number of neutrons added together. The number of protons is also known as the atomic number and can be found on the periodic table. Therefore, the number of neutrons is the mass number (238) less the number of protons (92), so there are 146 neutrons. The number of electrons always equals the number of protons in a neutral atom, so C is the correct answer.

5. C: TEKS Standard 7.13(A)

Student 3 correctly matches each body system to one of its main functions. Student 1 is correct about all systems except the integumentary system, as it is responsible for protecting the body from outside harm. Student 2 incorrectly identified the functions of every system mentioned. Student 4 has the functions of the excretory and endocrine systems switched.

6. D: TEKS Standard 8.6(E)

Step 6 of the experiment states the ingredients in the bottle are producing heat, which is a temperature change. A temperature change is a sign that a chemical reaction has happened. Adding dish soap, mixing the liquids, and combining mixtures do not, on their own, suggest a chemical reaction has occurred.

7. A: TEKS Standard 8.9(B)

The structure of the Milky Way galaxy is spiral, meaning it has curved "arms" stretching out from a central point. While spiral galaxies have a flat, disc-like appearance, elliptical galaxies are more three-dimensional and appear to be roughly the same shape regardless of the viewing angle.

8. C: TEKS Standard 8.12(B)

The main food source for the lizards in the garden was the grasshoppers. With the grasshoppers eliminated, the lizards had to move to a new area where the grasshoppers weren't affected by the farmer's actions. Therefore, the population of lizards in the garden decreased. The extra space did not help the lizards because the main food source was gone. The tomato plants were not affected in this scenario. In this situation, most lizards would not adapt their eating habits but would instead find a new location.

9. B: TEKS Standard 6.6(D)

The density of a homogeneous object, liquid, or gas is its mass divided by its volume, or the ratio of its mass to its volume. Density is inversely proportional to the volume and directly proportional to the mass. The ratio of the density of A to the density of B is 5 : 4 or $\frac{5}{4}$. Hence, the ratio of the volume of A to the volume of B is 4 : 5 or $\frac{4}{5}$. Alternatively, one could solve the equation $5V_A = 4V_B$.

10. TEKS Standard 8.9(A)

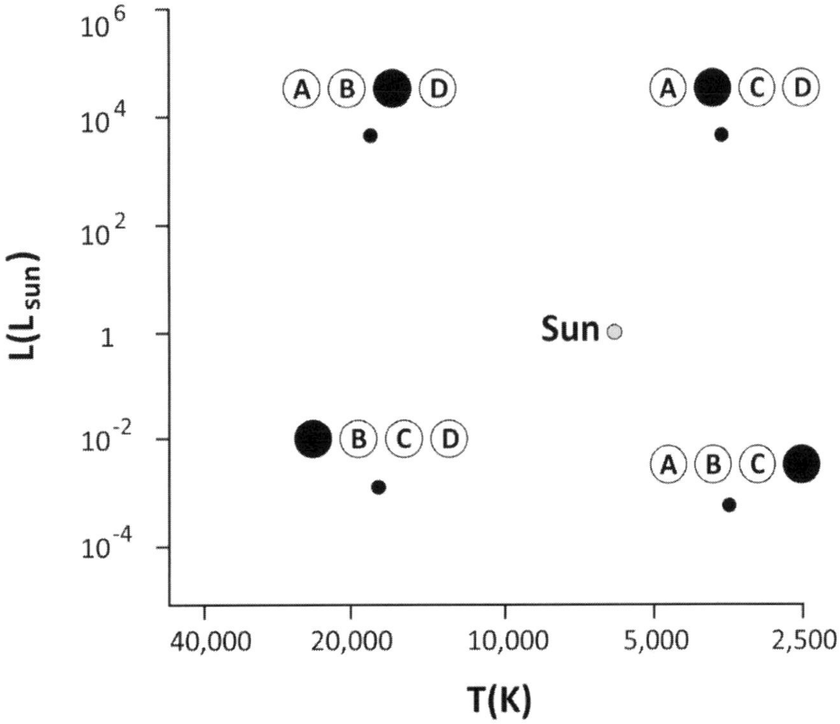

On the Hertzsprung–Russell diagram, a white dwarf that is hotter and less bright than the Sun would be located to the left and below the Sun. A supergiant that is cooler and has more luminosity would be located to the right and above the Sun. A main sequence star that is brighter and hotter than the Sun would be located above and to the left of the Sun. A main sequence star that is cooler and dimmer would be located to the right and below the Sun.

11. B: TEKS Standard 6.8(A)

There is more potential energy at position R than position T because it is a high point, and the potential of a gravitational pull downward is at its greatest. There is less kinetic energy at position Q than position S because the skier's speed is greater at S than at Q because of the downhill slope. Option A is incorrect because there is greater potential energy at position R than position S. Option C is incorrect because the kinetic energy is high at position T, but the potential energy is low. Option D is incorrect because the potential energy decreases from position R to position T.

12. TEKS Standard 6.6(C)

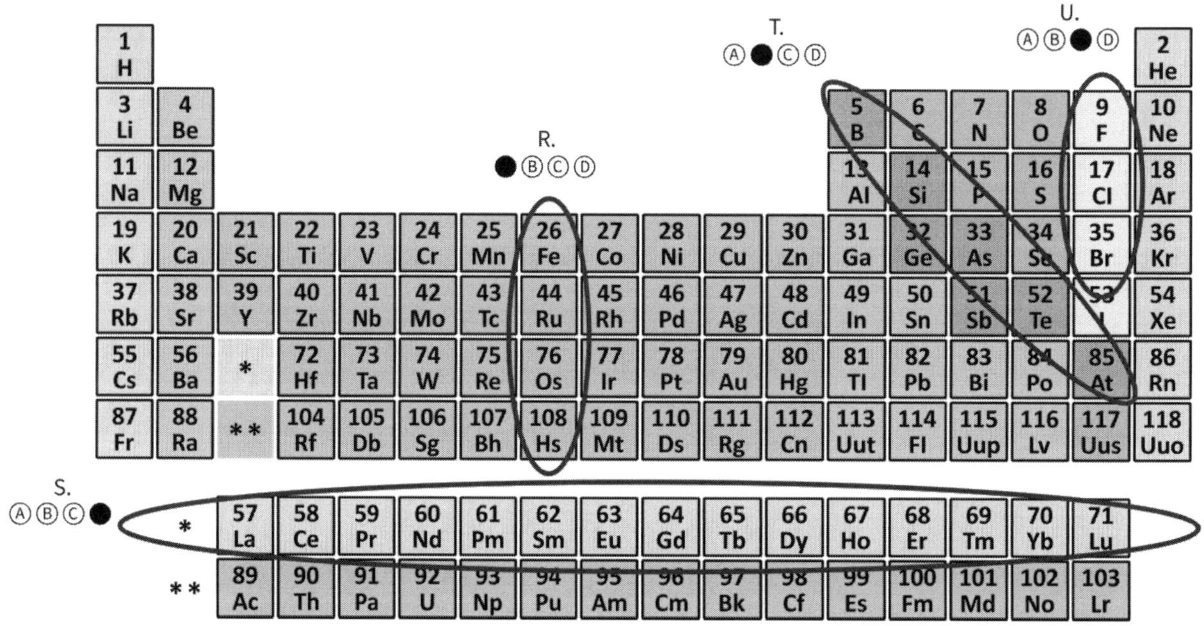

Elements in set R are all metals. Elements in set S are all rare earth metals. Elements in set T are all metalloids. Elements in set U are all nonmetals.

13. A: TEKS Standard 6.12(A)

Giraffes and ants both eat from the acacia tree, which is a biotic factor since it is living. They both also need warm temperatures, which is an abiotic, or nonliving, factor. The bears both interact with the same biotic factors. The shark and dolphins both interact with the same abiotic factors, as do the desert plants.

14. Third: TEKS Standard 8.7(B)

All three laws are operating, but the third law (forces come in equal and opposite pairs) best explains the motion. The first law (inertia) is shown from the fact that the balloon doesn't move until a force acts upon it. The second law (F = ma) is shown because you can see the force and the acceleration. The force comes from the contraction of the rubber balloon. The stretched rubber exerts a force on the air inside the balloon. This causes the air to accelerate in accordance with the second law. You can't see this acceleration because the air is invisible and because it is all the air in the room that the balloon is exerting a force on. However, the air in the room exerts an equal and opposite force on the balloon (this is Newton's third law), which causes the balloon to accelerate in the direction it did.

15. C: TEKS Standard 7.10(B)

The arrows in option C show the plates coming together, which would force one or both parts of land up to form a mountain. Option A shows the plates sliding past one another. Option B shows the plates moving away from each other. Option D shows the plates moving in the same direction.

16. D: TEKS Standard 7.10(B)

The boundary identified in the previous question that results in mountain formation is a convergent boundary. Referring to the options in the previous question, options A and D are both transform boundaries, and option B is a divergent boundary.

17. B: TEKS Standard 7.7(A)

Before comparing the average speed at which each student can throw the ball, the average speed of each student's throws must first be calculated. This is done by finding the speed of each throw and then finding the average of the speeds belonging to each student. The speed for each throw can be calculated by dividing the distance the ball traveled by the amount of time it took the ball to travel that distance. Then, to find the average speed, add up each speed and divide by 3. Student 2 can throw the football at an average speed of 12.75 m/s, which is faster than student 1, who throws an average of 11.9 m/s, and student 3, who throws an average of 11.17m/s. Option B correctly compares the average speed at which each student throws the ball.

18. B: TEKS Standard 6.9(A)

Texas and Bolivia are both located in the Western Hemisphere. In fact, Bolivia is almost directly south of Texas, which means that when Earth is rotating on its axis, both locations are receiving direct light from the Sun at the same time and, therefore, are experiencing day and night at similar times. Since Texas is in the Northern Hemisphere and Bolivia is in the Southern Hemisphere, seasons are the opposite of one another. When Texas experiences summer, it is winter in Bolivia, and the opposite is true as well.

19. B: TEKS Standard 8.10(C)

Hurricanes are primarily formed because of the temperature difference between the oceans and the atmospheric air. The oceans heat up during the summer months and once they climb above 80 degrees Fahrenheit, the conditions are ideal for a hurricane. Evaporation of the warm water forms clouds, which then expand into storm clouds. Atmospheric winds help push the storm over warmer waters, allowing it to grow. A hurricane will die if introduced to cold waters or cut off from a water source.

20. B: TEKS Standard 8.12(B)

The English ivy will overtake the trees and use the water and sunlight that the trees need to survive. Eventually, the trees will die under the cover of the English ivy, and the population of trees will decrease. The ivy will lead to animals losing shelter because the trees will die. The ivy will use the water that the trees need to live, not provide more water. The ivy chokes the trees and does not provide support.

21. TEKS Standard 7.7(C)

Between the time intervals of 0 to 2 seconds, the object is accelerating. From 2 to 8 seconds, the speed of the object remains constant, but from 8 to 16 seconds, the object begins to accelerate again. From 16 to 20 seconds, the object's speed is constant, but from 20 to 24 seconds, the speed decreases. At 24 seconds, the object has stopped moving.

22. D: TEKS Standard 7.12(A)

Option D is correct because it correctly lists the organisms from producers to consumers. Option A is incorrect because the zooplankton does not consume the sprat. Option B is incorrect because the herring does not consume the cod. Option C is incorrect it lists the organisms from consumers to producers.

23. D: TEKS Standard 6.6(C)

Silver is a great conductor of heat and electricity because it is made of metal. The only other listed element that is in the metal group on the periodic table is copper. Hydrogen (A), phosphorus (B), and krypton (C) are all nonmetals.

24. Three: TEKS Standard 7.6(B)

One molecule of citric acid is made up of 21 atoms. It contains 6 atoms of carbon, 8 atoms of hydrogen, and 7 atoms of oxygen, and $6 + 8 + 7 = 21$. One molecule of caffeine is made up of 24 atoms. It contains 8 atoms of carbon, 10 atoms of hydrogen, 4 atoms of nitrogen, and 2 atoms of oxygen, and $8 + 10 + 4 + 2 = 24$. Therefore, caffeine has three more atoms than citric acid.

25. B: TEKS Standard 8.13(A)

Argument 2 is correct because only plant cells have a cell wall, chloroplasts, and large vacuole. Argument 1 is incorrect because the cell is a plant cell, and plant cells also have mitochondria. Argument 3 is incorrect because only plant cells have a cell wall, and both plant and animal cells have mitochondria. Argument 4 is incorrect because neither statement is true about plant cells.

26. C: TEKS Standard 8.7(A)

The formula for net force is $net\ force = (mass \times acceleration)$. Substitute the values given in the problem to the formula. Then solve for the mass by isolating the variable to one side of the equation using inverse operations.

$$71 = (m)(12)$$
$$\frac{71}{12} = \frac{(m)(12)}{12}$$
$$m = \frac{71}{12}$$
$$m = 5.91\overline{6}$$

The answer to this is $5.91\overline{6}$ or 5.92 if rounded to the nearest hundredths place. Answer choice A is the value of net force, 71, and acceleration, 12, multiplied together, which is incorrect because acceleration times net force does not equal mass. Answer choice B is 12 divided by 71, which is also incorrect since acceleration divided by net force does not equal mass either. Answer choice D is simply an incorrect answer.

27. B: TEKS Standard 8.10(B)

The low-pressure system moving through Oklahoma will produce clouds and an overcast sky. The front moving through is a cold front, so lower temperatures are expected. The high-pressure system in Montana indicates sunny and clear conditions. There is no front moving through Montana, so the temperature cannot be predicted from the information on this map.

28. B: TEKS Standard 8.7(A)

If side 2 pulled a mass of 72 kg with an acceleration rate of 1.5 m/s^2, the net force needed would be 108 N because 72 kg $\times$ 1.5 $m/s^2 = 108$ N. Option A is incorrect because it shows a force calculated using the mass of 68 kg, but that was the mass of side 2, not the mass that side 2 was moving. Option C is incorrect because it shows a force calculated using the combined masses of both sides, but only the side being pulled should be used in the calculation. Option D is incorrect because it shows a force calculated by dividing the mass pulled by the acceleration rate instead of multiplying the two values.

29. A: TEKS Standard 7.11(A)

A watershed includes the water both above and below ground. Surface water is the water above ground, and groundwater is below ground. As the factory releases its waste into the surface water, chemicals from the waste will also leach into the groundwater. This means that the chemicals will be found in both the surface water and groundwater. Answer choice B is incorrect because the chemicals in the factory will most likely not be neutralized in the surface water. While there are ways to neutralize chemical waste, those involve scientific processes like reducing or increasing acidity, as well as the proper disposal of waste. Answer choice C is incorrect for the same reasons as choice B. It is incredibly unlikely that the water in the watershed will be able to neutralize chemicals. More likely, the watershed will become polluted. Answer choice D is incorrect because the chemicals found in the factory will most likely pollute the groundwater as well as the surface water.

30. C: TEKS Standard 8.7(B)

Newton's first law states that an object, like the girl, will continue to move in the same direction, in this case forward, unless a force stops it. The brakes caused the force that stopped the go-cart, but there was no force to stop the girl, so she continued to move forward until her seatbelt stopped her. Option A refers to Newton's second law, which could be applied to how fast the go-cart could move, but it would not explain why the girl continued to move forward even after the go-cart had stopped. Option B refers to Newton's third law, which does not explain why the girl moved forward in this scenario. Option D also refers to Newton's first law, which does explain what caused the go-cart and the girl to move, but it doesn't explain why the girl continued to move after the go-cart stopped.

31. D: TEKS Standard 6.9(A)

The diagram represents summer in the Southern Hemisphere because the Southern Hemisphere is tilted toward the Sun. The Northern Hemisphere is currently tilted away from the Sun. The Earth's tilt is responsible for the seasons, not the day-and-night cycle. The part of Earth that is facing the Sun is experiencing daytime, so parts of the Northern and Southern Hemisphere are both experiencing daytime at the same time.

32. C: TEKS Standard 6.8(B)

The solar panels are powered by the light energy of the Sun. The solar panels convert the light energy into electrical energy that provides power to the home. The oven converts electrical energy into thermal energy to cook the food. Although the Sun does provide thermal energy, the solar panels are not powered by heat. The Sun does not provide chemical energy. The home is powered by electrical energy, in the form of electricity, and not mechanical energy. Although an oven may have a light source, thermal energy is needed to cook the food.

33. 34 kg: TEKS Standard 8.7(A)

Net force is divided by the acceleration rate to find the mass. In this case, $85 \text{ N} \div 2.5 \text{ m/s}^2 = 34 \text{ kg}$.

34. C: TEKS Standard 7.6(C)

Chewing food into smaller pieces is a physical change, not a chemical change. Changing one substance to a different substance is an example of a chemical change, so choices A, B, and D are incorrect.

35. B: TEKS Standard 7.13(C)

Sexual reproduction allows the genetic information from two parents to mix. This encourages the creation of new genes. The production of new genes and of new gene combinations leads to more diversity within a population of organisms, which is a great advantage. The requirement of two parents is simply a characteristic of sexual reproduction. It is not an advantage beyond the fact that it promotes diversity, so choice A is incorrect. Choice C is incorrect because, for sexual reproduction, the number of offspring produced can depend on the species of the parents. Choice D is incorrect because some organisms that reproduce asexually have and pass down chromosomes.

36. D: TEKS Standard 7.10(A)

Evidence of plate tectonics is based on the shapes of the continents, which seem to fit together like a puzzle, as well as the fossils found along these edges. The Mid-Atlantic Ridge is the birthplace of new crust that is then destroyed in the subduction zones in the Pacific Ring of Fire, where most seismic activity takes place.

37. B, C: TEKS Standard 8.6(E)

When a chemical reaction occurs, the mass remains unchanged. Melting is a sign of a physical change. Temperature change (A), development of odor, bubbles (D), the formation of a precipitate (E), and a color change are all signs a chemical reaction could have happened.

38. TEKS Standard 6.6(C)

Classification	Conductivity	Observation 1	Observation 2	Observation 3
Metalloid	**Semiconductor**	**Not malleable & broke easily when hammered**	**Shiny, reflective luster**	**High melting point**

Since the object was not malleable, it cannot be a metal. Shiny luster and a high melting point are characteristics that both a metal and a metalloid can have. Metalloids are semiconductors of electricity, and metals are better conductors of electricity.

Practice Test #2

1. Before bed, a student set her battery-operated alarm clock, and, as expected, it went off promptly at 6:00 a.m. the next morning. What energy is being transformed in this simple action?

a. Chemical energy was converted to electrical energy, which was converted to sound energy.
b. Electrical energy was converted to chemical energy, which was converted to thermal energy.
c. Mechanical energy was converted to chemical energy, which was converted to sound energy.
d. Electrical energy was converted to light energy, which was converted to electrical energy.

2. Which correctly states the two main differences between vacuoles in plant cells and animal cells?

a. Vacuoles in animal cells are larger than in plant cells. The vacuoles in plant cells aid in photosynthesis, while the vacuoles in animal cells help retain water.
b. Vacuoles help to guard what comes into the animal cells but help to protect the plant cells. The vacuoles are thicker in animal cells than in plant cells.
c. Vacuoles in plants provide the support for the whole cell, and in animal cells they are where the cells grow. Vacuoles in animal cells are smaller than in plant cells.
d. Vacuoles are larger in plant cells than in animal cells. Vacuoles in animal cells store waste, while vacuoles in plant cells maintain water.

3. Which does NOT correctly explain a cause-and-effect relationship between tectonic plate boundaries and their effects on Earth?

a. The subduction boundary under the Pacific Ocean floor near Japan caused an underwater earthquake that led to a tsunami in 2011.
b. The Himalayas are a large mountain range in Asia that were formed long ago when tectonic plates of Eurasia and India collided at a convergent boundary.
c. The San Francisco Earthquake of 1906 was one of the deadliest earthquakes in US history and was located along a transform boundary.
d. The Rocky Mountains are a mountain range that runs through Colorado and were created by plate tectonics at a divergent boundary.

4. The map below shows the ocean currents. The dark, black arrows indicate warm ocean water, and the lighter, gray arrows indicate cool ocean water. Fill in the bubble next to the three locations that would be expected to have more precipitation and hurricane conditions than the other areas.

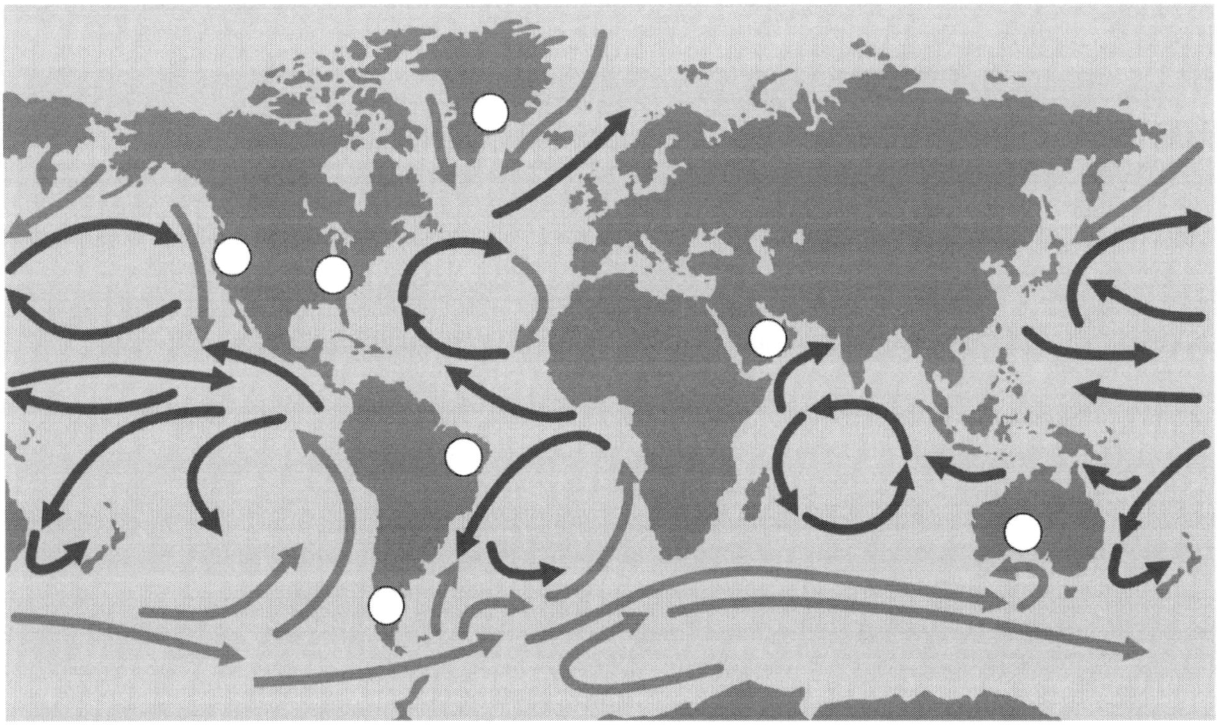

5. Students were asked to write about their observations after completing an experiment that involved a chemical reaction. Which of the following correctly describes the observations?

Chemical Reaction Observations:

1. The masses of the substances were the same before and after the chemical reaction occurred.
2. There was a color change indicating that a chemical reaction could have occurred.
3. The number of atoms increased in the new substance after the chemical reaction occurred.
4. The atoms in the first substance were regrouped to create a new substance.

a. Statements 1 and 4 are incorrect.
b. Only statement 2 is incorrect.
c. Only statement 3 is incorrect.
d. Statements 3 and 4 are incorrect.

6. Which of the following is an effect of the moon on the earth?

a. Tides
b. Landslides
c. Tornadoes
d. Seasons

7. A golf cart is accelerating at a rate of 5.8 m/s^2. The force moving the golf cart forward is 2,400 N. Wind, friction, and several other resistive forces are pulling against the golf cart with 350 N. What is the mass of the golf cart to the nearest kilogram? Write your answer in the blank below.

[ ] kg

8. A desert biome is depicted below showing the biotic factors organisms rely on for food.

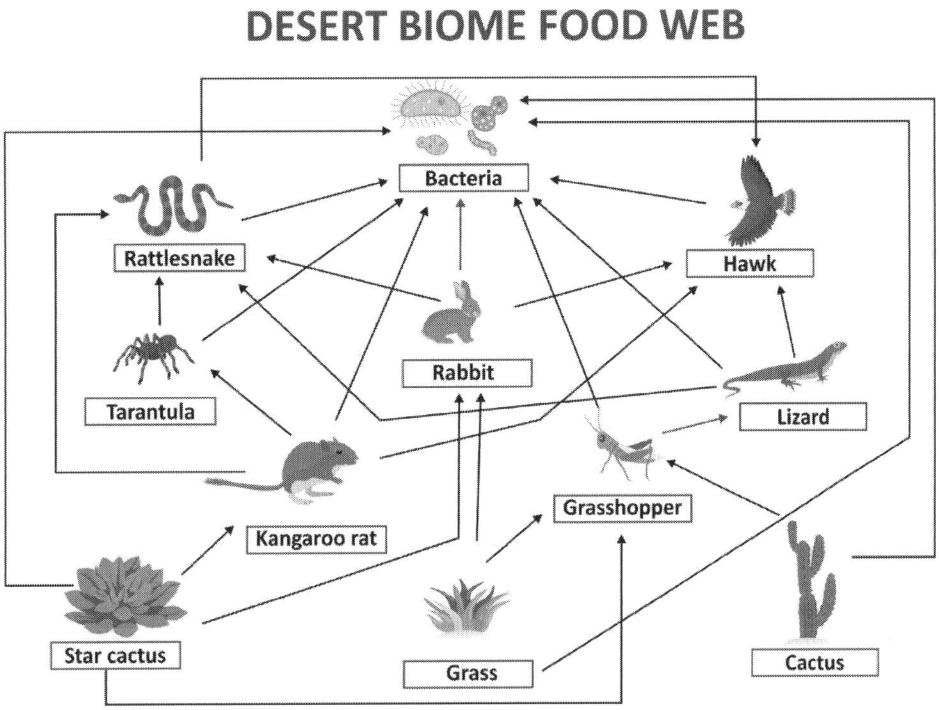

What would be the result if something happened to drastically decrease the grasshopper population in the desert biome?

a. The plants would not be eaten by another organism on the food web.
b. The kangaroo rat population would decrease since there would be fewer plants to eat.
c. The lizard population would drastically decrease as well.
d. The lizard population would increase since the population of one of its predators would have decreased.

9. Aubrey lives 200m from Brianna's house. If it takes her 100s to travel the distance, what is Aubrey's speed? Write your answer in the blank below.

[ ] m/s

10. Students created the energy web below to diagram the energy flow in an Arctic ecosystem.

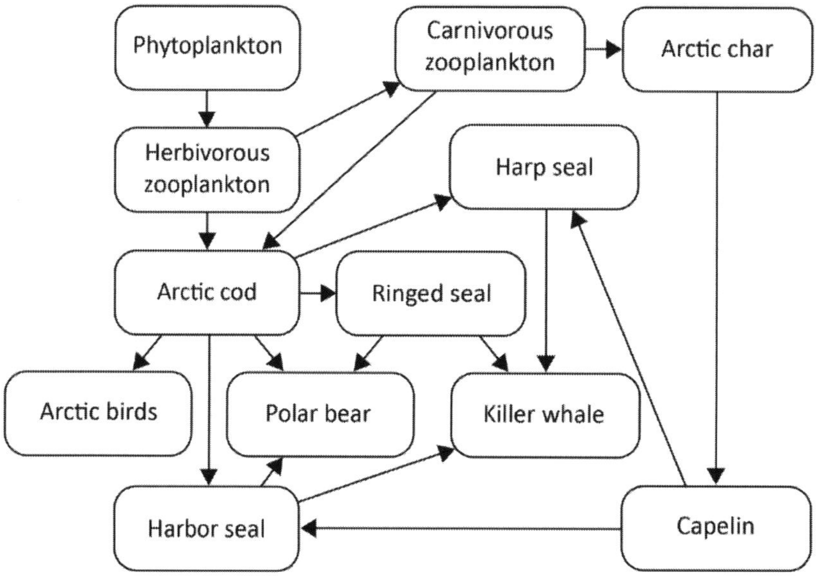

Based on the energy web, which statement is NOT true?

a. Harbor seals are the prey of polar bears and predators of arctic cod.
b. Killer whales prey on ringed seals and harp seals, but they do not have any predators.
c. Carnivorous zooplankton are the prey of arctic cod and herbivorous zooplankton but the predator of arctic char.
d. Polar bears are the predator of the ringed seal and the arctic cod, but they are not the prey of any other organism.

11. Which of the following is an example of a chemical change?

a. Salt dissolving in water
b. Water evaporating
c. Silver tarnishing
d. Dry ice sublimating

12. Students are playing a game in which one student throws a tennis ball against a wall while other students try to catch it before it hits the ground. Which statement below correctly describes the force of the tennis ball and the wall?

a. The tennis ball applies the same amount of force to the wall as the wall applies to the tennis ball.
b. The tennis ball applies more force to the wall than the wall applies to the tennis ball.
c. The tennis ball is the only object applying a force, because the wall does not move.
d. The tennis ball applies less force to the wall than the wall applies to the tennis ball.

13. Students played a game to see who could sort the descriptions of stars, nebulae, and galaxies the fastest. Write the term that matches each description in the blanks. The options are listed below.

Star	Nebula	Galaxy

Description	Term
A cloud of dust and gas that does not emit its own light	
Largest in size when compared to the other two	
Smallest in size when compared to the other two	
The Milky Way	
The Sun	
When it collapses, a star can form	
Makes its own light and rotates on its axis	
Made up of the other two terms	

14. This butterfly has markings on its wings that look like huge eyes. How does this physical adaptation help the butterfly stay alive and reproduce?

a. The eyespots help the butterfly fly.
b. The eyespots help the butterfly find food.
c. The eyespots help the butterfly scare off predators.
d. The eyespots help the butterfly smell.

15. A doctor checked a patient's reflexes by tapping on a specific area of the patient's knees. He then took the patient's blood pressure and listened to her lungs. What three body systems did the doctor examine?

a. Circulatory, respiratory, and skeletal systems
b. Circulatory, respiratory, and nervous systems
c. Respiratory, integumentary, and nervous systems
d. Muscular, circulatory, and integumentary systems

16. When a volcano erupts, the lava may flow for miles. When the lava cools, it can create a new rocky environment. Which of the following species would be the last to move into an area where this type of primary succession had occurred?

a. Plants with no roots like mosses
b. An oak tree that has deep roots
c. A fungus like a lichen
d. A willow tree that has shallow roots

17. A man is walking on a treadmill. The man is walking with 55 N of force, and the resistive force pushing the man in the opposite direction is 25 N. The man has a mass of 90 kg.

Which direction will the man move? What is his acceleration rate to the nearest hundredth? How was the acceleration rate calculated? Write your response to these questions on the lines below.

____

____

____

____

____

18. Which of the following is NOT true for all cells?

a. Cells are the basic structures of any organism
b. Cells can only reproduce from existing cells
c. Cells are the smallest unit of any life form that carries the information needed for all life processes
d. All cells are also called eukaryotes

19. Which of the following is an example of an experiment that shows a chemical change?

a. A clear liquid is poured into a beaker. A different clear liquid is poured into the same beaker. A wooden stir stick is used to mix the liquids together. Small, solid flecks begin to fall to the bottom of the beaker.
b. A liquid and a solid are combined in a beaker. The solid dissolves in the liquid. Heat is added. Eventually, only a solid remains at the bottom of the beaker.
c. A liquid and a solid are combined in a beaker. The beaker is shaken, and the solid dissolves. Then the beaker is placed in the freezer. Two hours later it is removed, and a solid has formed.
d. Two clear liquids are combined in a beaker. The beaker is then placed on a heater. Gas begins to rise from the beaker.

20. After studying Earth and space, students were asked to write one fact that they learned. The table below shows the statements that each student wrote.

Student	Written Statement
Student 1	The tilt of the Earth on its axis and the orbit of the Earth around the Sun are responsible for the seasons.
Student 2	The Earth revolves around the Sun in an elliptical shape, which results in the day-and-night cycle.
Student 3	When it is summer in the Northern Hemisphere, it is winter in the Southern Hemisphere.
Student 4	When the invisible axis at the North Pole is pointed away from the Sun, it is summer in the Northern Hemisphere.

Which students wrote a correct fact?

a. Student 1 only
b. Students 1, 2, and 3
c. Students 1 and 3
d. Students 2 and 4

21. On average, how many neutrons does one atom of bromine (Br) have?

a. 35
b. 44.90
c. 45
d. 79.90

22. Students conducted a series of tests on an unknown material to determine its density. Below are the steps the students took.

Step 1: The unknown material was placed on the left side of a balance scale. Two-gram weights were added to the right side of the balance scale one at a time. It was balanced when 24 grams were placed on the right side of the balance scale.
Step 2: The unknown material was placed in a beaker that contained 50 mL of water. Using the displacement method, the students found that the material's volume is 2 cm^2.
Step 3: The students calculated the density of the unknown material.

Based on the density the students calculated in step 3, what was the unknown material? Write your answer in the blank below.

Metal	Density (g/cm^3)
Silver	10.5
Lead	11.3
Palladium	12.0
Gold	19.3
Platinum	21.4

23. A student writes the clues about an element below.

Element Clues:

1. Has seven valence electrons
2. Has 10 neutrons
3. Has nine electrons
4. Has nine protons

What element is the student describing?

a. Neon, (Ne)
b. Argon, (Ar)
c. Silicon, (Si)
d. Fluorine (F)

24. A ball is thrown and the distance it traveled is measured. Which data set corresponds to the graph below?

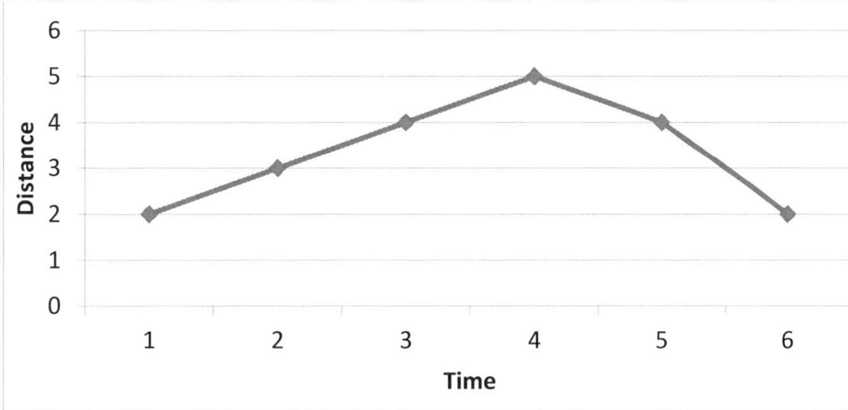

a.

Time	Distance
1	2
2	4
3	6
4	8
5	9

b.

Time	Distance
1	2
3	4
5	6
7	8
9	9

c.

Time	Distance
2	0
4	1
6	3
8	5
9	7

d.

Time	Distance
1	2
2	3
3	4
4	5
5	4
6	2

25. Which of the following situations would result in the generation of new crust?

a. Two crustal plates converge
b. Two crustal plates move apart
c. Two crustal plates slide past one another
d. A crustal plate is pushed down into the mantle

26. In the store, you are pushing a cart with no problem. However, as you are shopping, you add items to the cart that have varying masses. Which of Newton's Laws play a role in the amount of force needed to push the cart through the store?

a. Newton's First Law
b. Newton's Second Law
c. Newton's Third Law
d. Newton's Fourth Law

27. A student is performing an experiment to test whether an element is a metal, nonmetal, metalloid, or rare Earth element. She has narrowed down the options to a metal or a metalloid. Which answer choice best states a question she should ask to determine if the element is a metal or a metalloid?

a. Is the element malleable?
b. Is the element conductive?
c. Does the element have luster?
d. Is the element magnetic?

28. A seagull is a medium-sized bird that can be found flying above coastlines, bays, and lakes, and it is an omnivore. A hammerhead shark is a special category of fish and can grow to be over 500 pounds. It lives in the ocean and is a carnivore. Which is NOT a biotic factor that seagulls and hammerhead sharks compete for?

a. Cod fish
b. Seaweed
c. Mussels
d. Shrimp

29. The picture below illustrates the path of a golf ball that was hit by a golfer.

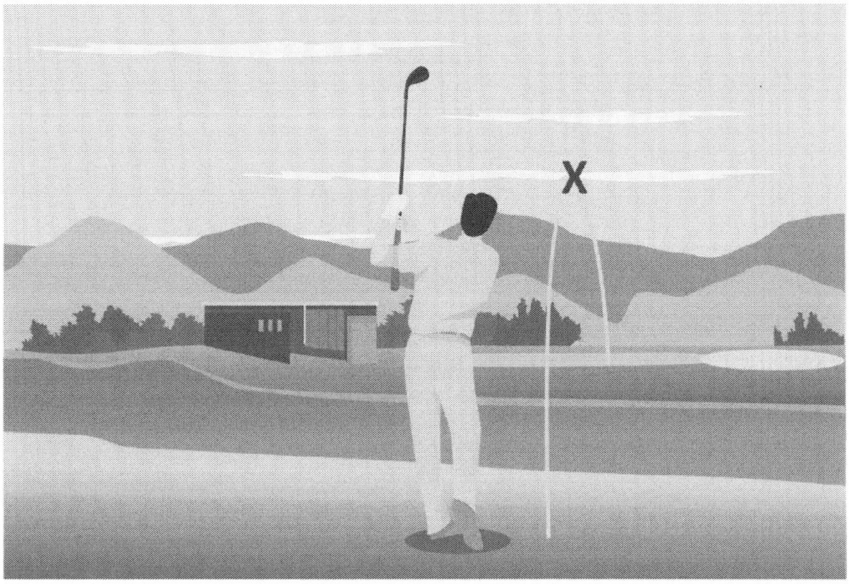

Which statement correctly describes what is happening right when the golf ball reaches its peak height (X)?

a. The golf ball's potential energy and kinetic energy are both decreasing.
b. The golf ball's potential energy is at its highest, and the golf ball's kinetic energy is also at its highest.
c. The golf ball's potential energy is at a low, and the golf ball's kinetic energy is at its highest.
d. The golf ball's potential energy is at its highest, and the golf ball's kinetic energy is at a low.

30. In the suburban neighborhood of Northwoods, there have been large populations of deer, and residents have complained about them eating flowers and garden plants. What would be a logical explanation, based on observations, for the large increase in the deer population over the last two seasons?

a. Increased quantity of food sources
b. Decreased population of a natural predator
c. Deer migration from surrounding areas
d. Increase in hunting licenses sold

31. What force keeps the years on Earth consistently the same length of time?

a. The revolution of Earth on its axis
b. The gravitational pull of the Sun on Earth
c. The gravitational pull of Earth on the Moon
d. The Moon's orbit around Earth

32. Students had to write an essay about the Earth and space as part of their science course. In the paragraph below the student wrote about the Sun.

The Sun

The Sun is a star that is located in a spiral arm of the Milky Way galaxy. It is a ball of burning gas. Although the Sun is closer to the Earth than many other stars, it is not the closest. The Sun is very bright because it is one of the largest stars in the galaxy. The Sun is the center of our solar system, and all planets in our solar system orbit the Sun.

There are two inaccurate statements in the paragraph above. On the lines below, identify the two incorrect statements and explain why these statements are false.

____

____

____

____

____

33. Radiation therapy is a common treatment for people with tumors and cancer that uses high-energy electromagnetic waves. Which electromagnetic waves are most likely used in this process?

a. Radio waves
b. Infrared
c. Microwaves
d. Gamma rays

34. Metals, nonmetals, and metalloids have many similarities and differences. In the blank next to each characteristic in the table, write the category that characteristic matches. The options are listed below.

Metals only	Nonmetals only	Metals and metalloids	Nonmetals and metalloids

Characteristic	Category
Can appear shiny	
Insulator of heat	
Low melting point	
Can appear dull	
Excellent conductor of electricity	
Can conduct thermal energy	

35. The image below shows Earth rotating on its axis as it orbits the Sun.

Which statement is most likely true about a student who lives in Texas based on this image of Earth?

a. The student is asleep in bed and covered up with two heavy blankets.
b. The student is swimming in a lake and getting ready to eat lunch.
c. The student is sleeping in a house with the air conditioner running.
d. The student is outside playing in the snow after eating breakfast.

36. Before a factory was built in town, the population of moths was 90 percent white and 10 percent gray. After the factory was built, the population of moths changed to 20 percent white and 80 percent gray. The factory releases smoke into the air, which leads to air pollution in town. Which answer choice best describes the change in the moths' colors?

a. The factory covered the white moths' wings in soot.
b. The gray color is better suited to the new smoke-polluted environment.
c. The moths decided to change color so that they would be less visible.
d. The gray moths are predators of the white moths.

37. Bluefin tuna are a species of fish that need ocean water below 68 degrees Fahrenheit to survive. Global warming is causing the oceans' temperatures to change. The graph below illustrates this change.

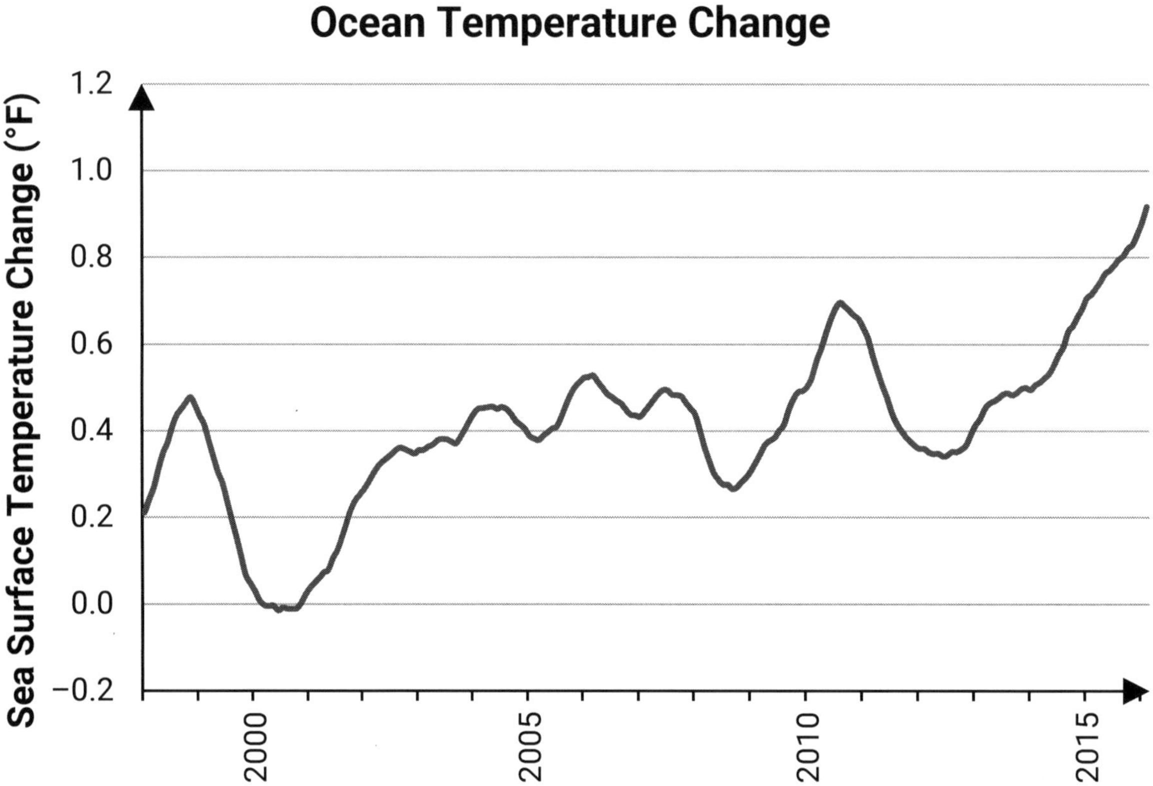

How might the population of bluefin tuna adapt to this environmental change?

a. The bluefin tuna will have to adapt to survive closer to the surface of the ocean water where the temperatures are warmer.
b. The bluefin tuna will have to move to bodies of freshwater where the water temperatures are colder than 68 degrees.
c. The bluefin tuna will have to decrease their daily movement to stay cooler in the warming water.
d. The bluefin tuna will have to adapt to survive at a deeper ocean depth where the water temperatures are cooler.

38. Which three substances below contain eight or more atoms? Select all that apply.

a. $2CaC_2$
b. $2C_2H_2$
c. $3CaCl_2$
d. H_3PO_4
e. H_2CO_3

Answer Key and Explanations for Test #2

1. A: TEKS Standard 6.8(B)

The alarm clock transforms the chemical energy in the battery to electrical energy as it closes the circuit, causing the alarm to use sound energy to wake the student up. Option B switched the transformation from electrical to chemical, and thermal energy is not created. The battery did not use mechanical energy as stated in option C. Option D did not mention the chemical energy used by the battery.

2. D: TEKS Standard 8.13(A)

The vacuole that appears in a plant cell is larger in size than the vacuole in an animal cell. In plants, vacuoles regulate water, while in animals, they store waste. The vacuoles' sizes are backward in option A, and the functions described are not correct. The part of the cell that guards what is coming in and out of an organism is the cell membrane, not the vacuoles. The thickness of the vacuole is not a difference between plant and animal cells. The functions described in option C are the functions of the cytoplasm.

3. D: TEKS Standard 7.10(B)

Divergent boundaries do not form mountains but instead cause the tectonic plates to move away from each other, often creating ocean ridges. Tsunamis like the one in Japan in 2011 are caused by underwater earthquakes at subduction boundaries. Mountains like the Himalayas are often formed at convergent boundaries, which appear where tectonic plates push together. The San Francisco Earthquake in 1906 happened along a transform boundary, and this type of boundary appears where tectonic plates slide past each other.

4. TEKS Standard 8.10(C)

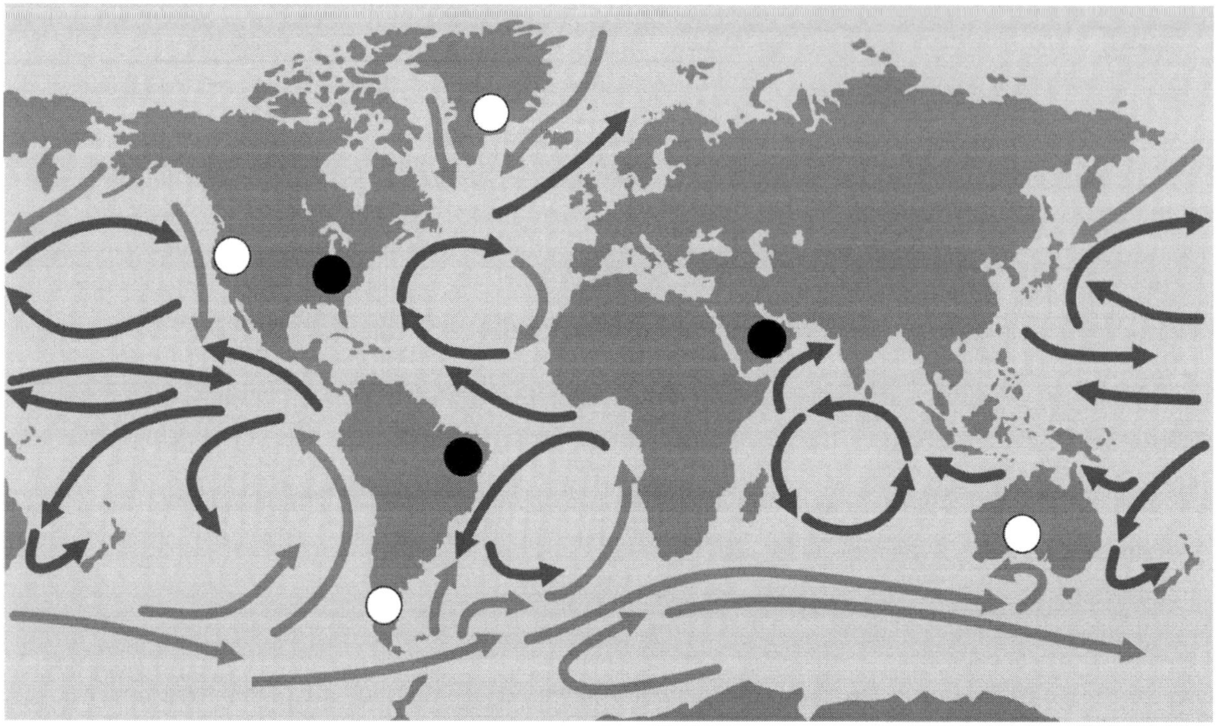

Warm ocean water evaporates quickly and fills the atmosphere with more water, which leads to precipitation. This warm ocean water and wet atmosphere create prime conditions for a hurricane.

5. C: TEKS Standard 8.6(E)

Only statement 3 is incorrect. The number of atoms always stays the same during a chemical reaction, so the number would not increase. Statement 1 is correct as the mass would stay constant. Statement 2 is correct as a color change is a common sign that a chemical reaction has occurred. Statement 4 is correct as atoms are grouped in different ways in a chemical reaction.

6. A: TEKS Standard 6.9(B)

Tides. The moon's gravity causes tides. The moon does not cause landslides, tornadoes, or seasons. Therefore, the correct choice is A.

7. 353 kg: TEKS Standard 8.7(A)

The net force of the golf cart can be found by subtracting the resistive force, 350 N, from the force moving the golf cart forward, 2,400 N. 2,400 N − 350 N = 2,050 N. To find the mass of the golf cart, divide the net force, 2,050 N, by the acceleration rate of 5.8 m/s^2. 2,050 N ÷ 5.8 m/s^2 = 353 kg.

8. C: TEKS Standard 6.12(A)

The lizard population would drastically decrease as well because the grasshopper is the main biotic factor the lizard depends on for food. The plants are still consumed by the rabbit and kangaroo rat. The kangaroo rats would have more plants to eat because they would no longer be competing with the grasshoppers. The grasshopper is not a predator of the lizard.

9. 2 m/s: TEKS Standard 7.7(A)

The formula to calculate speed is S=D/T. In this problem, divide 200m by 100s. This gives you 2 m/s, which is Aubrey's speed.

10. C: TEKS Standard 7.12(A)

Option C is the correct answer because according to the arrows in the diagram, carnivorous zooplankton are the prey of arctic char and arctic cod and predators of herbivorous zooplankton. Option A is not the correct answer because the arrows indicate that harbor seals are the prey of polar bears and the predators of arctic cod. Option B is not the correct answer because the arrows indicate that killer whales prey on ringed seals and harp seals, but they do not have a predator. Option D is not the correct answer because the arrows indicate that polar bears are predators of ringed seals and artic cod, but they do not have any predators.

11. C: TEKS Standard 7.6(C)

A chemical change involves a chemical reaction where new products are formed. When silver tarnishes, a thin layer of corrosion is formed, indicating a chemical change. A physical change does not produce new substances. Phase changes such as evaporation and sublimation are examples of physical changes. Salt dissolving in water is also a physical change because the ions just separate, and no new substances are formed.

12. A: TEKS Standard 8.7(B)

According to Newton's third law, the tennis ball applies the same force to the wall as the wall applies to the tennis ball. Options B and D are not true according to Newton's third law. Option C is incorrect because the wall does apply a force to the tennis ball.

13. TEKS Standard 8.9(A)

Description	Term
A cloud of dust and gas that does not emit its own light	Nebula
Largest in size when compared to the other two	Galaxy
Smallest in size when compared to the other two	Star
The Milky Way	Galaxy
The Sun	Star
When it collapses, a star can form	Nebula
Makes its own light and rotates on its axis	Star
Made up of the other two terms	Galaxy

Stars, like the Sun, are smaller than nebulae and galaxies. They make their own light and rotate on their own axis. Nebulae are clouds of dust and gas. They don't produce their own light and sometimes form stars when they collapse. Galaxies are the largest of the three terms and are made up of stars and nebulae, among other things. The Milky Way is our galaxy.

14. C: TEKS Standard 7.13(D)

The eyespots help the butterfly scare off predators. Butterflies with the two large eyespots will suddenly show them to predators to scare them off. The eyespots do not help them fly, find food, or smell. These spots help the butterfly stay alive and reproduce, and this trait then becomes more prevalent. The butterflies without the eyespots will begin to decrease in number. Thus, this is an example of natural selection.

15. B: TEKS Standard 7.13(A)

When the doctor tested the patient's reflexes, he was making sure the nerves were sending the right information to the brain, so he was testing the nervous system. Blood pressure is a function of the circulatory system, as it is one characteristic of blood flow. This means that the doctor examined the circulatory system. Lungs are used for breathing and are a part of the respiratory system, so this system was also tested by the doctor. Though the knee is a joint, reflexes are a function of the nervous system, so the skeletal system is not being examined and option A is incorrect. The integumentary system is not being examined in this scenario, so options C and D are incorrect. Additionally, the muscular system is used if the patient has the correct reflex, but the doctor is examining the response of the nervous system, so two of the systems listed in option D are incorrect.

16. B: TEKS Standard 8.12(B)

An oak tree would be the last of the species listed to move into the area. It would take a long time for the rocky terrain to break down enough to suit the deep root system of an oak tree. The other species listed would be suited to the environment sooner after it is created. The fungus and the plants with no root systems would appear before the oak tree because they can adapt to grow on rocks. It would still take much time for the environment to change to support a willow tree, but because its roots grow to cover a wide area rather than growing deep into the ground, this environment could still support a willow tree before it could support an oak tree.

17. TEKS Standard 6.7(B)

The man will continue to move forward on the treadmill because his net force is greater than the net force pushing him back. His acceleration rate rounded to the nearest hundredth is $0.33\ m/s^2$. This was calculated by dividing the net force of 30 N by the mass of 90 kg.

18. D: TEKS Standard 6.13(A)

Only cells with a membrane around the nucleus are called eukaryotes. Cells are the basic structure of all organisms (A), and they are the smallest unit of life (C). Additionally, they can only be produced by other cells (B).

19. A: TEKS Standard 8.6(E)

In option A, two liquids are combined, and a new solid substance is formed. This is an example of a chemical reaction. In option B, a solid is dissolved in a liquid. The liquid is then evaporated by the heat, and the solid remains. This experiment shows only physical changes. Options C and D also both involve a change of state of matter, which is not an indication that a chemical reaction occurred.

20. C: TEKS Standard 6.9(A)

Student 1 is correct, the tilt of Earth and its elliptical revolution about the Sun are responsible for the changing seasons. Student 3 is correct because the Northern Hemisphere and Southern Hemisphere experience opposite seasons because of the way Earth is titled. Student 2 is incorrect because Earth rotating on its axis is what is responsible for the day-and-night cycle, not Earth's orbit around the Sun. Student 4 is incorrect because the opposite would be true: when the invisible axis at the North Pole is pointed away from the Sun, it is winter in the Northern Hemisphere.

21. B: TEKS Standard 7.6(B)

To determine the average number of neutrons in one atom of an element, subtract the atomic number from the average atomic mass. For bromine (Br), subtract its atomic number (35) from its average atomic mass (79.9) to acquire the average number of neutrons, 44.9.

22. Palladium: TEKS Standard 6.6(D)

In step 1, the students found that the mass of the object was 24 g (12×2 g). In step 2, the students found the volume of the unknown material was 2 cm^3, since the water was displaced by 2 mL when adding the unknown material. The density can be found by dividing the mass of 24 g by the volume of 2 cm^3. Therefore, the density of the unknown material is 12 g/cm^3, which is equal to palladium.

23. D: TEKS Standard 7.6(B)

It is understood that fluorine has seven valence electrons since it is located in group 17 of the periodic table. It can be determined that fluorine has 10 neutrons by subtracting fluorine's atomic number (9) from its mass number (19). Since fluorine has an atomic number of 9, it can be determined that it contains nine protons, and, as a neutral atom, it must also have nine electrons.

24. D: TEKS Standard 7.7(C)

The graph represents a set of data. The line graph increases in distance from 1 second to 4 seconds and then begins decreasing. The only data set that shows distance increasing and then decreasing is set D.

25. B: TEKS Standard 7.10(A)

When two crustal plates move apart, magma welling up could result in the formation of new crust. This has been shown to be occurring on the ocean floor where places of the crust are weaker. The crust spreads apart at these trenches, pushing outward and erupting at the ridges. When two crustal plates converge, sublimation occurs as one plate runs under another pushing it up. Two crustal plates slide past one another, is an example of a transform fault, which does not create new crust. A crustal plate is pushed down into the mantle, does not form new crust but perhaps recycles the old one.

26. B: TEKS Standard 8.7(B)

Newton's Second Law states that the acceleration of an object is increased by the force applied and decreased by its mass. As the cart becomes heavier through the store, the shopper must apply more force when pushing it to achieve its acceleration. Newton's First Law states if an object is at rest, it will stay at rest until a force is acted upon it. Newton's Third Law states that any object that exerts a force will be met by an equal opposing force. There is no Fourth Law.

27. A: TEKS Standard 6.6(C)

Metals and metalloids have specific defining characteristics. Metals are conductive, malleable, lustrous, and ductile. Metalloids are also conductive and lustrous, but they are not malleable or ductile. Instead, they are brittle and nonductile. Since only metals are malleable, this question can help determine if the element is a metal or metalloid. If the answer is yes, the element is a metal, and if not, it is a metalloid. Answer choice B, on the other hand, does not work as a determining question because both metals and metalloids are conductive. Answer choice C does not help since both metals and metalloids are lustrous. Answer choice D cannot work because magnetism is not a determining factor. Magnetism is typically a trait of rare elements.

28. B: TEKS Standard 6.12(A)

Seagulls are omnivores, meaning they eat plants and animals, but hammerhead sharks are carnivores, meaning they only eat meat. This means seagulls and hammerhead sharks would not compete for seaweed, since it is a plant. They both eat cod fish, mussels, and shrimp, so they would compete for these biotic factors.

29. D: TEKS Standard 6.8(A)

When the golf ball reaches its peak height, it stops moving for a split second, so its kinetic energy is at a low. However, since it is at its peak height, it has the most potential energy. While the kinetic energy decreased, the potential energy increases as the ball travels higher.

30. B: TEKS Standard 8.12(B)

A decrease in a natural predator, such as a wolves, coyotes, bobcat, or wild dogs, would allow the population to become out of control. In a population of deer that has increased, there would be a natural decrease in a food source for the nutritional needs for the animals. Although deer have been known to share a human's developed habitat, it is often forced by reduced territory and food sources. An increase in hunting licenses would be used by local officials to try to control the population, helping to decrease the number of adults of breeding age.

31. B: TEKS Standard 7.9(B)

An Earth year occurs each time Earth makes a revolution around the Sun. The consistent revolution of Earth around the Sun is due to the Sun's gravitational pull on Earth. Option A is incorrect because Earth does not revolve on its axis. It rotates, causing day and night. Option C is incorrect because the gravitational pull on the Moon does not affect the length of the year. Option D is incorrect because the Moon's orbit is not a force. It is caused by gravity, which keeps the Moon in orbit around Earth.

32. TEKS Standard 8.9(B)

The first false statement is that the Sun is not the closest star to the Earth, as it is the closest star to the Earth. The second false statement is that the Sun is one of the largest stars in the galaxy because the Sun is just a medium-sized star.

33. D: TEKS Standard 8.8(B)

In the prompt, it says that radiation uses high-energy waves to treat patients. The question asks which electromagnetic waves are most likely used, and gamma rays are the only high-energy waves mentioned in the answer choices. Gamma rays have the highest energy of all waves on the electromagnetic spectrum, and they are incredibly dangerous. Answer choice A is incorrect because radio waves are very low-energy waves. They are used for things like broadcasting radio and television programs. Answer choice B is incorrect because infrared waves are also low-energy waves. They are still below the range of visible light and transmit heat. Answer choice C is incorrect because microwaves are also low-energy waves. These waves are used for cooking and for communication via phones.

34. TEKS Standard 6.6(C)

Characteristic	Category
Can appear shiny	Metals and metalloids
Insulator of heat	Nonmetals only
Low melting point	Nonmetals only
Can appear dull	Nonmetals and metalloids
Excellent conductor of electricity	Metals only
Can conduct thermal energy	Metals and metalloids

Only metals are excellent conductors of electricity, but metals and metalloids can conduct thermal energy and can be shiny in appearance. Only nonmetals insulate heat and have a low melting point, but nonmetals and metalloids can appear dull. Metalloids can appear either shiny or dull.

35. C: TEKS Standard 6.9(A)

Since the Northern Hemisphere is titled toward the Sun, it is summertime in Texas, and since Texas is on the part of Earth that has rotated away from the Sun, it is night. A student would be sleeping with the air conditioner on during a summer night. The student would not be covered with two heavy blankets in the summer. The student would not be getting ready for lunch or have just finished breakfast at night. It would not be snowing in Texas during the summer.

36. B: TEKS Standard 8.13(C)

After the factory was built, it began polluting the town with smoke, making the environment grayer. In the new environment, it is likely that the gray moths would have an evolutionary advantage because they cannot be seen as well by predators as the white moths. Even without knowing the specifics, the change in numbers of white and gray moths can be attributed to environmental adaptation because the change happened after an environmental occurrence. Answer choice A is incorrect. While it is possible for a moth's wings to become covered in soot from the smoke, this is not something that would carry through generations. There is a difference between a physical change and a genetic change. A genetic change is passed through generations, whereas a physical change is not. Answer choice C is incorrect because genetic changes cannot occur based on want. Just as a person cannot decide to change eye color, a moth cannot decide to change the color of its wings. Answer choice D is incorrect because moths are not predators in the first place. Furthermore, these moths are different color variations of the same species, so they would not prey on each other.

37. D: TEKS Standard 8.12(B)

The ocean waters are warming. The bluefin tuna population will have to adapt to survive at a deeper ocean depth where the waters are cooler. The waters at the surface of the ocean will be warmer, so that would not help the bluefin tuna. Bluefin tuna are saltwater fish and will not survive in freshwater. Decreasing movement will not affect temperature change enough.

38. B, C, D: TEKS Standard 7.6(B)

The first option contains only six atoms, so it is incorrect. The second option contains eight atoms, so it is correct. The third option contains nine atoms and is correct. The fourth option contains eight atoms and is correct. The fifth option contains only six atoms and is incorrect.

Practice Test #3

1. Periodic tables are useful for many reasons. One way they can be used is to help classify elements.

Element	Classification
____________	Metalloid
____________	Metal
____________	Noble Gas
____________	Nonmetal

Match each element to its classification using knowledge of the periodic table.

Rn – Radon	Cl – Chlorine
Co - Cobalt	B - Boron

2. In Lake Erie, a species of fish called the Blue Pike was overfished one year. The following year, there was a pollution incident that killed off another large portion of the population. These events, combined with the previous year's overfishing of adult fish, led to the extinction of the Blue Pike species—none of the other species were affected. What happened to other fish species in the lake over time after the Blue Pike became extinct?

a. They became extinct
b. They were not affected by the other species' fate
c. Their numbers increased due to lack of competition
d. Their numbers decreased due to lack of competition

3. Scientists studied a forest ecosystem where most of the plants were dying and only a few were still living. Below are some notes the scientists took.

Dying Plants	**Living Plants**
Number of plants: 50-60 Root depth: shallow (1-2 ft) Other observations: • Dried-up leaves • Dying plants clumped together	Number of plants: 5-6 Root depth: deep (6-8 ft) Other observations: • Roots are spread out • Plants not near each other

Based on the notes, why might most of the plants be dying while only a few are living?

a. The lack of oxygen is causing plants to die. The living plants have deeper roots, which give them more access to oxygen below the soil, but the dying plants have less access to oxygen because of the shallow roots.
b. The lack of Sun is causing the plants to die. The shallow root system of the dying plants doesn't allow as much access to the Sun as the deep root system of the living plants.
c. The increase in insects is causing the plants to die. Since the dying plants are all clumped together, there are more insects living in those plants eating the stems and leaves.
d. The lack of water is causing the plants to die. The large number of plants with shallow roots is causing too much competition for water. There are only a few plants with a deeper root system, and those plants are far apart, so there is little competition among them.

4. Many fishermen will watch the tide report for the local area and get up very early or stay out late in order to have the best fishing opportunity. Which factor affects the fisherman's fishing opportunities?

a. The gravitational relationship between the earth and moon
b. The gravitational relationship between the earth and sun
c. The earth's gravity
d. The moon's phases

5. The San Andreas Fault runs for over 800 miles along the California coastline and is a transform boundary. Which statement below is true about California due to its location along the San Andreas Fault?

a. California is home to over 25 active volcanoes.
b. There are many earthquakes in California.
c. California is home to many hurricanes.
d. The land in California is home to many valleys.

6. All living things have:

a. Organelles
b. Cells
c. Tissues
d. Cell walls

7. How many electrons are in an uncharged atom of $^{45}_{20}Ca$?

a. 20
b. 45
c. 65
d. 25

8. There are annual remote-controlled car competitions around the country. The winning car at a recent competition had an acceleration rate of 20 m/s2. Which two of the following cars has a higher acceleration rate than that car? Select all that apply.

Car Number	Net Force of the Motor (N)	Mass of the Car (kg)
Car 1	35	2.8
Car 2	58	3.5
Car 3	42	2.0
Car 4	61	3.1
Car 5	54	2.3

a. Car 1
b. Car 2
c. Car 3
d. Car 4
e. Car 5

9. In a pond, eutrophication, the pollution of water by plant nutrients, can occur, causing chemical, biological, and ecological changes to the pond. As plant material begins to decompose and carbon dioxide begins to increase, what would happen to the fish in the pond?

a. They would flourish
b. They would relocate to another area
c. They would die off
d. They would not be affected

10. A group of researchers in Antarctica discovered an organism belonging to an undiscovered species. Below are some characteristics of the organism.

Characteristics:
• Has many cells • Has no cell wall • Is heterotrophic

To which kingdom does the organism belong?

a. Bacteria
b. Protista
c. Fungi
d. Animalia

11. In which situation does the squirrel have the most potential energy with the least kinetic energy?

a. The squirrel is climbing around a sycamore tree looking for acorns.
b. The squirrel is sitting in the 10-foot oak tree watching another squirrel in a smaller adjacent tree.
c. The squirrel is climbing up the 10-foot oak tree chasing after another squirrel.
d. The squirrel is sitting on the grass behind a tree trying to hide from a cat.

12. Energy pyramids show different organisms in each trophic level of an ecosystem.

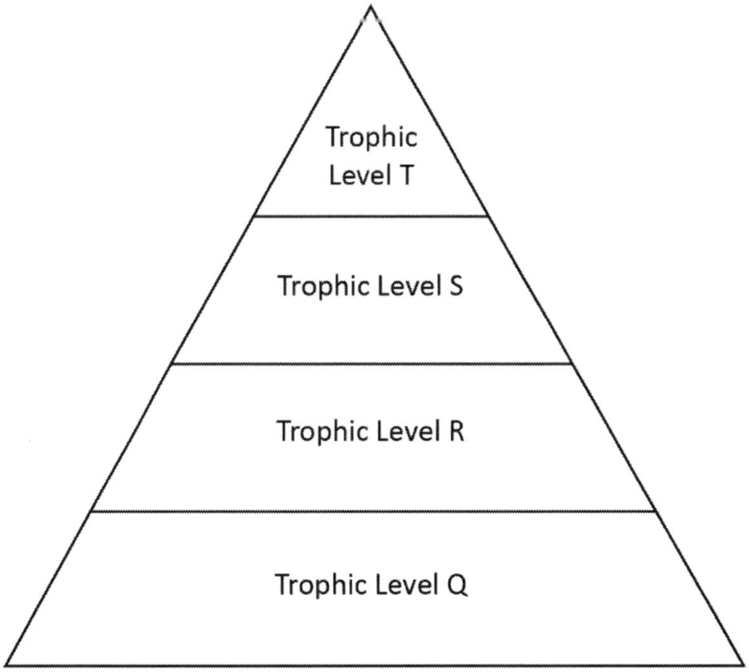

In the energy pyramid for the northern Pacific Ocean, which trophic level would algae and seaweed belong in? Which tropic level would killer whales belong in? Why would those organisms could belong in the trophic levels you chose? Write your response to these questions on the lines below.

____

____

____

____

____

13. Write the missing term from each sentence below in the blank beneath the sentence.

All elements in groups 3 to 12 in the periodic table can be classified as ____________.

Since these elements share that property, it can also be determined that these elements are good ____________ of heat and electricity.

14. How does the law of conservation of mass relate to the substances in a chemical reaction? Write your response to this question on the lines below.

____

____

____

____

____

15. Which of the following does not represent a physical change?

a. Salt dissolved in water
b. A spoiling apple
c. Sugar dissolved in water
d. Pulverized rock

16. Which of the following apparent colors of stars indicates the coolest temperature?

a. Orange red
b. Yellow orange
c. Yellow white
d. Blue white

17. The model below shows the tilt of Earth and its location relative to the Sun.

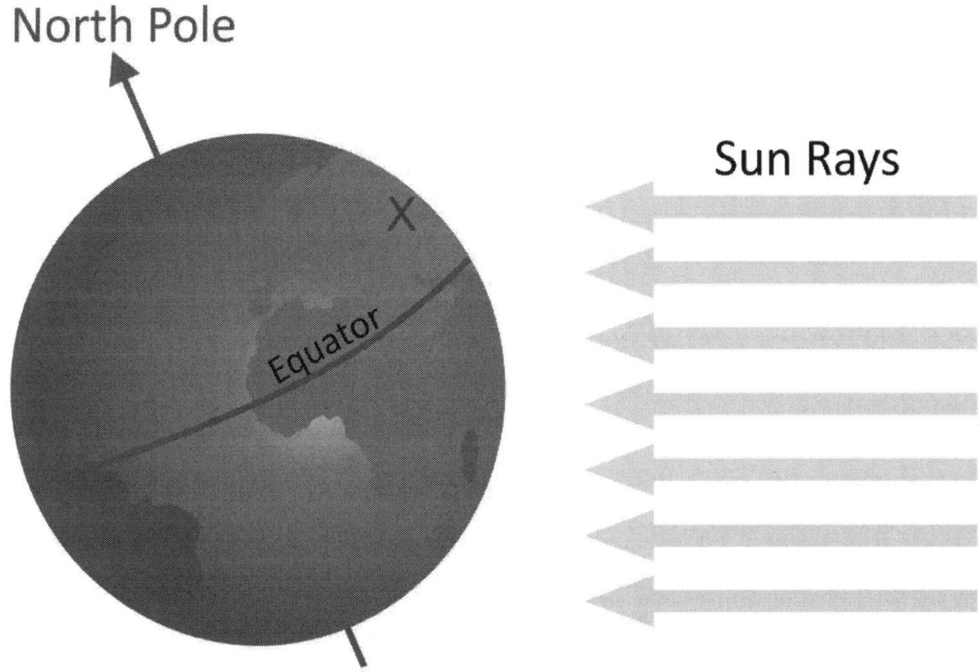

According to the model, which statement correctly describes the time of day in Asia, which is marked with an X, and correctly states the reason that it is that time of day?

a. It is daytime in Asia because the tilt of Earth puts the Northern Hemisphere closer to the Sun, causing it to be brighter.
b. It is daytime in Asia because Earth is rotating on its axis, and Asia is on the part of the Earth that is currently facing the Sun.
c. It is nighttime in Asia because the tilt of Earth is causing that part of the Earth to be farther away from the Sun.
d. It is nighttime in Asia because Earth is rotating on its axis, and Asia is north of the equator.

18. How are the mitochondria in an animal cell and the chloroplasts in a plant cell similar?

a. They both protect the cell from outside materials.
b. They are both responsible for energy to maintain the function of the cell.
c. They are both responsible for storing the DNA in a cell.
d. They both store nutrients the organism needs to survive.

19. Oxygen is an element that is found in many different substances. Oxygen is found in the balanced equation that the student wrote below.

$$2Fe_2O_3 + 3C \rightarrow 4Fe + 3CO_2$$

Which balanced equation shows a reaction that has the same number of oxygen atoms as the balanced equation the student wrote above?

a. $6Fe + 3O_2 \rightarrow 2Fe_3O_3$
b. $4Ca + 4CO_3 \rightarrow 2Ca_2 + 2C_2O_6$
c. $8Fe + 4O_2 \rightarrow 4Fe_2O_2$
d. $4Ca_3 + 2CO_2 \rightarrow 6Ca_2 + C_2O_4$

20. Which trait of a child is NOT a trait that would be stored in the genes within the chromosomes of the parents?

a. The child is tall and has brown hair like his father.
b. The child is color blind like her mom and dad.
c. The child speaks Spanish like her mother.
d. The child has many freckles on her face like her dad.

21. While driving in a car as a passenger, your mother stops abruptly in order to avoid hitting a hubcap in the road. After she slams on her brakes, you both move forward and then back once the seatbelt is activated. This is an example of which of Newton's Laws? Write your answer in the blank below.

22. You are watching the Olympic ice skating championships and see the pairs are up next. They begin their routine facing each other with their palms up and against each other. When the music starts they push themselves apart with their palms. What type of force is this?

a. Magnetic
b. Balanced
c. Action and reaction force
d. Centripetal force

23. For the organs in the muscular system and the circulatory system to function at their best, the body must be given proper nutrients. Which two systems of the body are most involved in the process of absorbing nutrients and removing waste?

a. Digestive and excretory systems
b. Digestive and endocrine systems
c. Excretory and integumentary systems
d. Endocrine and integumentary systems

24. A farmer noticed that his cornfield was being destroyed by grasshoppers. He researched many ways to eliminate grasshoppers from his fields and noticed several good options. Which option would most negatively affect the quality of the water in his area?

a. Removing weeds and other overgrowth from the area so only soil and corn stalks remain
b. Using a commercial pesticide
c. Spraying the plants with a water and garlic solution
d. Lightly dusting the corn plants with flour

25. Which statement below correctly explains the cause of wind?

a. Wind is produced when the temperatures in the ocean change quickly.
b. Cold air moves across the ocean creating high wind as it progresses.
c. The Sun heats the Earth unevenly, which powers convection and leads to wind.
d. An increase in clouds creates wind as the atmosphere is fuller.

26. What changes would occur if Earth did not have a tilt and if Earth rotated on its axis at a speed double the current rotation rate?

a. The world would only have winter and summer, and the days and nights would last about 12 hours each.
b. The world wouldn't have any seasons, and the days and nights would last about six hours each.
c. The world wouldn't have any seasons, and the days and nights would last about 24 hours each.
d. The world would only have winter and summer, and it would always be daytime.

27. Which of the following descriptions concerning air masses is true?

a. Maritime tropical air masses bring warm, dry weather.
b. Continental polar air masses bring warm, moist weather.
c. Continental tropical air masses bring cold, dry weather.
d. Maritime polar air masses bring cold, moist weather.

28. The two people in the figure below are pushing the box in opposite directions. The person on the left is pushing at 65 N and the person on the right is pushing at 87 N. What is the net force on the box?

a. The box is moving to the right at 22 N.
b. The box is not moving at 0 N.
c. The box is moving to the left at 22 N.
d. The box is moving to the left at 25 N.

29. You are driving to your grandmother's house for her birthday. She lives 582 miles away. The average speed limit is 65mph. About how long will it take you to get to your grandmother's house? Round your answer to the nearest hour and write it in the blank below.

[ ] hours

30. Which of the following scenarios is NOT an example of a chemical reaction?

a. The eggs, oil, and brownie powder were mixed and placed in the hot oven. The batter began rising as more heat was added.
b. The banana sitting on the counter began developing black spots all over its surface.
c. The puddle on the ground evaporated, and the concrete was no longer wet.
d. A tablespoon of vinegar was poured into a container of baking soda, and then bubbles and foam formed and spilled out onto the table.

31. Which force is responsible for the curved orbits of the planets in the solar system?

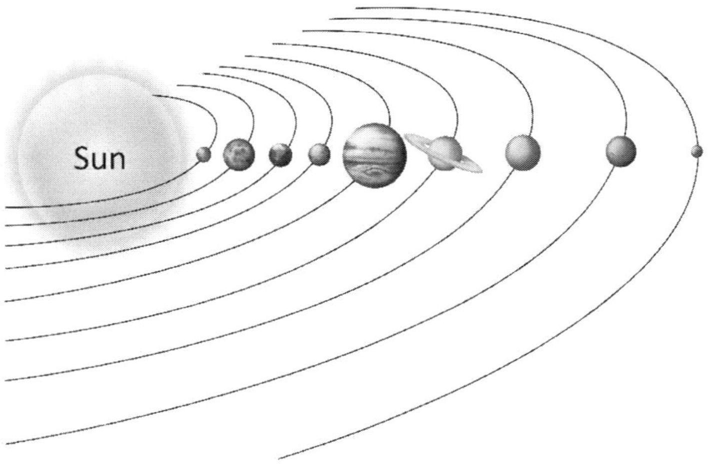

a. Inertia of the center of every planet
b. Gravity from the Sun
c. Gravity from the center of every planet
d. Inertia of the Sun

32. An electromagnetic spectrum is shown below.

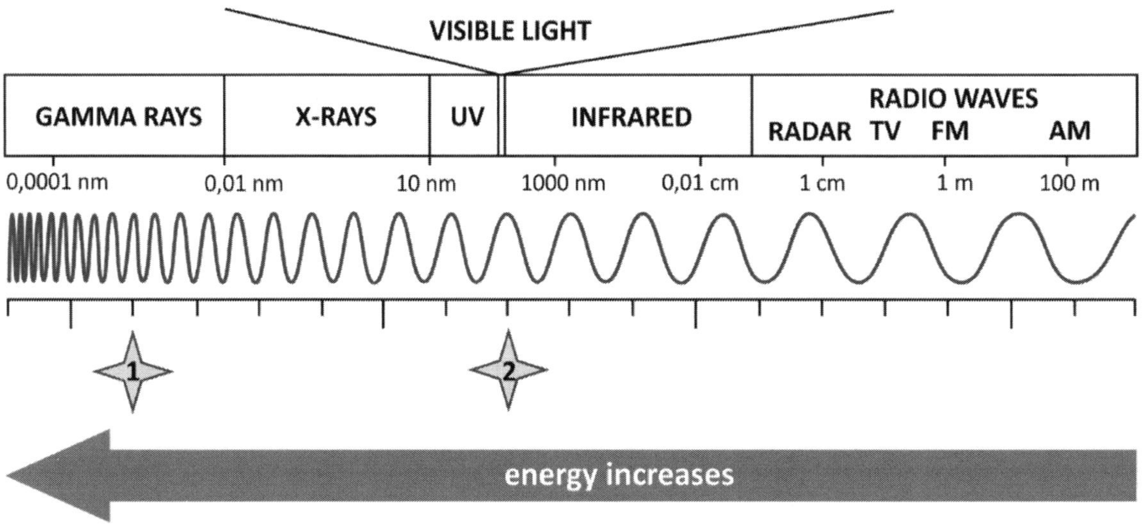

Which statement correctly compares celestial object 1 and celestial object 2, according to the electromagnetic spectrum?

a. Celestial object 1 has more energy than celestial object 2.
   Celestial 2 has shorter wavelengths than celestial object 1.
b. Celestial object 1 has shorter wavelengths than celestial object 2.
   Celestial object 2 can be seen by a human without the use of a telescope.
c. Celestial object 1 has less energy than celestial object 2.
   Celestial object 2 emits ultraviolet light, visible light, and infrared light.
d. Celestial object 1 can only be seen with a telescope that can detect gamma rays.
   Celestial object 2 can only be seen with a telescope that can detect ultraviolet rays.

33. Copper has a density of 8.96 g/cm^3. Silver and gold both have densities that are greater than copper. Which two of the metals below could be gold or silver? Select all that apply.

Metal	Volume	Mass
Metal 1	4.2 cm^3	20.5 g
Metal 2	2.4 cm^3	25.0 g
Metal 3	6.8 cm^3	50.0 g
Metal 4	2.1 cm^3	40.5 g
Metal 5	3.5 cm^3	10.5 g

a. Metal 1
b. Metal 2
c. Metal 3
d. Metal 4
e. Metal 5

34. The diagram below shows how a dam can be used to transform energy. When the intake door is opened, the water is pushed through the opening, which causes the turbine to spin and the generator to operate.

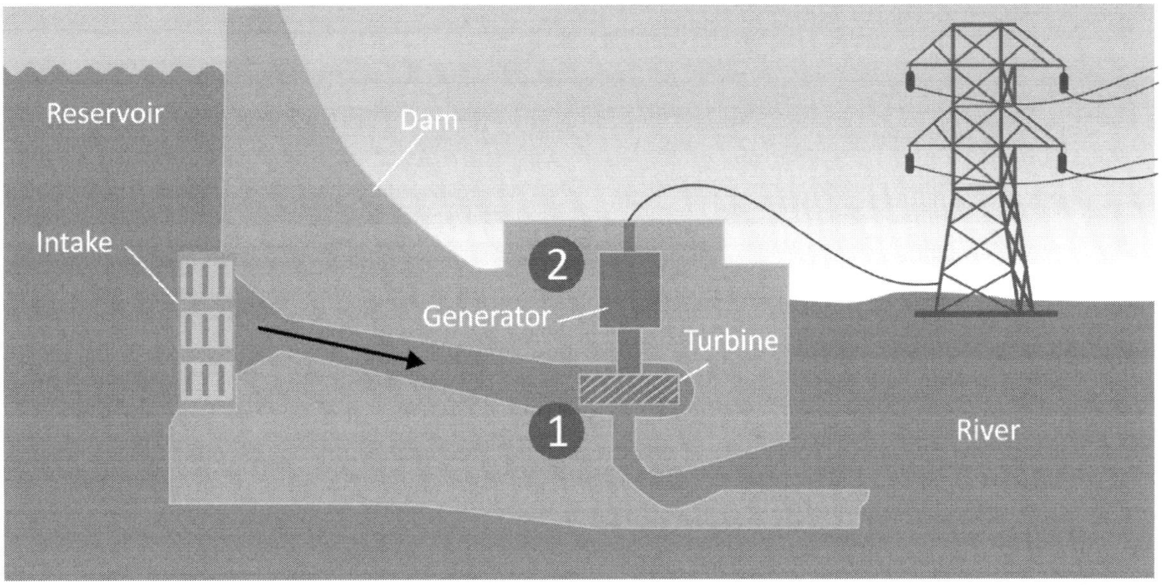

Which type of energy transformation has occurred?

a. Chemical to electrical
b. Mechanical to chemical
c. Chemical to mechanical
d. Mechanical to electrical

35. Two students are working together to move a box. The first student pulls the box with a force of 15 N while his friend pushes the box with a force of 25 N. The friction of the floor is providing a resistive net force of 8 N. If the mass of the box is 25 kg, what is the rate of acceleration for the box in meters/second^2?

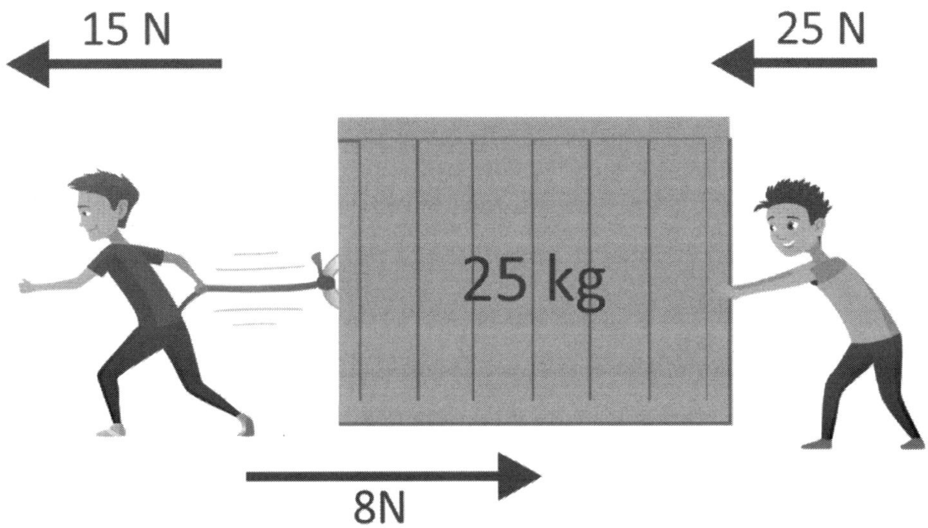

a. 1.28 m/s^2
b. 1.92 m/s^2
c. 1.6 m/s^2
d. 0.68 m/s^2

36. Which of the following is the most likely explanation for the reason finches on separate islands within an archipelago have differently shaped beaks?

a. Each bird evolved from a pre-existing ancestor on each island
b. The finches spread among the islands, but in small numbers, so genetic drift caused beak shape to change
c. Natural selection shaped the beaks in accordance with food availability on each island
d. The different finches were introduced by ancient humans

37. Students are making observations about different elements. In the table, write the classification that best fits each element, based on its location on the periodic table. The options are listed below.

Metal	Nonmetal	Noble Gas

Element	Classification
Nickel (Ni)	
Xenon (Xe)	
Radon (Rn)	
Neon (Ne)	
Silicon (Si)	

38. Gazelles are an important biotic factor in the life of an African lion because they are one of the lion's main sources of food. The graph below shows the gazelle population compared to the lion population.

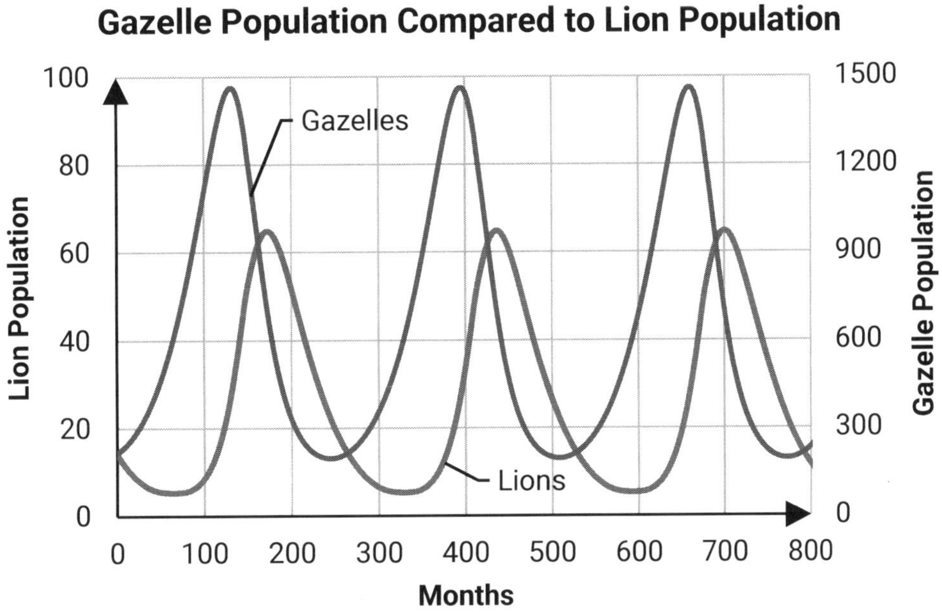

What is true about the gazelle population when the lion population is low? What is true about the gazelle population when the lion population is high? What is the reason for this? Write your response to these questions on the lines below.

Answer Key and Explanations for Test #3

1. TEKS Standard 6.6(C)

Element	Classification
B - Boron	Metalloid
Co - Cobalt	Metal
Rn - Radon	Noble Gas
Cl – Chlorine	Nonmetal

Boron is located in group 13 of the periodic table. It falls in the "stair-step" portion of the table, so it is a metalloid. Cobalt is located in group 9 of the periodic table. Most of the elements in groups 1 through 12 are metals. Radon is located in group 18. This group houses all the noble gases. Chlorine is located in group 17 above the "stair-step" portion of the table, so it is a nonmetal.

2. C: TEKS Standard 8.12(B)

In an ecosystem, when one species is affected by overfishing or pollution, other species will either thrive due to a lack of competition or become extinct for the same reasons. The question states that the other species were not impacted by the overfishing or pollution. Thus, their populations would not have decreased for those reasons. Once extinct, the other species were no longer the potential prey of the Blue Pike or competing against them for similar food sources and so had the opportunity to increase their population numbers.

3. D: TEKS Standard 6.12(A)

Since there are so many plants with a shallow root system, the plants are all competing for water, which is creating a water deficit. There are only a few plants with deep roots, and there is much less competition for water among them. The shallow root system does not result in less oxygen or less sunlight for plants, so that is not the cause of the plants dying. There is no evidence in the notes of an increase in the number of insects or signs of insect damage on the dying plants.

4. A: TEKS Standard 6.9(B)

The rising and falling of the ocean's tides are directly influenced by the gravitational pull of the moon on the earth. High tide is found in areas closest and farthest from the moon because the moon pulls the water and earth toward it, leaving the water on the other side of the earth behind. Low tide occurs in the areas not affected by high tide. There are two tides each day.

5. B: TEKS Standard 7.10(B)

The San Andreas Fault is a transform boundary, and transform boundaries often cause earthquakes. Therefore, there are many earthquakes in California. Convergent boundaries are responsible for volcano formation and can also cause earthquakes, but California only has seven active volcanoes, and these were not formed due to California's location along the San Andreas Fault. Hurricanes are caused by weather and not plate boundaries. Valleys are caused by divergent boundaries.

6. B: TEKS Standard 6.13(A)

Cells are the basic units of life, and all organisms have them. Some organisms like bacteria have just a single cell, while complex organisms like humans have hundreds of trillions. Prokaryotes do not have organelles Not all organisms have tissues, groups of cells that make up connective tissue, muscle tissue, etc. Finally, only some types of cells, including plant cells, have cell walls.

7. A: TEKS Standard 7.6(B)

Since the atomic number is 20, which represents the number of protons in the atom, there must be an equal number of electrons in a neutral atom. Protons have a positive charge and electrons are negative. Equal numbers of protons and electrons will result in a neutral atom, or zero charge.

8. C, E: TEKS Standard 8.7(A)

To find the acceleration, divide the force of the motor by the mass of the car. Car 1 has an acceleration rate of 12.5 m/s^2, so it is incorrect. Car 2 has an acceleration rate of 16.57 m/s^2, so it is incorrect. Car 3 has an acceleration rate of 21 m/s^2, so it is correct. Car 4 has an acceleration rate of 19.68 m/s^2, so it is incorrect. Car 5 has an acceleration rate of 23.48 m/s^2, so it is correct.

9. C: TEKS Standard 8.12(B)

In a pond, plants produce oxygen as a byproduct of photosynthesis. During eutrophication, plants die and decompose, causing increased levels of carbon dioxide. Fish cannot relocate from the pond, and they cannot live without oxygen, so they would die.

10. D: TEKS Standard 6.13(B)

The organism must be an animal belonging to kingdom Animalia, as organisms in this kingdom are heterotrophic and have many cells, none of which have cell walls. Choices A and B are incorrect because organisms in kingdoms Bacteria and Protista only have one cell. Choice C is incorrect because organisms in kingdom Fungi have cells with cell walls.

11. B: TEKS Standard 6.8(A)

The squirrel sitting in the 10-foot tree has the most potential energy because of the height of the tree. The squirrel has the least kinetic energy because it is not moving. The squirrel in options A and C is moving, so it has much kinetic energy and little potential energy. The squirrel in option D has the least kinetic energy, but it is on the ground, so it has less potential energy than the squirrel in the tree.

12. TEKS Standard 7.12(A)

Energy pyramids show how energy is distributed in an ecosystem. Producers often have the most energy, so they are usually represented at the bottom of the pyramid. Trophic level Q represents organisms that are producers, so algae and seaweed would belong in that level. Each tier or level has less energy than the one beneath it, so the organisms represented at the top of the pyramid are consumers. In this pyramid, the top level represents tertiary consumers. Trophic level T represents tertiary consumers, which are predators of secondary consumers, so a killer whale would belong in that level.

13. metals, conductors: TEKS Standard 6.6(C)

All the elements located in groups 3 to 12 are metals. Metals have properties that make them good conductors of heat and electricity.

14. TEKS Standard 8.6(E)

The law of conservation of mass states that matter cannot be created or destroyed. This means that in a chemical reaction, new matter is not created, which would result in a greater mass, nor destroyed, which would result in a lower mass. In a chemical reaction, a new substance is formed, but no matter is created or destroyed in this process. The atoms have just been grouped in a new way. Therefore, the mass of the new substance would be the same as the mass of the previous substance.

15. B: TEKS Standard 7.6(C)

A spoiling apple has undergone a chemical change (one substance is changed into another). Dissolving both sand and salt in water, refers to a physical change, since the salt and water and the sand and water can be separated again by evaporating the water, which is a physical change. Pulverized rock is also an example of a physical change where the form has changed but not the substance itself

16. A: TEKS Standard 8.9(A)

Orange red stars have temperatures less than 3,700 K. Yellow orange stars range between 3,700 and 5,200 K. Yellow white stars range between 5,200 and 6,000 K. Blue white stars range between 10,000 and 30,000 K.

17. B: TEKS Standard 6.9(A)

The diagram illustrates daytime in Asia because Earth is rotating on its axis, and that side of Earth is currently facing the Sun. The tilt of Earth is responsible for the seasons and not the day-and-night cycle, and the Northern Hemisphere is actually tilted away from the Sun in the image. It is nighttime in North and South America, which are on the side of the world that has rotated away from the Sun.

18. B: TEKS Standard 8.13(A)

The mitochondria in an animal cell make the chemical energy needed for the cell, and the chloroplasts in a plant cell turn energy from the Sun into food for the plant. Option A describes the cell wall, option C describes the nucleus, and option D describes vacuoles.

19. A: TEKS Standard 7.6(B)

The balanced equation in the example contains six oxygen atoms on both sides of the arrow. Option A is a balanced equation that has six oxygen atoms on both sides. Option B contains 12 oxygen atoms. Option C contains eight oxygen atoms. Option D contains 4 oxygen atoms.

20. C: TEKS Standard 8.13(B)

Speaking Spanish is a skill that is not genetic, as it is learned, and would therefore not be stored in the genes within the chromosomes of the parents. Height, hair color, freckles, and color blindness are all genetic traits children can inherit from their parents.

21. First: TEKS Standard 8.7(B)

Newton's First Law is the law of inertia, which states an object will continue in the direction that it was traveling until acted upon. In this case, your body continued to move forward until your seatbelt stopped you, acting as an unbalanced force.

22. C: TEKS Standard 8.7(B)

The ice skaters are applying Newton's Third Law to create an equal and opposite reaction force, causing both partners to move. Although each skater is pushing the other, they each move due to the force they applied and the opposite force. Magnets are not at play in this scenario, so choice A is incorrect. The forces are equal, but balanced forces do not cause movement, so choice B is incorrect. The skaters' path due to this event will be straight, not curved or circular, so choice D is incorrect.

23. A: TEKS Standard 7.13(A)

The digestive system is responsible for breaking consumed food down into parts that can be absorbed by the body. The excretory system removes any unnecessary waste that remains after food has been converted to energy. The endocrine system relates to hormones, and the integumentary system involves the skin.

24. B: TEKS Standard 7.11(A)

Commercial pesticides have chemicals that can get into groundwater and pollute area streams and lakes. Removing weeds and overgrowth would not affect the water in the area. The water and garlic solution and the flour would enter the water supply, but since neither contain harsh chemicals, they would not be harmful.

25. C: TEKS Standard 8.10(A)

Wind is produced by convection, the process of warm, less dense air rising and cold, more dense air sinking. Convection is powered by the Sun. The change in ocean temperature alone does not create wind. Cold air moving across the ocean is wind and is not the cause of wind. Clouds do not produce wind.

26. B: TEKS Standard 6.9(A)

Without the tilt of Earth, there would be no seasons because both the Northern and Southern Hemispheres would remain at the same distance from the Sun all year. A complete rotation of Earth on its axis currently takes 24 hours, so if it doubled in speed, it would only take 12 hours, leaving about six hours of day and six hours of night. The days and nights would no longer last 12 hours each if the rotation rate of the Earth was doubled(A), and the rotation rate would have to slow down for the days and nights to last 24 hours each (C). There would still be day and night because the Earth would still be rotating (D).

27. D: TEKS Standard 8.10(B)

Air masses are named for the areas over which they form. Since maritime polar air masses form over oceans in frigid regions, they bring cold, moist weather. Since maritime tropical air masses form over oceans in warmer regions, they bring warm, moist weather. Since continental polar air masses form over northern Canada or Alaska, they bring cold, dry weather. Since continental tropical air masses form over deserts, they bring warm, dry weather.

28. C: TEKS Standard 6.7(B)

The person on the right is pushing with more force than the person on the left. If the person on the right pushes towards the left with 87 N, and the person on the left pushes to the right with 65 N, the net force on the box is 22 N. This means the box will move to the left. Answer choice A is incorrect because the difference between the two opposing forces must be calculated to determine the direction and force. In this case, the force pushing to the left is greater than the force pushing to the right. Answer choice B is incorrect because the person on the right is pushing harder than the person on the left. Therefore, the force is not balanced, and the box will move. Answer choice D is incorrect because, while the box is moving to the left, it is being moved with 22 N, not 25 N.

29. 9 hours: TEKS Standard 7.7(A)

The formula for calculating speed is S=D/T. However, you are looking for time, so you would divide distance (D) by speed (S) to get the time (T). Since $582 \div 65 = 8.95$ and the question asks for the nearest number of hours, the answer is 9 hours.

30. C: TEKS Standard 8.6(E)

Evaporation is a physical change and does not result in a chemical reaction. The ingredients of the brownie were mixed, and when heat was added, a new substance was formed, which is evidence of a chemical reaction (A). Any rotting fruit is an example of a chemical reaction (B). Over time, air reacts with the yellow banana skin to create a chemical reaction that results in the black, rotting spots. When vinegar and baking soda are combined, new substances are formed, which is evidence that a chemical reaction occurred. The bubbles are also an indicator of a chemical reaction (D).

31. B: TEKS Standard 7.9(B)

Gravity from the Sun is the force mostly responsible for maintaining the orbits of planets in the solar system. Gravity is the force of an object to draw another object to its center. The more mass an object has, the greater its gravitational pull. The Sun is the object with the most mass in the solar system, so it has the great gravitational pull and draws all the planets toward it. This pull prevents the planets from flying off into space, and it creates the curved orbit of the planets as they move. Answer choice A is incorrect because inertia is the tendency of an object to either stay at rest or keep moving unless acted on by an outside force. In the solar system, inertia is important because it helps keep the planets moving in orbit; however, inertia is not the main force maintaining the planets' orbits but simply the force responsible for their movement. Answer choice C is incorrect because gravity from the Sun is what holds the solar system together, not gravity from the center of every planet. Answer choice D is incorrect because while the Sun does have inertia that keeps it spinning, the inertia of the Sun is not responsible for the orbit of planets.

32. B: TEKS Standard 8.8(B)

Option B is correct because celestial object 1 has shorter wavelengths than celestial object 2, and celestial object 2 is under the visible light section of the spectrum, so it can be seen without the use of a telescope. Option A is incorrect because, although celestial object 1 does have more energy than celestial object 2, celestial object 2 has longer wavelengths than celestial object 1. Option C is incorrect because celestial object 1 has more energy than celestial object 2. However, it is true that celestial object 2 emits ultraviolet light, visible light, and infrared light. Option D is incorrect because, although celestial object 1 can only be seen with a gamma-ray telescope, celestial object 2 is under the visible light section of the spectrum, so it can be seen by the naked human eye.

33. B, D: TEKS Standard 6.6(D)

The density of metal 1 is found by dividing 20.5 g by 4.2 cm^3, which equals 4.9 g/cm^3 and is not greater than the density of copper. The density of metal 2 is found by dividing 25.0 g by 2.4 cm^3, which equals 10.4 g/cm^3 and is greater than the density of copper. The density of metal 3 is found by dividing 50.0 g by 6.8 cm^3, which equals 7.4 g/cm^3 and is not greater than the density of copper.

The density of metal 4 is found by dividing 40.5 g by 2.1 cm^3, which equals 19.3 g/cm^3 and is greater than the density of copper. The density of metal 5 is found by dividing 10.5 g by 3.5 cm^3, which equals 3 g/cm^3 and is not greater than the density of copper.

34. D: TEKS Standard 6.8(B)

The moving water causes the turbine to spin, which is an example of mechanical energy. The mechanical energy of the spinning turbine powers the generator, which in turn provides electrical energy through the lines to the electrical tower. There is no chemical energy used in this situation because no chemical reaction is used to generate energy.

35. A: TEKS Standard 8.7(A)

The students are moving the box forward with a combined force of 40 N: $15\text{ N} + 25\text{ N} = 40\text{ N}$. The floor gives a resistive force of 8 N, so the total net force moving the box forward is 32 N: $40\text{ N} - 8\text{ N} = 32\text{ N}$. To find the rate of acceleration, divide the net force by the mass of the box. $32\text{ N} \div 25\text{ kg} = 1.28\text{ m/s}^2$. Option B is incorrect because it shows what the acceleration would be if all forces were combined instead of showing the acceleration if the resistive net force was subtracted. Option C is incorrect because it shows what the acceleration would be if the the resistive force was not considered at all. Option D is incorrect because it shows what the acceleration would be if the calculation did not include the net force provided by the student pulling the box.

36. C: TEKS Standard 7.13(D)

Finches with beaks well-suited for the types of food available on an island had an evolutionary advantage. As a result, these finches survived and reproduced, a phenomenon known as natural selection. The finches share a common ancestor, regardless of the island on which they now live. Genetic drift refers to genetic changes that occur due to random chance; this would not account for different beaks on different islands. Introduction by humans would not account for different beaks, since phenotypes change over time.

37. TEKS Standard 6.6(C)

Element	Classification
Nickel (Ni)	Metal
Xenon (Xe)	Noble Gas
Radon (Rn)	Noble Gas
Neon (Ne)	Noble Gas
Silicon (Si)	Nonmetal

Nickel is a metal. Xenon, radon, and neon are noble gasses. They are also nonmetals, but they are more specifically noble gasses. Silicon is a nonmetal, but it is not a noble gas.

38. TEKS Standard 6.12(A)

When the lion population is low, the gazelle population is high. The lion is a predator of the gazelle. When there are fewer lions, fewer gazelles will become prey, so more gazelles will live. When the lion population is at its highest, the gazelle population decreases because there are more lions to prey on the gazelles.

How to Overcome Test Anxiety

Just the thought of taking a test is enough to make most people a little nervous. A test is an important event that can have a long-term impact on your future, so it's important to take it seriously and it's natural to feel anxious about performing well. But just because anxiety is normal, that doesn't mean that it's helpful in test taking, or that you should simply accept it as part of your life. Anxiety can have a variety of effects. These effects can be mild, like making you feel slightly nervous, or severe, like blocking your ability to focus or remember even a simple detail.

If you experience test anxiety—whether severe or mild—it's important to know how to beat it. To discover this, first you need to understand what causes test anxiety.

Causes of Test Anxiety

While we often think of anxiety as an uncontrollable emotional state, it can actually be caused by simple, practical things. One of the most common causes of test anxiety is that a person does not feel adequately prepared for their test. This feeling can be the result of many different issues such as poor study habits or lack of organization, but the most common culprit is time management. Starting to study too late, failing to organize your study time to cover all of the material, or being distracted while you study will mean that you're not well prepared for the test. This may lead to cramming the night before, which will cause you to be physically and mentally exhausted for the test. Poor time management also contributes to feelings of stress, fear, and hopelessness as you realize you are not well prepared but don't know what to do about it.

Other times, test anxiety is not related to your preparation for the test but comes from unresolved fear. This may be a past failure on a test, or poor performance on tests in general. It may come from comparing yourself to others who seem to be performing better or from the stress of living up to expectations. Anxiety may be driven by fears of the future—how failure on this test would affect your educational and career goals. These fears are often completely irrational, but they can still negatively impact your test performance.

Elements of Test Anxiety

As mentioned earlier, test anxiety is considered to be an emotional state, but it has physical and mental components as well. Sometimes you may not even realize that you are suffering from test anxiety until you notice the physical symptoms. These can include trembling hands, rapid heartbeat, sweating, nausea, and tense muscles. Extreme anxiety may lead to fainting or vomiting. Obviously, any of these symptoms can have a negative impact on testing. It is important to recognize them as soon as they begin to occur so that you can address the problem before it damages your performance.

The mental components of test anxiety include trouble focusing and inability to remember learned information. During a test, your mind is on high alert, which can help you recall information and stay focused for an extended period of time. However, anxiety interferes with your mind's natural processes, causing you to blank out, even on the questions you know well. The strain of testing during anxiety makes it difficult to stay focused, especially on a test that may take several hours. Extreme anxiety can take a huge mental toll, making it difficult not only to recall test information but even to understand the test questions or pull your thoughts together.

Effects of Test Anxiety

Test anxiety is like a disease—if left untreated, it will get progressively worse. Anxiety leads to poor performance, and this reinforces the feelings of fear and failure, which in turn lead to poor performances on subsequent tests. It can grow from a mild nervousness to a crippling condition. If allowed to progress, test anxiety can have a big impact on your schooling, and consequently on your future.

Test anxiety can spread to other parts of your life. Anxiety on tests can become anxiety in any stressful situation, and blanking on a test can turn into panicking in a job situation. But fortunately, you don't have to let anxiety rule your testing and determine your grades. There are a number of relatively simple steps you can take to move past anxiety and function normally on a test and in the rest of life.

Physical Steps for Beating Test Anxiety

While test anxiety is a serious problem, the good news is that it can be overcome. It doesn't have to control your ability to think and remember information. While it may take time, you can begin taking steps today to beat anxiety.

Just as your first hint that you may be struggling with anxiety comes from the physical symptoms, the first step to treating it is also physical. Rest is crucial for having a clear, strong mind. If you are tired, it is much easier to give in to anxiety. But if you establish good sleep habits, your body and mind will be ready to perform optimally, without the strain of exhaustion. Additionally, sleeping well helps you to retain information better, so you're more likely to recall the answers when you see the test questions.

Getting good sleep means more than going to bed on time. It's important to allow your brain time to relax. Take study breaks from time to time so it doesn't get overworked, and don't study right before bed. Take time to rest your mind before trying to rest your body, or you may find it difficult to fall asleep.

Along with sleep, other aspects of physical health are important in preparing for a test. Good nutrition is vital for good brain function. Sugary foods and drinks may give a burst of energy but this burst is followed by a crash, both physically and emotionally. Instead, fuel your body with protein and vitamin-rich foods.

Also, drink plenty of water. Dehydration can lead to headaches and exhaustion, especially if your brain is already under stress from the rigors of the test. Particularly if your test is a long one, drink water during the breaks. And if possible, take an energy-boosting snack to eat between sections.

Along with sleep and diet, a third important part of physical health is exercise. Maintaining a steady workout schedule is helpful, but even taking 5-minute study breaks to walk can help get your blood pumping faster and clear your head. Exercise also releases endorphins, which contribute to a positive feeling and can help combat test anxiety.

When you nurture your physical health, you are also contributing to your mental health. If your body is healthy, your mind is much more likely to be healthy as well. So take time to rest, nourish your body with healthy food and water, and get moving as much as possible. Taking these physical steps will make you stronger and more able to take the mental steps necessary to overcome test anxiety.

Mental Steps for Beating Test Anxiety

Working on the mental side of test anxiety can be more challenging, but as with the physical side, there are clear steps you can take to overcome it. As mentioned earlier, test anxiety often stems from lack of preparation, so the obvious solution is to prepare for the test. Effective studying may be the most important weapon you have for beating test anxiety, but you can and should employ several other mental tools to combat fear.

First, boost your confidence by reminding yourself of past success—tests or projects that you aced. If you're putting as much effort into preparing for this test as you did for those, there's no reason you should expect to fail here. Work hard to prepare; then trust your preparation.

Second, surround yourself with encouraging people. It can be helpful to find a study group, but be sure that the people you're around will encourage a positive attitude. If you spend time with others who are anxious or cynical, this will only contribute to your own anxiety. Look for others who are motivated to study hard from a desire to succeed, not from a fear of failure.

Third, reward yourself. A test is physically and mentally tiring, even without anxiety, and it can be helpful to have something to look forward to. Plan an activity following the test, regardless of the outcome, such as going to a movie or getting ice cream.

When you are taking the test, if you find yourself beginning to feel anxious, remind yourself that you know the material. Visualize successfully completing the test. Then take a few deep, relaxing breaths and return to it. Work through the questions carefully but with confidence, knowing that you are capable of succeeding.

Developing a healthy mental approach to test taking will also aid in other areas of life. Test anxiety affects more than just the actual test—it can be damaging to your mental health and even contribute to depression. It's important to beat test anxiety before it becomes a problem for more than testing.

Study Strategy

Being prepared for the test is necessary to combat anxiety, but what does being prepared look like? You may study for hours on end and still not feel prepared. What you need is a strategy for test prep. The next few pages outline our recommended steps to help you plan out and conquer the challenge of preparation.

Step 1: Scope Out the Test

Learn everything you can about the format (multiple choice, essay, etc.) and what will be on the test. Gather any study materials, course outlines, or sample exams that may be available. Not only will this help you to prepare, but knowing what to expect can help to alleviate test anxiety.

Step 2: Map Out the Material

Look through the textbook or study guide and make note of how many chapters or sections it has. Then divide these over the time you have. For example, if a book has 15 chapters and you have five days to study, you need to cover three chapters each day. Even better, if you have the time, leave an extra day at the end for overall review after you have gone through the material in depth.

If time is limited, you may need to prioritize the material. Look through it and make note of which sections you think you already have a good grasp on, and which need review. While you are studying, skim quickly through the familiar sections and take more time on the challenging parts.

Write out your plan so you don't get lost as you go. Having a written plan also helps you feel more in control of the study, so anxiety is less likely to arise from feeling overwhelmed at the amount to cover.

Step 3: Gather Your Tools

Decide what study method works best for you. Do you prefer to highlight in the book as you study and then go back over the highlighted portions? Or do you type out notes of the important information? Or is it helpful to make flashcards that you can carry with you? Assemble the pens, index cards, highlighters, post-it notes, and any other materials you may need so you won't be distracted by getting up to find things while you study.

If you're having a hard time retaining the information or organizing your notes, experiment with different methods. For example, try color-coding by subject with colored pens, highlighters, or post-it notes. If you learn better by hearing, try recording yourself reading your notes so you can listen while in the car, working out, or simply sitting at your desk. Ask a friend to quiz you from your flashcards, or try teaching someone the material to solidify it in your mind.

Step 4: Create Your Environment

It's important to avoid distractions while you study. This includes both the obvious distractions like visitors and the subtle distractions like an uncomfortable chair (or a too-comfortable couch that makes you want to fall asleep). Set up the best study environment possible: good lighting and a comfortable work area. If background music helps you focus, you may want to turn it on, but otherwise keep the room quiet. If you are using a computer to take notes, be sure you don't have any other windows open, especially applications like social media, games, or anything else that could distract you. Silence your phone and turn off notifications. Be sure to keep water close by so you stay hydrated while you study (but avoid unhealthy drinks and snacks).

Also, take into account the best time of day to study. Are you freshest first thing in the morning? Try to set aside some time then to work through the material. Is your mind clearer in the afternoon or evening? Schedule your study session then. Another method is to study at the same time of day that you will take the test, so that your brain gets used to working on the material at that time and will be ready to focus at test time.

Step 5: Study!

Once you have done all the study preparation, it's time to settle into the actual studying. Sit down, take a few moments to settle your mind so you can focus, and begin to follow your study plan. Don't give in to distractions or let yourself procrastinate. This is your time to prepare so you'll be ready to fearlessly approach the test. Make the most of the time and stay focused.

Of course, you don't want to burn out. If you study too long you may find that you're not retaining the information very well. Take regular study breaks. For example, taking five minutes out of every hour to walk briskly, breathing deeply and swinging your arms, can help your mind stay fresh.

As you get to the end of each chapter or section, it's a good idea to do a quick review. Remind yourself of what you learned and work on any difficult parts. When you feel that you've mastered the material, move on to the next part. At the end of your study session, briefly skim through your notes again.

But while review is helpful, cramming last minute is NOT. If at all possible, work ahead so that you won't need to fit all your study into the last day. Cramming overloads your brain with more information than it can process and retain, and your tired mind may struggle to recall even previously learned information when it is overwhelmed with last-minute study. Also, the urgent nature of cramming and the stress placed on your brain contribute to anxiety. You'll be more likely to go to the test feeling unprepared and having trouble thinking clearly.

So don't cram, and don't stay up late before the test, even just to review your notes at a leisurely pace. Your brain needs rest more than it needs to go over the information again. In fact, plan to finish your studies by noon or early afternoon the day before the test. Give your brain the rest of the day to relax or focus on other things, and get a good night's sleep. Then you will be fresh for the test and better able to recall what you've studied.

Step 6: Take a Practice Test

Many courses offer sample tests, either online or in the study materials. This is an excellent resource to check whether you have mastered the material, as well as to prepare for the test format and environment.

Check the test format ahead of time: the number of questions, the type (multiple choice, free response, etc.), and the time limit. Then create a plan for working through them. For example, if you have 30 minutes to take a 60-question test, your limit is 30 seconds per question. Spend less time on the questions you know well so that you can take more time on the difficult ones.

If you have time to take several practice tests, take the first one open book, with no time limit. Work through the questions at your own pace and make sure you fully understand them. Gradually work up to taking a test under test conditions: sit at a desk with all study materials put away and set a timer. Pace yourself to make sure you finish the test with time to spare and go back to check your answers if you have time.

After each test, check your answers. On the questions you missed, be sure you understand why you missed them. Did you misread the question (tests can use tricky wording)? Did you forget the information? Or was it something you hadn't learned? Go back and study any shaky areas that the practice tests reveal.

Taking these tests not only helps with your grade, but also aids in combating test anxiety. If you're already used to the test conditions, you're less likely to worry about it, and working through tests until you're scoring well gives you a confidence boost. Go through the practice tests until you feel comfortable, and then you can go into the test knowing that you're ready for it.

Test Tips

On test day, you should be confident, knowing that you've prepared well and are ready to answer the questions. But aside from preparation, there are several test day strategies you can employ to maximize your performance.

First, as stated before, get a good night's sleep the night before the test (and for several nights before that, if possible). Go into the test with a fresh, alert mind rather than staying up late to study.

Try not to change too much about your normal routine on the day of the test. It's important to eat a nutritious breakfast, but if you normally don't eat breakfast at all, consider eating just a protein bar. If you're a coffee drinker, go ahead and have your normal coffee. Just make sure you time it so that the caffeine doesn't wear off right in the middle of your test. Avoid sugary beverages, and drink enough water to stay hydrated but not so much that you need a restroom break 10 minutes into the test. If your test isn't first thing in the morning, consider going for a walk or doing a light workout before the test to get your blood flowing.

Allow yourself enough time to get ready, and leave for the test with plenty of time to spare so you won't have the anxiety of scrambling to arrive in time. Another reason to be early is to select a good seat. It's helpful to sit away from doors and windows, which can be distracting. Find a good seat, get out your supplies, and settle your mind before the test begins.

When the test begins, start by going over the instructions carefully, even if you already know what to expect. Make sure you avoid any careless mistakes by following the directions.

Then begin working through the questions, pacing yourself as you've practiced. If you're not sure on an answer, don't spend too much time on it, and don't let it shake your confidence. Either skip it and come back later, or eliminate as many wrong answers as possible and guess among the remaining ones. Don't dwell on these questions as you continue—put them out of your mind and focus on what lies ahead.

Be sure to read all of the answer choices, even if you're sure the first one is the right answer. Sometimes you'll find a better one if you keep reading. But don't second-guess yourself if you do immediately know the answer. Your gut instinct is usually right. Don't let test anxiety rob you of the information you know.

If you have time at the end of the test (and if the test format allows), go back and review your answers. Be cautious about changing any, since your first instinct tends to be correct, but make sure you didn't misread any of the questions or accidentally mark the wrong answer choice. Look over any you skipped and make an educated guess.

At the end, leave the test feeling confident. You've done your best, so don't waste time worrying about your performance or wishing you could change anything. Instead, celebrate the successful completion of this test. And finally, use this test to learn how to deal with anxiety even better next time.

Review Video: Test Anxiety
Visit mometrix.com/academy and enter code: 100340

Important Qualification

Not all anxiety is created equal. If your test anxiety is causing major issues in your life beyond the classroom or testing center, or if you are experiencing troubling physical symptoms related to your anxiety, it may be a sign of a serious physiological or psychological condition. If this sounds like your situation, we strongly encourage you to seek professional help.

Online Resources

Due to our efforts to try to keep this book to a manageable length, we've created a link that will give you access to all of your online resources:

mometrix.com/resources719/staarg8sci

It's Your Moment, Let's Celebrate It!

Share your story @mometrixtestpreparation